SAN JOSE DEL BADO

THE 1803 LAND GRANTEES

Henrietta Martinez Christmas

Nancy Anderson

Foreword by Malcolm Ebright

ISBN: 978-1-942626-343

Library of Congress Control Number

2016950990

Published by:
New Mexico Genealogical Society
P O Box 27559
Albuquerque, NM 87125-7559

Cover Picture of San Jose Church furnished by Henrietta Martinez Christmas

Table of Contents

Introduction

Land grants and projects entail using many types of documents to recreate the settlers who first acquired the land and is a difficult process. Most New Mexicans with at least knowledge of five generations of their family can say they descend from a community or person who owned a piece of a land grant.

The San Miguel del Bado land grant was called the El Vado del Rio Pecos and consisted of two settlements, San Miguel del Bado and the San Jose del Bado. Pedro Bautista Pino described his action in 1803 with the following words. "I was commissioned to found at El Vado del Rio Pecos two settlements, and to distribute lands to more than 200 families.[1]"

This book contains those who were allotted or granted land within the San Jose del Bado settlement.

After much study of the El Vado land grant and the two settlements, it became evident that San Miguel's grantees came mostly from Santa Fe. San Jose's grantees consisted of people from Tome to Abiquiu and beyond, with the majority from Cochiti.

What happened to San Jose over the last 200+ years? It grew and many of the people ended up moving to other land grants such as Anton Chico, Las Vegas, Chaperito, Tecolote, San Geronimo and began the process of an eastern migration within New Mexico.

After reviewing the list of the San Jose del Bado allotments, double checking church records, visiting county clerk's offices and archives, we believe we have put forth the best possible family group sheets of those from the San Jose del Bado settlement.

---

[1] John L. Kessell, *Kiva, Cross and Crown* (Washington, D. C.: National Park Service, U. S. Department of Interior, 1979), p. 418-419

Acknowledgments

The New Mexico State Records Center & Archives houses the majority of the material we used in this book when it comes to the land.

Our thanks to Rick Hendricks, State Historian, Rob Martinez, Assistant State Historian, Robert Torrez, former State Historian and Malcolm Ebright. All of the above "put meat on the bones" and helped make this book more complete. The Center of the Southwest Research at University of New Mexico, the Genealogy Center of Albuquerque Public Library, the San Miguel County Clerk's office and Highlands University Library were also great resources.

It takes more than research of church and land records to put together a good book. We appreciate the help from Patricia Rivera Wallace in locating censuses, indexing and editing and editing suggestions made by Karen Daniel.

With all of the help, we hope this book explains the settlement of San Jose del Bado and brings the families to life.

San Jose valley

Foreword

The San Miguel del Bado Grant and the 1803 Allotments at San José del Bado

By Malcolm Ebright

The San Miguel del Bado grant was the first major community land grant to expand the periphery of Spanish settlement on the eastern frontier of New Mexico around Pecos Pueblo. After the Comanche Peace Treaty was signed by Governor Juan Bautista Anza in 1786, the entire area of Spanish settlement from Abiquiú to Ojo Caliente to Picuris, Las Trampas, Truchas, and Pecos was opened up for expansion of Hispanic settlements.[2] New Mexico population figures begin to show a rapid increase in the number of Spaniards in the late 1790s, as new settlements were formed within land grants in the Taos and Pecos areas.[3] It is within this expanding of the edge of Spanish settlement that the San Miguel del Bado Grant was made in 1794.

In late November of that year, Lorenzo Marquez, for himself and on behalf of fifty-one other families, asked Governor Fernando Chacón to make them a grant of lands at the place called El Vado, and the surrounding area.4 Marquez was living in Santa Fe at the time he presented his petition to Governor Chacón, but was familiar with the area around Pecos Pueblo, possibly as a presidio soldier stationed there.5 Lorenzo Marquez described the fifty-one men who joined him in the petition as having large families and small amounts of land in Santa Fe, insufficient for their support due to "the great scarcity of water which owing to the great number of people [in

[2] For further discussion see, Ebright and Hendricks, *The Witches of Abiquiú: The Governor, the Priest, the Genízaro Indians, and the Devil* (Albuquerque: University of New Mexico Press, 2006), 277, note 35 and Pekka Hämäläinen, *The Comanche Empire* (New Haven: Yale University Press, 2008), p.8 and n. 35, p. 277.

[3] For Pecos Valley, the population figures for Spaniards and Pecos Pueblo Indians are:

Year	Spaniards	Pecos Indians
1799	178	118
1804	437	125

Frances Levine, *Our Prayers Are in This Place: Pecos Pueblo Identity Over the Centuries*, (Albuquerque: University of New Mexico Press, 1999), p. 44.

[4] "In 1792, Lorenzo Márquez, the original petitioner for the neighboring El Vado land grant, was *padrino* at one of the two baptisms at Pecos for the year. In 1793 *padrinos* at four of the five baptisms at Pecos Pueblo were El Vado settlers names on the 1803 list of settlers. Lorenzo Marquez was a *padrino* in three of these," Levine, *Our Prayers Are in This Place, p.* 87. The mission center was moved from Pecos to San Miguel del Bado prior to 1818, due to the "expertly prepared petition of Comanche *genízaro* José Cristóbal Guerrero," Levine, *Our Prayers Are in This Place,* 95. Ebright and Hendricks, *The Witches of Abiquiú*, pp. 76-77.

[5] Marquez and one of his co-grantees Domingo Padilla, "show up in the 1780s in the Pecos books as godfathers and marriage witnesses. John Kessell, *Kiva, Cross, and Crown: The Pecos Indians and New Mexico, 1540-1840* (Albuquerque: University of New Mexico Press, 1987), p. 418.

Santa Fe] we cannot all enjoy."[6] The petition states that thirteen of the fifty-two petitioners were Indians, and it is likely that a large portion of the fifty-one families were either Genízaros, Indians or mestizos.[7] Three decades earlier the population of Santa Fe was said to have been fourteen percent Genízaro.[8] The best description of the makeup of the settlers of the San Miguel del Bado Grant is by Fray Angélico Chávez, an early authority on Genízaros:

"San José and San Miguel del Vado were settled by Spanish military personnel and the genízaro colony of Santa Fe; also by Indians of other pueblos, including the more progressive Pecos Indians, who entered into a genízaro status and thus contributed to the depopulation of their pueblo; the San José and San Miguel Genízaros also assimilated many converts from the Comanche and other Plains tribes."[9]

Marquez and his co-petitioners asked for land described as follows: "On the north the Rio de la Vaca, from the place called the Rancheria to the Agua Caliente, on the south the Cañon Blanco, on the east the Cuesta, with the little hills of Bernal, and on the west the place commonly called the Guzano."[10]

The petitioners said they had twenty-five guns among them and they promised to "enclose ourselves in a plaza well fortified with bulwarks and towers," as well as supply themselves with more firearms and ammunition. They told the governor there was room enough on the land for themselves and "for everyone in the province not supplied." It is clear from the petition that protection against Indian raids (mostly Comanche and Apache) was one of the primary concerns of the settlers.[11]

Governor Fernando Chacón made the grant to the petitioners on November 25, 1794 and directed *Alcalde* Antonio José Ortiz to put the grantees in possession of the land.[12] On November 26, 1794 *Alcalde* Ortiz brought the fifty-two petitioners to El Vado (today's San Miguel del Bado), and performed the traditional ceremonies of delivery of possession to the grantees, though he did not allot specific tracts of land at that time. The list of individual petitioners attached to the petition has been lost, as was often the case, so other than Lorenzo Marquez, we do not know

---

[6] Petition of Lorenzo Marquez et al. for the San Miguel del Bado Grant, SG 119, Roll 24, fr. 599 (Spanish original), 664-65 (translation).

[7] Petition of Lorenzo Marquez et al. for the San Miguel del Bado Grant, SG 119, Roll 24, fr. 599 (Spanish original), 664-65 (translation).

[8] Ebright and Hendricks, *The Witches of Abiquiú*, p. 30.

[9] Fray Angelico Chavez, *Archives of the Archdiocese of Santa Fe, 1678-1900* (Academy of American Franciscan History: Washington, D.C., 1951), p. 205.

[10] Petition of Lorenzo Marquez, et al for the San Miguel del Bado grant, November 1794, San Miguel del Bado grant, SG 119, Roll 24, fr. 599 (Spanish original), 627 (translation).

[11] *Conformas a una prometemos el amurallarnos en una plaza bien fortificada con baluarteles y torreones, para todos quantos en la provincía haiga desacomodados.* Petition of Lorenzo Marquez, et al for the San Miguel del Bado grant, November 1794, San Miguel del Bado grant, SG 119, Roll 24, fr. 599 (Spanish original), 627 (translation).

[12] Grant by Governor Fernando Chacón, November 26, 1794, San Miguel del Bado grant, SG 119, Roll 24, fr 600 (Spanish original), 628 (translation).

who the grantees of the San Miguel del Bado grant were. The *alcalde* notified the grantees of five conditions, hat had to be followed:
"**First.** That the tract aforesaid has to be in common.

Second. They shall have to keep themselves equipped with firearms, and bows and arrows, in which they shall be inspected ... provided that after two years ... all the arms they have must be firearms, under the penalty that all who do not comply with this requirement shall be sent out of the settlement.

Third. That the plaza they may construct shall be according as expressed in their petition.

Fourth. That to the *alcalde* ... they shall set apart a small, separate piece of these lands for him to cultivate ... without their children or successors making any objection thereto.

Fifth. That the construction of their plaza, as well as the opening of *acequias*, and all other work that may be deemed proper for the common welfare, shall be performed by the community."[13]

Finally, Alcalde Ortiz notified the grantees of the boundaries, indicating that the pastures and watering places were to be held in common, and he performed the traditional ceremony followed in all Spanish and Mexican land grants, whereby title passed from the king to the grantees. Alcalde Ortiz "led them over said lands, and they plucked up grass, cast stones, and shouted 'Long live the king!' taking possession of said land quietly and peaceably, without any objection."[14] It is likely that the grantees started digging *acequias* and building their houses as soon as the grant was made if not before, but formal allotments of land were not made until 1803.

On March 12, 1803, seven years after the grant was made, Pedro Bautista Pino, an official of the *cabildo* of Santa Fe, traveled to San Miguel del Bado to distribute "the lands under cultivation to all the individuals who occupy said settlement." Pino, whose family would become heavily involved in land speculation in the Pecos/San Miguel del Bado area,[15] measured the lands from north to south and attempted to divide them equally between the fifty-eight families then living in the community. Pino had the settlers draw lots to determine both the location of the individual tract along the ditch and the amount of land each would get. Because of the numerous *ancones* or bends in the river "measuring the total was a pain," according to Pino. Most received fifty or sixty-five *varas*, a few received between 100 and 150 *varas*, and Juan José Sandoval received 230 *varas*. This may have been the tract set aside in the granting decree for the current *alcalde*.

---

[13] Act of possession by Alcalde Antonio José Ortiz, San Miguel del Bado grant, November 26, 1794, SG 119, Roll 24, fr. 600 (Spanish original), 627-28 (translation).

[14] Los friasee por dichas tierras, arrancaron sacate, tiraron piedras y dieron voces diciendo viva el rey, tomando posesion de dichas tierras quieta y pacificamente sin contradicion alguna. Act of Possession by Alcalde Antonio José Ortiz, [San Miguel] del Bado grant, November 26, 1794, SG 119, Roll 24, fr. 600 (Spanish original), 608-616 (transcription) fr. 627-28 (translation).

[15] G. Emlen Hall, "Juan Estevan Pino, '*se les coma*': New Mexico Land Speculation in the 1820s" *NMHR* 57 (January 1982).

Additional irrigated land was set aside to be worked in common, the products of which were "to be applied annually to the payment of three masses for the benefit of the blessed souls in purgatory."[16] The allotted lands stretched from "a hill situated at the edge of the river above the mouth of the ditch which irrigates said lands [on the north], and on the south the point of the hill of the pueblo and the valley called *Temporales*." A large amount of irrigable land remained to the south, to be distributed to new settlers with the consent of the *alcalde*. After the allotments at San Miguel, Alcalde Ortiz gathered the settlers together and told them they must "erect mounds of stone on their boundaries," and they could not sell their allotted tracts for ten years from that date.[17]

San Miguel Grant survey of 1896

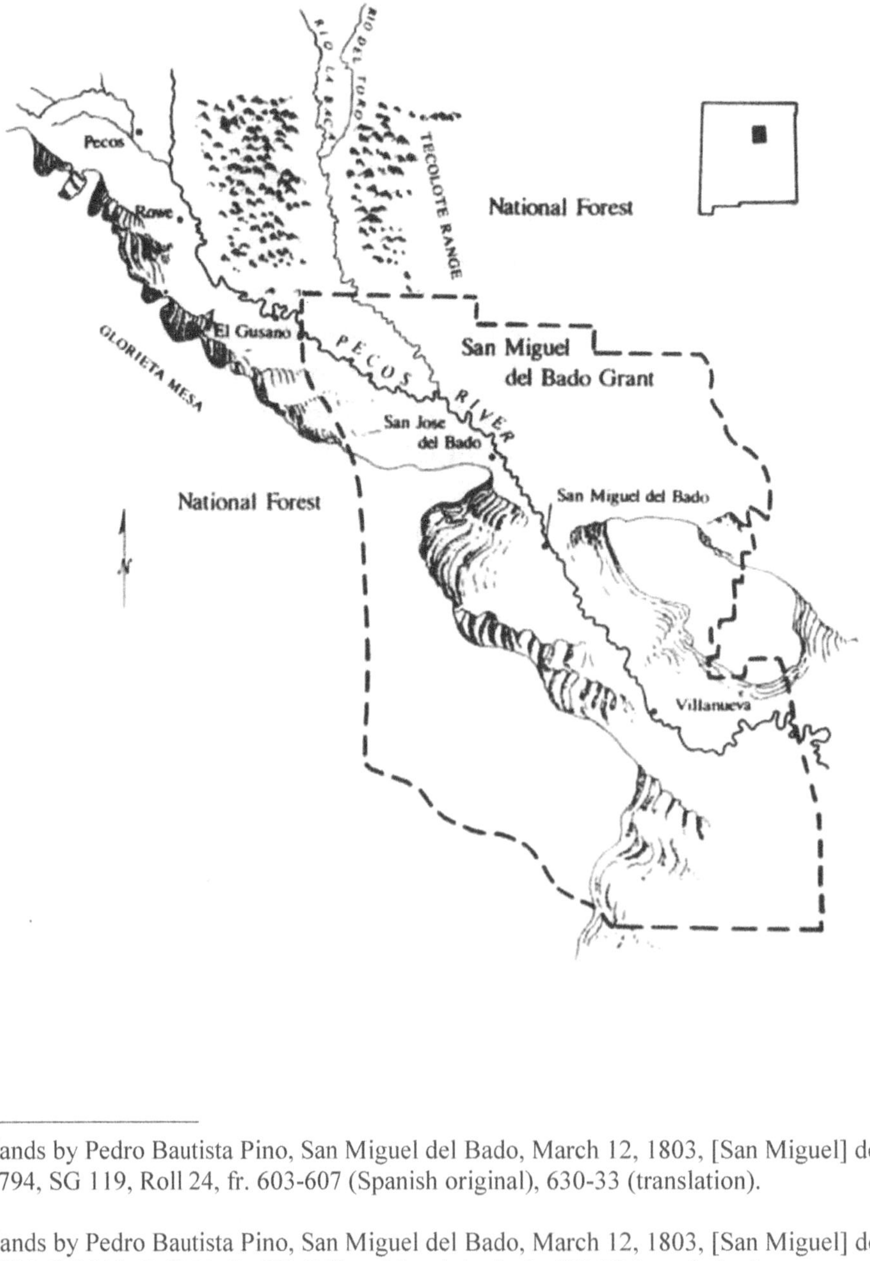

[16] Allotment of lands by Pedro Bautista Pino, San Miguel del Bado, March 12, 1803, [San Miguel] del Bado grant, November 26, 1794, SG 119, Roll 24, fr. 603-607 (Spanish original), 630-33 (translation).

[17] Allotment of lands by Pedro Bautista Pino, San Miguel del Bado, March 12, 1803, [San Miguel] del Bado grant, November 26, 1794, SG 119, Roll 24, fr. 603-7 (Spanish original), fr. 630-33 (translation).

Allotments at San José del Bado

Two days later, Pedro Bautista Pino made additional allotments of land to forty-five men and two women at the community of San José del Bado, two miles upstream from San Miguel. The procedures and conditions were similar to those at San Miguel del Vado. It appears that the settlers at San José had constructed their *acequia* but had not been living there, because Pino later said that he founded both San Miguel and San José. The even numbers (50, 100, 150, 200) of *varas* measuring the width of the tracts also indicates that Pino was establishing new boundaries rather than measuring existing ones. The following diagram of the *vara* strips at Vadito near Picuris and Peñasco show how the land was measured and allotted in most settlements, including San Miguel and San José.[18]

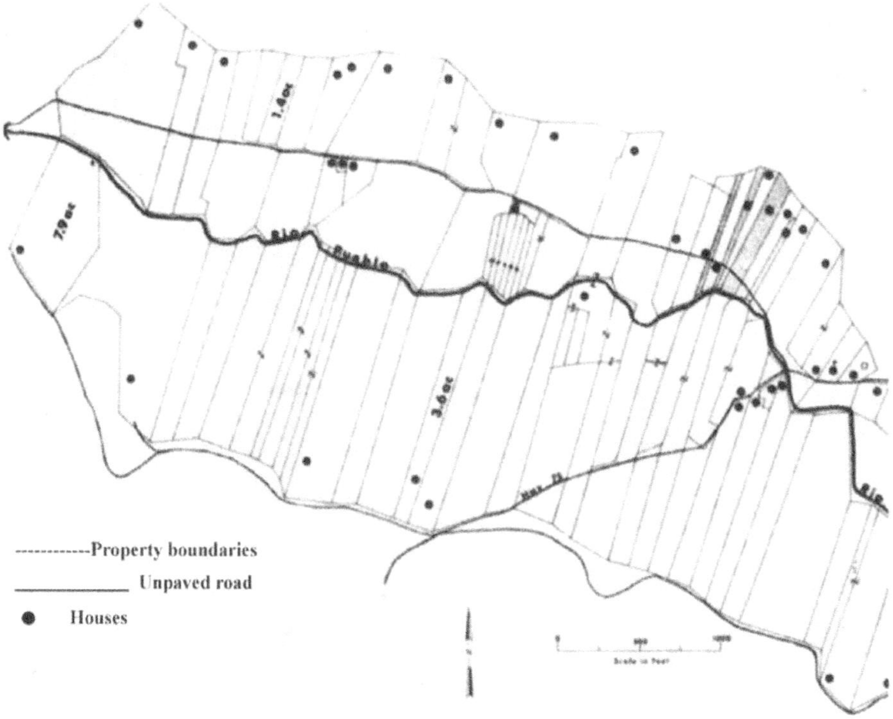

Allotment of lands at Vadito within the Picuris Grant

The measurements were usually made along the *acequia* so that the total number of varas measured would approximate the length of the *acequia*. The strips were of varying lengths, running from the river to the *acequia* and sometimes beyond. Houses and farmsteads, including barns and corrals, were usually built at the end of strip, leaving the remainder for irrigated fields. When the *vara* strips were laid out at San José, Pino had the gathered settlers draw lots to determine both for the size of the strip and its location along the *acequia*. The practice of drawing lots was typical of the ritual of the delivery of possession and allotment or *vara* strips, thus the word *suerte* (lot, drawing lots[19]) was sometimes applied to the strips themselves. The list

[18] Alvar Carlson, "El Rancho and Vadito: Spanish Settlement on Indian Lands," *El Palacio* 85 (Spring 1979): pp. 29-39, diagram at 37.

[19] *Simon and Shuster's International Spanish Dictionary* (New York: Simon and Shuster, 1973), p. 1519.

of forty-seven settlers who received allotments reveals that the first ten individuals received an average allotment of 165 *varas*, substantially more than the average of 104 *varas* for the rest of the settlers. Since many of this first group were leaders of the community, like Ygnacio Durán, who was "in charge of San José" in 1805, or José Antonio Ulibarri, a member of the important Ulibarri family and his brother, Santiago Ulibarri, it appears that they may have been put in possession first. The rest of the list is more random since Santiago Ulibarri, who would later consolidate his holdings by purchasing the tracts of other allottees, was listed near the end of the list with fifty *varas*, near his brothers, José Antonio, and José de Jesús Ulibarri. Lots may have been drawn only by the remaining settlers to determine their location along the *acequia*.[20] It was not unusual for the leaders of the community to receive larger tracts and be placed at the head of the list.

Recent surveys of allotted *vara* strips at Guadalupita show a similar pattern of strips running from the *acequia* to the river.

1910 C.H. Miller Survey - Guadalupita, New Mexico

[20] Kessell, *Kiva, Cross, and Crown*, 424; Allotment of lands at San José del Bado, March 14, 1803, and Approval by Governor Fernando Chacón, SANM I: p. 887. Santiago Ulibarri, patriarch of the Ulibarri family, would later in the 1820s and 1830s, purchase tracts of land at San José from Manuel Durán, Antonio Estrada, and Francisco Ulibarri (all allottees at San José in 1803), among others. Santiago Ulibarri became a militia captain in the Fifth Cavalry company, served in the Territorial Delegation, and was *juez de paz* of San Miguel del Bado in which capacity he made small land grants near the Las Vegas grant. Even as he was expanding his holdings and acquiring land grants by virtue of his position, in 1825 he signed a petition protesting the large land holdings of Juan Estévan Pino in the Pecos-San Miguel del Bado area. Malcolm Ebright, *Land Grants and Lawsuits in Northern New Mexico* (Albuquerque: University of New Mexico Press, 1994), pp. 189-90, 334 n. 92 and 93.

One of the best ways to visualize what the *vara* strips may have looked like is through an aerial photo. The following aerial photograph of Las Trampas shows the typical pattern of a mountain valley with *acequias* diverting water from each side of a river which runs through the center of the valley, and the *vara* strips running from the river to the *acequia*.[21]

Aerial photograph of the village of Las Trampas and surrounding lands, showing the Trampas River flowing through the center. The acequias on each side form a clear dividing line between the wooded common lands on one side and the irrigated private tracts on the other.

On March 30, 1803 Governor Fernando Chacón approved the allotments of land made at San José del Bado.[22] In his 1812 book *The Exposition on the Province of New Mexico*, Pedro Bautista Pino singled out the experience of these two distributions of land, one at San Miguel del Bado the other at San José del Bado, for special mention. He recalled that "during the administration of Señor Chacón, I was commissioned to found at El Vado de[l Rio] Pecos two settlements, and to distribute lands to more than 200 families [an exaggeration since there were about 105 families in the two settlements]. After I concluded this operation, and upon taking leave of them (having refused the fee they were going to give me for my labor), my heart, at that moment as never before, was overcome with joy. Parents and little children surrounded me, all of them expressing,

---

[21] Ebright, Land Grants and Lawsuits, p. 153.

[22] Allotment of lands at San José del Bado, March 14, 1803, and Approval by Governor Fernando Chacón, SANM I: 887.

even to the point of tears, their gratitude to me for having given them lands for their subsistence."[23]

Settlement on the San Miguel del Bado Grant

In addition to San Miguel del Bado and San José del Bado, several other settlements grew up on the San Miguel del Bado grant in the early decades of the nineteenth century. The village of Villanueva was initially called La Cuesta and though it was founded after San Miguel and San José it soon surpassed those villages in the number of baptism of children from the village as listed in the Pecos baptism books.[24] The village of La Cuesta was named after the landmark describing the eastern boundary of the San Miguel del Bado grant: "on the east La Cuesta and Los Cerritos de Bernal."[25] La Cuesta is said to have been founded in 1808 the first appearance of a baptism from La Cuesta in the Pecos baptismal books was in 1819. By 1835 La Cuesta had surpassed San Miguel and San José in the number of baptisms recorded.[26]

La Cuesta, along with El Cerrito, was the furthest village away from the political and military center of San Miguel and therefore the settlers there had to rely primarily on themselves for protection against Plains Indian attacks. La Cuesta was, like Abiquiú, Las Trampas and Truchas, a buffer community on the frontier acting as the first line of defense against Indian raids. Like the other communities in the area, it was a place where trade with Plains Indians took place, often trade in captives or *genízaros*. In the period between 1810 and 1828 four Indian captives were baptized from La Cuesta.[27]

By 1835 La Cuesta had surpassed San Miguel and San José in the number of baptisms recorded with forty-one for La Cuesta, thirty-four for San Miguel and thirty-five for San José. This trend continued for the next four years except 1836 when San Miguel exceeded Cuesta in the number of baptisms (San Miguel 31, Cuesta 23, total 161). Other communities in the 1836 baptisms include: Puertecito [Sena], El Pueblo, El Cerrito, Antón Chico, El Gusano, Las Mulas, Garambullo, Rio de la Baca, La Entranosa, Pecos, Cañon de Pecos, Los Trigos.[28] The map on page 440 of *Kiva, Cross, and Crown* by John Kessell shows the location of most of these communities strung along the Pecos River from El Cerrito on the south to Cañon de Pecos on the north, well within the Pecos League.

---

[23] Don Pedro Baptista Pino, *The Exposition on the Province of New Mexico, 1812*, Adrian Bustamante and Marc Simmons, eds. and trans. (Santa Fe and Albuquerque: El Rancho de las Golondrinas and the University of New Mexico Press, 1995) p. 7, n. 2, translation; p. 5-6, n. 2, Spanish facsimile.

[24] Archives of the Archidiocese of Santa Fe, books B-19 (Box 22) and B-20 (Box 22).

[25] Petition of Lorenzo Marquez, et al for the San Miguel del Bado grant, November 1794, San Miguel del Bado grant, SG 119, Roll 24, fr. 599 (Spanish original), 627 (translation).

[26] Robert Julyan, *The Place Names of New Mexico* (Albuquerque: University of New Mexico Press, 1996), 373 and T. M. Pearce, ed. *New Mexico Place Names: A Geographical Dictionary* (Albuquerque: University of New Mexico Press, 1965), p. 176.

[27] Levine, *Our Prayers Are in This Place*, p. 105.

[28] Levine, *Our Prayers Are in This Place*, p. 145.

1836, the year before the remaining Pecos Pueblo Indians moved to Jemez, is the last year baptisms were recorded for inhabitants from Pecos Pueblo (two) and Cañon de Pecos also recorded two baptisms. As the Pecos Pueblo members moved to Jemez, a few remained in the area. In 1849 a Pecos Indian at Jemez named "Hosta" identified as the governor of Pecos told Lieutenant James H. Simpson that of the remaining eighteen Pecos Indians fifteen were living at Jemez, one was at Cañon de Pecos, one at Santo Domingo, and one at La Cuesta. The inclusion of a Pecos Indian living at La Cuesta in 1849 shows the diverse nature of the community and probably indicates its greater preparedness for frontier defense.[29] The La Cuesta church was built around 1831 made of native stone. The church, dedicated to Our Lady of Guadalupe, still stands today.[30]

---

[29] James H. Simpson, Journal of a Military Reconnaissance from Santa Fé, New Mexico, to the Navajo Country (Philadelphia: Lippincott, Grambo, and Company, 1852); Levine, Our Prayers Are in This Place, p. 115.

[30] The license for the building of the La Cuesta (then called La Cuesta del Vado) church was issued May 18, 1831. Fray Angélico Chavez, Archives of the Archdiocese of Santa Fe, 1678-1900 (Washington, D.C.: Academy of American Franciscan History: 1957), p. 140.

Alcaldes of del Bado

When San Miguel del Bado and San Jose del Bado were handed over to the grantees, they were to form a municipal council, mayor, alderman, attorney and secretary.[31] When Congress began approving the various land grants, it was noted that the *Alcaldes* were given the right to give land to new settlers moving into the area.

List of known *Alcaldes*

1803	Don Pedro B. Piño Santa Fe, 2nd District[32]
1804	Juan Antonio Anaya Almazan[33]
1805-1808	Juan Antonio Alarí – *Teniente de justicia*, Pecos/El Vado subdistrict[34]
1809	Manuel Baca (San Jose) interm deputy justice[35]
1814	Juan Antonio Anaya – *Alcalde* of Pecos[36]
Nov 1820	Santiago Ulibarri[37]
Dec 1820	Luis Maria Cabeza de Baca[38]
Oct 1825	Tomas Sena[39]
Mar 1826	Jose Ramon Alarid
May 1832	Jose de Jesus Ulibarri[40]
Nov 1835	Vicente Rivera[41]

[31] SANM Series I, PLC 25, frame 659
[32] SANM Series I, SG 119, frames 603-604
[33] Christmas, Joe and Diane Stein Collection, folder 2
[34] Kessel, Kiva, Cross & Crown, p. 435
[35] Kessel, Kiva, Cross & Crown, p. 424
[36] Ibid, p. 441
[37] Christmas, Jose and Diane Stein Collection, folder 4
[38] Ibid, folder 5
[39] Ibid, folder 7
[40] Ibid, folder 12
[41] Ibid, folder 16

San Miguel-San Jose Church and Census Records

The first land grantees of 1803, both San Miguel del Bado and San Jose del Bado settlements, were combinations of Spanish, *genizaros*, Indians and *mestizos*. The land 'grant' did not stop in 1803 as the Governor gave the *alcaldes* of the two areas the right to grant land to new arrivals as land was available. New arrivals between 1803 and 1824 were not recorded, but references to them can be found in the 1901 enumeration of current land holders and how they acquired the land. The 1901 enumeration can only be used for clues, however, as those surveyed in 1901 tried to remember who inherited or purchased the land over a 98 year period.[42]

In the 1820 Ecclesiastical Report for Nuestra Señora de los Angeles de Pecos, there were 28 Indian men and 30 Indian women, for a total of 58. Under Spaniards and others, there were 356 men and 379 women for a total of 735. The total number of "souls" was 793.[43]

Life was not easy living in the San Miguel and San Jose del Bado area. The area was an outpost to help protect Santa Fe from Indian raids, but they did not have much of a military presence with only a few soldiers from the Santa Fe Presidio. The men from the area made up the auxiliary militia. They had to supply their own weapons and ammunition, were not trained and never paid. They fought against the Indian raids and were able to hold off the Texans in 1841 who supposedly came in peace, but were planning on making New Mexico a part of the Texas holdings. Finally, by 1842, the Second Regiment Cavalry from Mexico, was stationed in del Bado for better protection against invasions.

> "A Matter of Honor"[44]
> In October of 1843, during a dance at the home of Ramon Lopez, a young officer of the Cavalry, Manuel Garcia de Lara, murdered Antonio Moya who was from Tome, but in the area visiting relatives and friends. During the ensuing inquiries into the murder, the following people were involved in different ways.
>
> Santiago Ulibarri was the Justice at the time. Julio Garcia, age 22, a nephew of Ramon Lopez, was a witness. Nepomuceno Archuleta and Jose Miguel Sanchez examined the body and determined the cause of death which was stabbing by a saber. The parish priest, Jose Francisco Leyba, was called to attend to the deceased. Others were Manuel Sena, age 40; Miguel Geronimo Baca, age 41; Felix Montoya, age 38, a native of El Paso and living in del Bado for ten years; and finally don Damasio Salazar, captain of the auxiliary militia in Bado who was put in charge of the investigation.

---

[42]Spanish Archives of New Mexico; *San Miguel del Bado Land Grant*, Land Distribution, PLC 25, Roll 35, frame 654-1021.

[43]Kessell, *Kiva, Cross and Crown*, p. 429.

[44]Jill Mocho, *Murder and Justice in Frontier New Mexico, 1821 - 1846* (Albuquerque, NM: University of New Mexico Press, 1997), pp. 86 - 96.

The outcome of the investigation was murder, but the why was never understood except that Lara thought that Moya had insulted him by taking his chair at the dance. Lara was "held' for trial, but the outcome is unknown as those papers are missing.

One side note was made about the parish priest, Leyba, that he was not the "best example of priestly virtues." He was noted for his gambling and suspected of "enjoyed his whiskey." Leyba served the San Miguel del Bado parish from 1829 to 1832 and from 1839 to 1851.

Using the above material as well as history gives us a picture of a group of settlers who were on the front lines of New Mexico after 1800. They were an outpost to protect Santa Fe and then the first outpost the Texans came to in 1841. They witnessed the Anglos coming from the east and may have been in charge of collecting tariffs before the start of the Santa Fe Trail. They were the second community to witness Kearny's troops in New Mexico.

The Santa Fe Trail went through their communities and brought more people from the east. During the Civil War, troops were regular visitors and the San Miguel/San Jose area became the staging area for the battles of Glorieta and Pigeon Ranch in 1862. The coming of the railroad in the 1880s brought some much needed employment for the young men.

Church Records

As we look at the parish records, baptisms, marriages and burials in San Miguel del Bado, we know there are many that are incorrect. In some records, the mother's grandmother's maiden name is used instead of the mother's. In others, it appears the priest either wrote down the incorrect information to take back to write in the book and guessed the names of the principals in the record. But the godparents might also have made the mistake in giving the information. We may never know, but in the 52 years of records, from 1798 to 1850, many records have to be examined for incorrect information in baptismal or marriage record. Add to that records that were misplaced and never written into the baptismal, marriage, or burial books.

Baptisms, marriages and burials of Pecos Indians and settlers of the El Vado district:[45]

	Baptisms		Marriages		Burials	
	Pecos	El Vado	Pecos	El Vado	Pecos	El Vado
1793	5	0	2	0	9	0
1800	2	8	1	4	18	2
1805	0	14	1	12	2	11
1810	1	30	1	11	5	14
1815	0	24	0	5	3	12
1820	1	35	0	8	Not available	Not available
1825	1	176	1	40	1	97

[45]Kessell, *Kiva, Cross and Crown,* p. 420

Baptisms

Baptisms were done with only the godparents and the baby present and with the mother staying home to recuperate and the father tending to work. Most of the time, godparents were relatives and some were very distant relatives. In a few records, there is a feeling the godparents didn't even know the mother/father and didn't care what information was given. There are times when the grandparents are also given in the baptismal records, but they are sparse before 1832.

Marriages

Marriage records are usually the best for recording the parents of the bride or groom, except when the parents are given as unknown. Some marriage records are missing for San Miguel del Bado parish. Before 1853, there are quite a few marriages deduced from baptismal records of children of the couple.

Many marriages were arranged by parents and while the males may have known their brides for years, most of the time brides knew their grooms for a year or less. One statistic given for the San Miguel del Bado parish states seven out of ten women married between 1829 and 1833 had known of their groom for one year or less.

Length of Time Spouses had known each other
Before marriage in two parishes

San Miguel between 1829 and 1833[46]

	Males		Females	
	No	Percent	No	Percent
1 yr or less	16	23.8%	20	76.8%
2-3 yrs	15	22.3%	3	11.6%
4-10 yrs	28	41.8%	3	11.6%
Many years	8	12.1%	--	--

Burials

Burial records are very sparse and not every burial was recorded. The priest was not normally in attendance at burial and would bless the grave when he came to the area. One priest complained that he was not notified of a death.

---

[46] Ramon A. Gutierrez, *When Jesus Came, the Corn Mothers Went Away, Marriage, Sexuality, and Power in New Mexico, 1500-1846* (Stanford, CA: Stanford University Press, 1992), p. 236.

Census Records

The census records for 1841 and 1845 missed many people living in the area, which makes them incomplete, but still a valuable resource. The 1845 census gives Las Vegas and the surrounding area, but the San Miguel area is completely missing.

The 1850 census was done by J. D. Robinson who had no knowledge of how to spell Hispanic names and the best guess was he did not travel to each home, but got information from neighbors. Ages in some cases are off by 15 years for both the adults and the children. While age differences can be expected of many census records, they are not usually as incorrect as seen in the 1850 San Miguel County census. There are also many people are missing in the 1850 census.

This book has been put together using the church records as well as other book and archival materials. While we believe some of the people are related, we cannot prove it through any of the records researched. We tried to use census records in 1841, 1845, and 1850 and after to show if the land grantees or their children stayed in the San Jose area. According to the 1901 survey, some of the children were allotted land in the 1816-1824 period in both San Jose and San Miguel.

Other land grantees or their children were grantees of the Las Vegas land grant and Anton Chico land grant. Those lists are in the addendum.

SAN JOSE CEMETERY

Map of San Jose del Bado Settlement

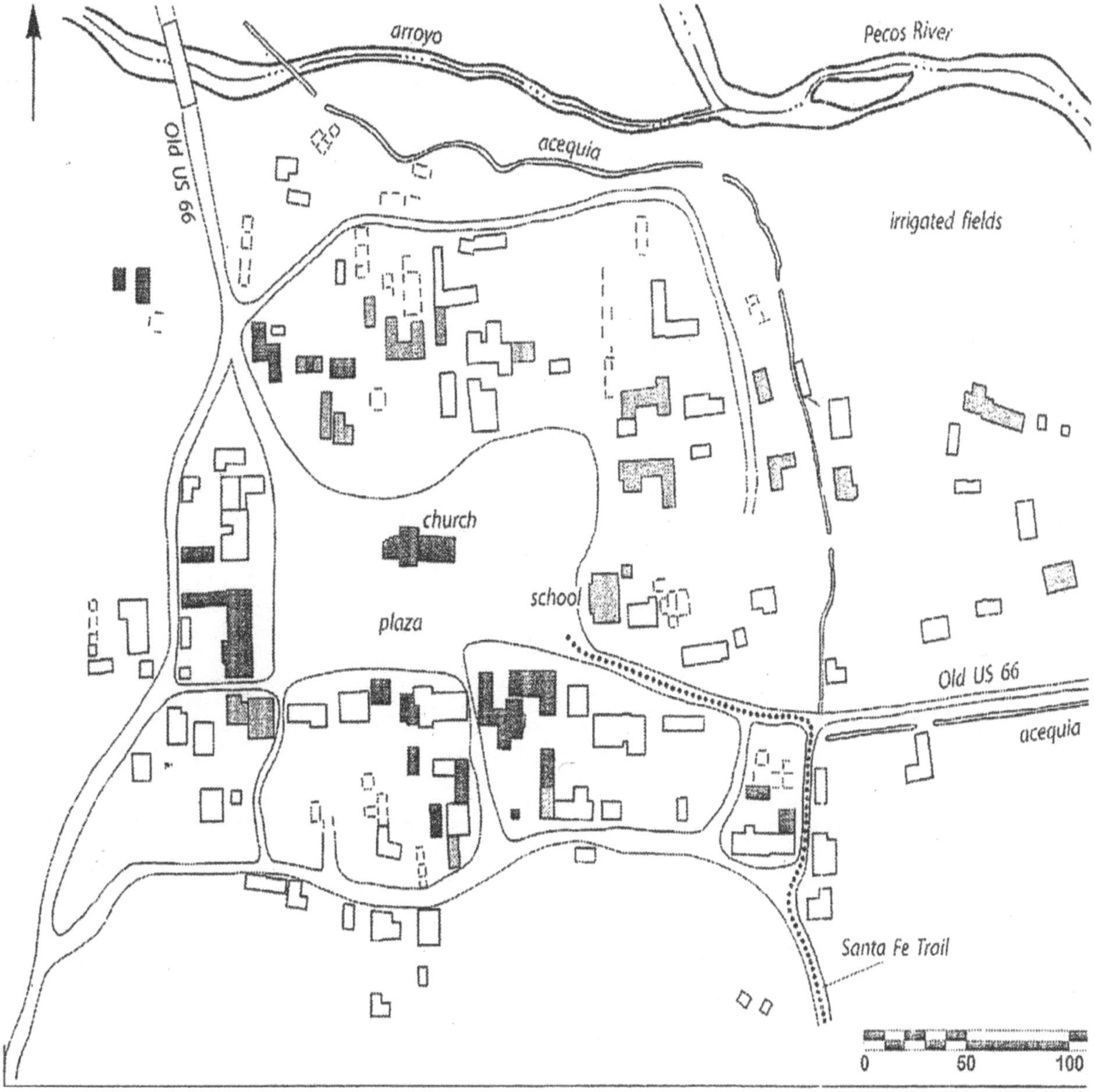

San Jose Plaza Structures

The above map was drawn for the Historic American Buildings Survey map of San Jose del Bado in 1974.[47]

---

[47]Thomas C. Windes, "A Dendrochronological Study of Nineteenth-Century San Miguel del Vado and San José del Vado in Northeastern New Mexico," *New Mexico Historical Review*, 86 (Fall 2011), p. 497.

Definitions

Acequia madre –main ditch for irrigation.

Alcalde - traditional Spanish municipal magistrate, who had both judicial and administrative functions.

Ancon - inlet of water

Color quebrado – very dark skin or part African and part Spanish

Coyote - mixture of Spanish and New Mexico Indian.[48]

Genizaro - an Indian who became a part of the Spanish community and adopted the Spanish way of life.[1]

Mestizo - a mixture of Spanish and Mexican Indian.[1]

Mulato - indicate a mixture of Spanish and Indian.[1]

Vara - unit of linear measure, equal to about 33 inches. 50 varas would equal 137.5 feet.

Parvulo/a (*parbulo/a*) – child under ten years of age

Natural daughter/son – not legitimate or no known father

Peso - Peso was a name in Hispanic America to the 8-royal coin or *real de a ocho*, a large silver coin. This *real de a ocho* or *peso* was minted in Spanish America, in the mines of Mexico and Peru. It was originally known as the "piece of eight" in English, due to the nominal value of 8 *reales*.[49]

Reales – 8 reales equal one peso

Quartilla – ¼ reale

el Teniente general – military lieutenant general

El tambor - drummer

La Castrense – military chapel in Santa Fe

Presidio –military fort

Parroquia – parish or parish church

Sala - room

---

[48] Olmsted, Virginia Langham. New Mexico Spanish and Mexican Colonial Census, 1790 * 1823 * 1845, (Albuquerque, NM: New Mexico Genealogical Society, 1975), p. 1

[49] Wikipedia, definition of peso, https://en.wikipedia.org/wiki/Peso.

Serca (*cerca*) – to live nearby

Sabania - sheet

Latas – small peeled or unpeeled poles for fencing or beams

Metate – stone used to grind wheat or corn

Retablo – alter piece

List of San Jose del Bado Grantees[50]

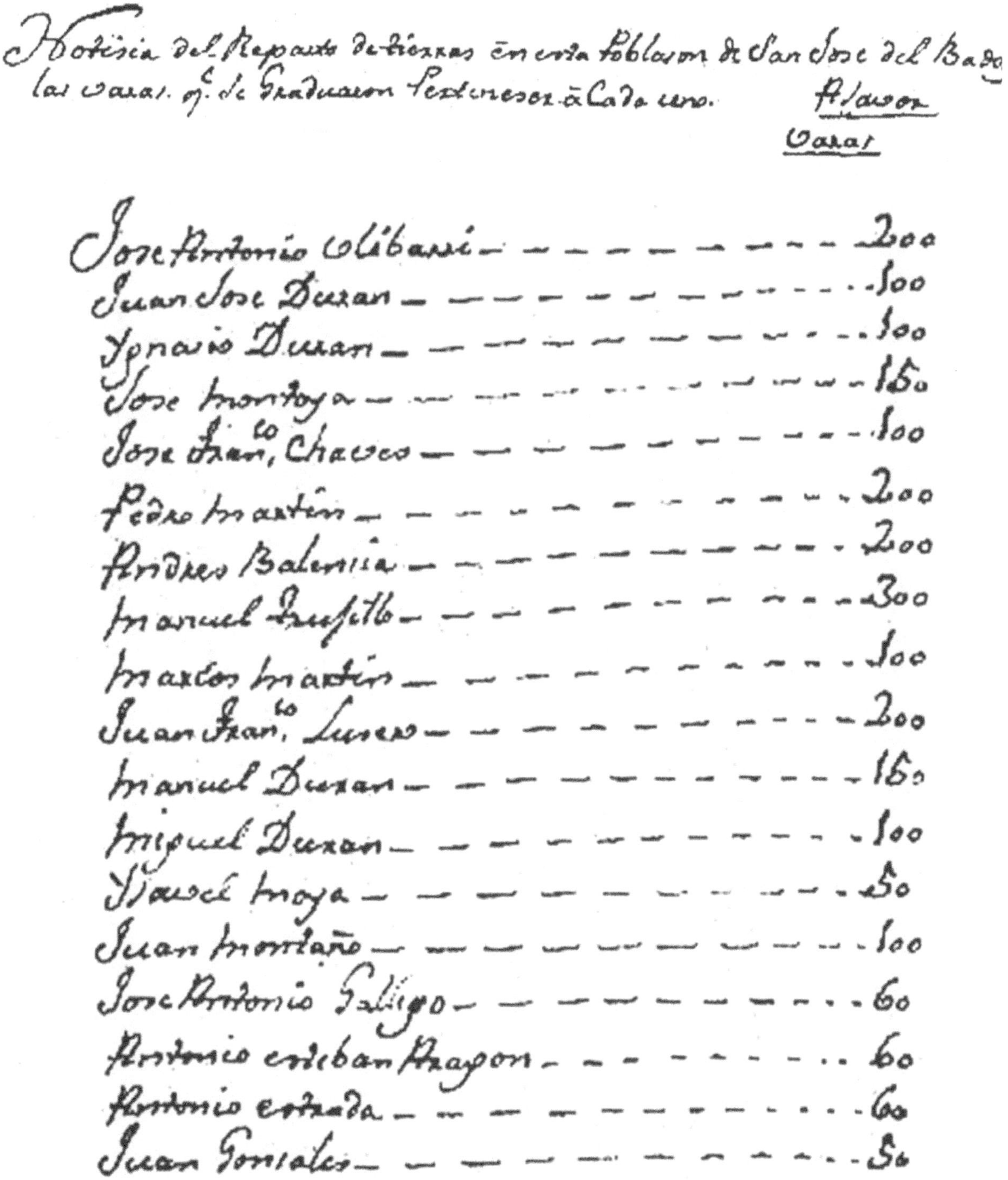

Noticia del Repartimiento de tierras en esta Poblacion de San Jose del Bado las varas q.e se Graduaron Pertenecer a Cada uno.

	Varas
Jose Antonio Olibari	200
Juan Jose Duran	100
Ygnacio Duran	100
Jose Montoya	150
Jose Fran.co Chaves	100
Pedro Martin	200
Andres Balencia	200
Manuel Trujillo	300
Marcos Martin	100
Juan Fran.co Lucero	200
Manuel Duran	150
Miguel Duran	100
Marcel Moya	50
Juan Montaño	100
Jose Antonio Gallego	60
Antonio Esteban Aragon	60
Antonio Estrada	60
Juan Gonzales	50

[50] State Archives of New Mexico, *Spanish Archives of New Mexico, Series I: San Miguel del Bado Land Grant*; TW #887; Roll 5, frames 244-247.

Ysidro Duran	50
Thoribio Gallego	125„
Alexandro Martin	100
Julian Roybal	150
Jose de Jesus Trujillo	50
Miguel Gonzales	178„
Jose Tenorio	150
Bernardo Martin	100
Santiago Apodaca	140
Nicolas Apodaca	100
Jose Juan, Lucero	150
Miguel Maese	117„
Benito Aragon	100
Thoribio Candelaria	76„
Salbador Tapia	200
Juan Christobal Tapia	126„

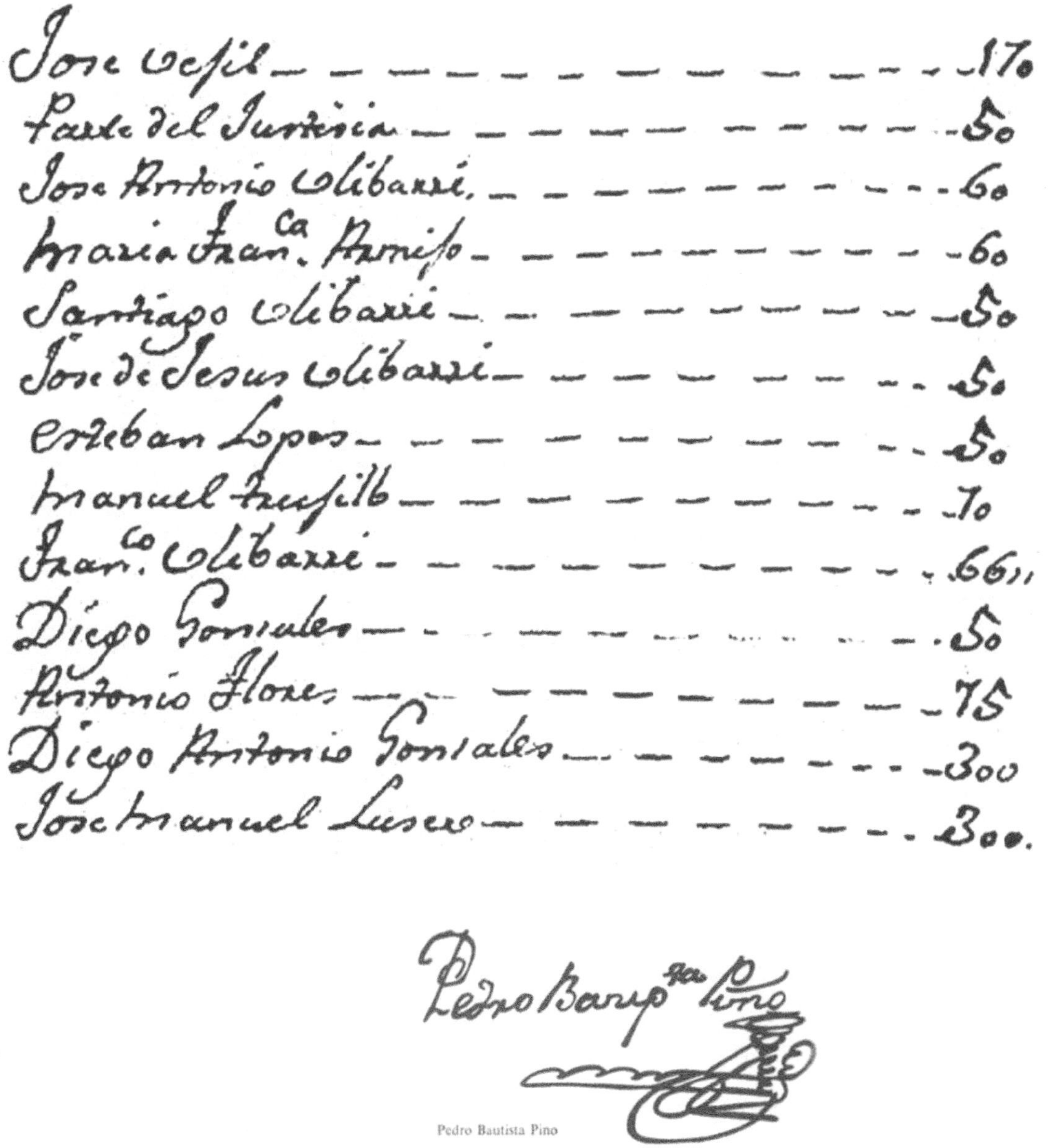

Jose Vejil	170
Parte del Justicia	50
Jose Antonio Olibarri	60
Maria Fran.ca Armijo	60
Santiago Olibarri	50
Jose de Jesus Olibarri	50
Esteban Lopes	50
Manuel Trujillo	70
Fran.co Olibarri	66"
Diego Gonsales	50
Antonio Flores	75
Diego Antonio Gonsales	300
Jose Manuel Lusero	300

Pedro Bautista Pino

Possession and distribution of the new settlement at El Bado on the Pecos River, in the year 1803.

Nicolas Apodaca

1. Nicolas Apodaca, son of Marcos Lorenzo Apodaca and Monica de Jesus Valverde, was baptized on September 10, 1753, in Santa Fe, and godparents were Nicolas Gonzales and Bernarda Casillas. (The mother of Nicolas is given as Feliciana Balverde.)[51]

Nicolas married Maria Rosa Gutierrez on October 14, 1782, in Cochiti, both Spanish. Maria Rosa was the widow of Vicente Aragon.[52]

In 1803, Nicolas was named as one of the grantees of the San Jose del Bado settlement and was allotted 100 *varas* of land.[53]

He died on May 24, 1818, in San Miguel del Bado at age 64, husband of Rosa Gutierrez.[54]

No children have been found for Nicolas Apodaca and Rosa Gutierrez, but Rosa and her first husband, Vicente Aragon, had several children, of which two sons, Antonio Estevan and Benito, were also grantees of San Jose del Bado settlement.

(See chapters on Antonio Estevan Aragon and Benito Aragon, also grantees of the San Jose del Bado settlement.)

---

[51]Margaret L. Windham and Evelyn L. Baca, compiler, *Baptisms of Santa Fe, Parroquia de San Francisco de Asis, Vol. 1, 5 September 1747 to 17 July 1791* (Albuquerque, NM: New Mexico Genealogical Society, 2002), p. 33.

[52]Luis Gilberto Padilla y Baca, *New Mexico Marriages - Pueblo Missions: San Felipe, Santa Ana, Santo Domingo y vecindario, Cochiti, Jemez* (Albuquerque, NM: Hispanic Genealogical Research Center of New Mexico, 2000), p. 23.

[53] State Archives of New Mexico, *Spanish Archives of New Mexico, Series I: San Miguel del Bado Land Grant*; TW #887; Roll 5, frames 244-247.

[54]NMGS Volunteers, compiler, *Pecos, San Miguel del Bado & Ribera Burials, 1796 - 1850* (Albuquerque, NM: New Mexico Genealogical Society, 2014), p. 16.

Jose Santiago Apodaca

1. Santiago Apodaca, son of Gregorio Apodaca and Diega Antonia Griego, married (1st) Maria Micaela Encinas.

Santiago married (2nd) Maria de la Luz Aragon, daughter of Vicente Aragon and Maria Rosa Gutierrez, on June 3, 1782, in Cochiti, both Spanish and residents of La Cañada de Cochiti.[55]

Maria de la Luz Aragon was baptized on December 1, 1767, in Cochiti; all Spanish and godparents were Santiago Saez and Maria Ysidora de Armijo, also Spanish.[56]

Maria Luz died on September 23, 1825, in Pecos at age 57.[57]

Santiago was named as one of the grantees of the San Jose del Bado settlement and was allotted 140 *varas* of land.[58]

Santiago died on December 2, 1830, in San Miguel del Bado.[59]

There were no known children of Santiago Apodaca and Maria Micaela Encinas.

Known children of Santiago Apodaca and Maria de la Luz Aragon were as follows:

i. Diego Antonio Apodaca was baptized on June 13, 1785, in Cochiti, age twelve days and godparents were Laureano Lucero and Antonia Rosa Lujan.[60]

He died on December 27, 1790, in Cochiti at age five.[61]

ii. Feliciano Lorenzo Apodaca was baptized on May 27, 1786, in Cochiti, age eight days and godparents were Francisco Bruno Apodaca and Maria Antonia Montoya.[62]

---

[55] Padilla y Baca, *New Mexico Marriages - Pueblo Missions: San Felipe, Santa Ana, Santo Domingo y vecindario, Cochiti, Jemez*, p. 22.

[56] Donald Dressen and Evelyn L. Baca, *San Buenaventura de Cochiti Church Baptisms, 1736-1873* (Albuquerque, NM: New Mexico Genealogical Society, 2000), p. 26.

[57] NMGS Volunteers, compiler, *Pecos, San Miguel del Bado & Ribera Burials, 1796 - 1850*, p. 22.

[58] State Archives of New Mexico, *Spanish Archives of New Mexico, Series I: San Miguel del Bado Land Grant*; TW #887; Roll 5, frames 244-247.

[59] NMGS Volunteers, compiler, *Pecos, San Miguel del Bado & Ribera Burials, 1796 – 1850*, p. 44.

[60] Dressen and Baca, *New Mexico Baptisms, San Buenaventura de Cochiti Church, 1736-1873*, p. 59.

[61] Christmas, *Cochiti Burials, 1776 - 1873*. AASF Roll 35: frame 428.

[62] Dressen and Baca, *New Mexico Baptisms, San Buenaventura de Cochiti Church, 1736-1873*, p. 60.

iii. Maria Manuela Apodaca was baptized on October 20, 1788, in Cochiti, age five days and godparents were Juan Jose Aragon and Maria Manuela Dominguez.[63]

Manuela died on January 3, 1791, in Cochiti at age two.[64]

iv. Maria Manuela Apodaca was baptized on February 12, 1791, in Cochiti, five days old resident of la Cañada, and godparents were Domingo Antonio Lucero and Maria Ygnacia Salas.[65]

v. Antonio Jose Apodaca was baptized on March 3, 1795, in Cochiti, age eight days and godparents were Antonio Jose Gonzales and Maria de los Reyes Gonzales.[66]

Antonio Jose married Maria Victoria Gallegos, daughter of Jose Eleuterio Gallegos and Maria Josefa Aragon.

Maria Victoria Gallegos was baptized on December 24, 1796, in San Ildefonso, born on the 16th and godparents were Andres Coca and Maria Dolores Aragon.[67]

In the 1845 Tecolote census, Jose was 28 and his wife, Vitoria Gallego, was 25. Children were Antonio Abad, 12; Maria Paula, 10; Jose Andres, 8; Maria Ynes, 6; Santiago, 4 and Maria Peregrina, 2. It is apparent that whoever took this census did not talk to someone who actually knew the ages of these people. Antonio Jose and Victoria were closer to 50; Antonio Abad was baptized in 1822; Maria Paula baptized in 1816; Maria Ynes baptized in 1820; Santiago baptized in 1831; and Maria Peregrina baptized in 1835.[68]

vi. Juana Maria Apodaca was baptized on April 28, 1797, in Cochiti, age five days and godparents were Felipe Santiago Hurtado and Juana Lorenza Baca.[69]

Juana Maria died on August 21, 1802 in Pecos at age 5.[70]

vii. Francisco Anselmo Apodaca was baptized on April 30, 1799, age eight days and godparents were Antonio Lucero and Maria Jacinta Ortega.

In later records, Francisco was called Francisco de Jesus.[71]

---

[63]Dressen and Baca, *New Mexico Baptisms, San Buenaventura de Cochiti Church, 1736-1873*, p. 66.

[64]Christmas, *Cochiti Burials, 1776-1873*, AASF Roll 35, frame 428.

[65]Dressen and Baca, *New Mexico Baptisms, San Buenaventura de Cochiti Church, 1736-1873*, p. 75.

[66]Dressen and Baca, *New Mexico Baptisms, San Buenaventura de Cochiti Church, 1736-1873*, p. 89.

[67]Nancy Anderson, *San Ildefonso Baptisms, 1726-1834*, Roll 9, p. 22B (frame 310).

[68]Virginia L. Olmsted, *New Mexico Spanish & Mexican Colonial Censuses, 1790 * 1823 * 1845.* (Albuquerque, NM: New Mexico Genealogical Society, 1975), p. 243.

[69]Dressen and Baca, *New Mexico Baptisms, San Buenaventura de Cochiti Church, 1736-1873*, p. 100.

[70]NMGS Volunteers, *Pecos, San Miguel del Bado & Ribera Burials, 1796 – 1850,* p. 4.

[71]Dressen and Baca, New Mexico Baptisms, San Buenaventura de Cochiti Church, 1736-1873, p. 109.

Francisco Anselmo married (1st) Maria de Jesus Mares, daughter of Jose Antonio Mares and Teodora Martin, on November 14, 1818, in San Miguel del Bado. Francisco was single and 24 years old. Maria de Jesus was single and 17 years old.[72]

In the 1845 Tecolote census, Francisco was 50 and his wife, Maria de Jesus, was 42. Children in the home were Concepcion (f), 15; Feliciana, 12; Jacinta, 10; Nicolasa, 9; Soledad, 7; Vitalia, 5; Altagracia, 3 and Santiago, 1. (Many of these do not match in either name or age to Francisco and Maria de Jesus's children that were baptized in San Miguel del Bado.).[73]

Enumerated in the 1860 Las Vegas census, Francisco was age 60, a laborer with real estate valued at $50. His wife, Jesus Mares, was 51. They were living next door to daughter, Maria Soledad, and her husband, Gregorio Pineda.[74]

Francisco Anselmo married (2nd) Maria Dominga de Jesus Ortega, daughter of Jose Ortega and Ana Maria Vigil, on January 11, 1862, in San Miguel del Bado. Francisco was the widower of Maria de Jesus Mares of San Jose.[75]

Maria Dominga de Jesus Ortega[76] was baptized on August 7, 1825, in Santa Fe, age three days. Godparents were Antonio Loreto Lopes and Juana Griego. (The baptismal record gives the Incorrect information on her grandmothers: paternal grandmother as Nicolasa Ortiz and maternal grandmother as Alarid.).[77]

Francisco was still alive when the 1880 Las Vegas census was enumerated. The census gives his age as 99, but he would have been 81 according to his baptismal record. The census also stated he was a laborer. Dominga was given as age 60, but would have been age 55. They are shown with two sons: Eulogio, 14 and Pablo Siriaco, age 13. No baptismal record for either boy has been found.[78]

---

[72]Luis Gilberto Padilla y Baca, *New Mexico Marriages & Marriage Investigations; San Miguel del Vado, 1802-1865* (Albuquerque, NM: Hispanic Research Center of New Mexico, ca 2000), p. 6.

[73]Olmsted, *NM Spanish & Mexican Colonial Censuses, 1790 * 1823 * 1845*, p. 242.

[74]1860 United States Federal Census, Territory of New Mexico. M653-713; Fco Apodaca; San Miguel County, Las Vegas, family #344, p. 334. Ancestry, www.ancestry.com, Provo, UT

[75]Arellanes, Windham and Baca, *San Miguel del Bado Marriages, 1829-1878*, p. 129.

[76]Ella Louise May and Virginia L. Olmsted, extractor, Margaret Leonard Windham and Evelyn Lujan Baca, compilers, *New Mexico Baptisms of Santa Fe, Parish of Saint Francis of Assisi, Vol. III, 1 January 1823 to 26 June 1833; Castrense Register, June 1798 to 26 June 1833*, (Albuquerque, NM: New Mexico Genealogical Society) p. 119.

[77]May and Olmsted, Windham and Baca, *Santa Fe Baptisms, Vol. III*, p. 119.

[78]1880 United States Federal Census, Territory of New Mexico. Roll 803; J. Francisco Apodaca; San Miguel County, Upper Las Vegas, p. 337A, ED 033. Ancestry, www.ancestry.com, Provo, UT.

viii. Pablo Antonio Apodaca was baptized on April 12, 1801, in Cochiti, age eight days, Spanish, and godparents were Pablo Antonio Montoya and Maria de la Encarnacion Montoya.[79]

Pablo Antonio married (1st) Maria del Refugio Lovato, daughter of Tomas Lovato and Maria Rosa Chavez, before May 1825.

Maria del Refugio Lovato was baptized on June 13, 1809, in Santa Fe, age two days and godparents were Alejandro Lovato and Josefa Martin, her paternal grandparents.[80]

Pablo Antonio married (2nd) Maria dela Cruz Griego, daughter of Miguel Griego and Maria Guadalupe Quintana, on November 16, 1841, in San Miguel del Bado. Pablo was the widower of Maria Refugio Lovato and Maria de la Cruz was single.[81]

When enumerated in the 1850 Tuckeleta, San Miguel County census, Pablo was listed in the household of Ignacio Sisneros and about 20 other people other than Pablo's family. Pablo was age 60, a laborer and had real estate worth $50. His wife, Cruz, was 25 and children at home were Jose Felis, 7; Miguel, 3 and Santiago, just born. His son, Jose de Jesus and his wife, Lorenza, were living with them, also. Jose was 20 and a laborer and Lorenza was 17.[82]

In the 1870 San Geronimo, San Miguel County, census, Pablo was 80 years old, a farm worker and no other information was shown. His wife, Cruz, was 45. A son was also listed, Miguel, age 25 and then Magdalena, age 4, but her relationship is unclear[83]

Santiago married (3rd) Maria Guadalupe Gallegos, daughter of Francisco Gallegos and Maria Francisca Estrada on February 11, 1830, in San Miguel del Bado. Santiago was the widower of Maria Micaela Encinas (1st marriage) and Maria de la Luz Aragon (2nd marriage). He was 50 years old when he married Maria Guadalupe, who was 29 years old and single. The marriage record gives his age as 50, but he was probably closer to 80. [84]

---

[79]Dressen and Baca, *New Mexico Baptisms, San Buenaventura de Cochiti Church, 1736-1873*, p. 118.

[80]May, Windham and Baca, compilers, *New Mexico Baptisms of Santa Fe, Parroquia de San Francisco de Asis, Vol. II, 15 August 1796 to 30 December 1822,* p. 133.

[81]Arellanes, Windham and Baca, *San Miguel del Bado Marriages, 1829-1878*, p. 31.

[82]1850 United States Federal Census, Territory of New Mexico. Roll M432-469; Pablo Apodacca; San Miguel County, Tuckeleta, family #1516, p. 78A. Ancestry, www.ancestry.com, Provo, UT.

[83]1870 United States Federal Census, Territory of New Mexico. Roll M593-895; Pablo Apodaca; San Miguel County, San Geronimo, family #78, p. 201A. Ancestry, www.ancestry.com, Provo, UT.

[84]Eloise Arellanes, Margaret L. Windham and Evelyn L. Baca, *New Mexico Marriages, San Miguel del Bado Church, 12 November 1829 to 10 November 1878* (Albuquerque, NM: New Mexico Genealogical Society, 1997), p. 1. Fr. Angelico Chavez, compiler, *New Mexico Roots Ltd., A demographic perspective from genealogical, historical and geographic data found in the Diligencias Matrimoniales or Pre-Nuptial Investigations (1678-1869) of the Archives of the Archdiocese of Santa Fe* (Santa Fe: Museum of New Mexico Press, 1982), p. 52.

There were no known children of Santiago Apodaca and Maria Guadalupe Gallegos.

San Jose

This picture shows the outline of the main plaza with the church in the middle.– Google maps[85]

[85]Google maps. Http//www.google.com/maps/ San Jose, NM.

Antonio Estevan Aragon

1. Antonio Estevan Aragon, son of Vicente Aragon and Maria Rosa Gutierrez, was born circa 1771 and married Juana Maria de los Reyes Lucero on June 13, 1791, in Cochiti, both Spanish.[86]

Antonio Estevan Aragon was named as a grantee of the San Jose del Bado settlement and was allotted 60 *varas* of land.[87]

In the 1850 San Miguel census, Antonio Estevan was 89 years old and a farmer with real estate valued at $400. His wife, Reyes, was 70 years old. Victor Aragon, age 16, was a laborer with real estate valued at $50.[88]

Juana Maria de los Reyes Lucero died on July 18, 1856, in San Miguel del Bado.[89]

Known children of Antonio Estevan Aragon and Juana Maria de los Reyes Lucero were as follows:

i. Soledad Aragon was baptized on March 18, 1792, in Cochiti, age eight days and godparents were Juan Esteban Gaona and Maria Josefa Jaramillo.[90]

Soledad married Julian Gonzales, son of Miguel Gonzales and Maria Manuela Garcia.

Enumerated in the 1850 San Miguel County census, in the community of San Miguel, Julian was 60, a farmer with real estate worth $600. His wife, Soledad, was 50. Their daughter, Maria Esquipula, was 17. They had one servant, Nicolas Ribera, age 18.[91]

Soledad died on November 12, 1851, in San Miguel del Bado at age 59.[92]

---

[86]Luis Gilberto Padilla y Baca, *New Mexico Marriages - Pueblo Missions: San Felipe, Santa Ana, Santo Domingo y vecindario, Cochiti, Jemez* (Albuquerque, NM: Hispanic Genealogical Research Center of New Mexico, 2000), p. 27.

[87]Spanish Archives of New Mexico, Series I, *San Miguel del Bado Land Grant*; TW #887; Roll 5; frames 244-247.

[88]1850 United States Federal Census, Territory of New Mexico. Roll M432-469; Anto Cest Aragon; San Miguel County, San Miguel, p. 67A; dwelling/household #1307. Ancestry, www.ancestry.com, Provo, UT.

[89]Nancy Anderson extractor, *Ribera/San Miguel del Bado Burials, 1848-1955*, AASF/FHL Film 0016879, Albuquerque Genealogy Center, Albuquerque.

[90]Dressen and Baca, *San Buenaventura de Cochiti Church Baptisms, 1736-1873*, p. 79.

[91]1850 United States Federal Census, Territory of New Mexico. Roll 432-469, Estevan Aragon; San Miguel County, San Miguel, p. 67A. Ancestry, www.ancestry.com, Provo, UT.

[92]Anderson, *San Miguel/Ribera Burials, 1848-1955*, AASF/FHL Film 0016879.

ii. Manuel Cristobal Aragon was baptized on April 5, 1795, in Cochiti, age eight days and godparents were Cristobal Lucero and Beatriz Lucero.[93]

Manuel Cristobal married Josefa Martin(ez) before December 25, 1813, when they were godparents for the son of Jose Maria Trujillo and Maria Andrea Montoya in San Miguel del Bado.

iii. Maria Agreda de Jesus Aragon was baptized on January 12, 1796, in Cochiti, age seven days and godparents were Juan Domingo Apodaca and Juana de la Cruz Jaramillo.[94]

She died January 26, 1800, in Cochiti, legitimate daughter of Antonio Esteban Aragon and Maria de los Reyes Lucero, Spanish and residents of la Cañada.[95]

iv. Jose Manuel Aragon was baptized on March 19, 1798, in Cochiti, age six days and godparents were Jose Manuel Lucero and Maria Felipa Lucero.[96]

Jose Manuel married Maria Teodora Rael, daughter of Alonzo Rael and Maria Manuela de Jesus Armijo.

Maria Teodora Rael was baptized on April 6, 1807, in Santa Fe, age two days and godparents were Antonio Jose Armijo and Guadalupe Garcia.[97]

In the 1850 San Miguel census, Jose Manuel was age 50, a farmer, and had $800 in real estate. His wife, Teodora, was 40. Others in the home were: Ignacio, 25; Ignacia, 20; 'Donno' (Donaciana), 14; Luis, 8; Ricardo, 5; and Rumaldo, just born.[98]

He died on January 30, 1853, in North San Ysidro at age 54, adult, widower of Teodora Rael. He was buried in the San Ysidro Catholic Cemetery (Manuelitas), but the date on the tombstone is given as January 1852.[99]

Teodora died on April 24, 1851, in North San Ysidro, San Miguel County, at age 44 and was buried in the San Ysidro Catholic Cemetery (Manuelitas).[100]

---

[93]Dressen and Baca, New Mexico Baptisms, San Buenaventura de Cochiti Church, 1736-1873, p. 90.

[94]Dressen and Baca, New Mexico Baptisms, San Buenaventura de Cochiti Church, 1736-1873, p. 94.

[95]Christmas. *Cochiti Burials, 1776 - 1873.* AASF Roll 35, frame 477.

[96]Dressen and Baca, New Mexico Baptisms, San Buenaventura de Cochiti Church, 1736-1873, p. 103.

[97]Ella Louise May, extractor, Margaret Leonard Windham and Evelyn Lujan Baca, compilers, *New Mexico Baptisms of Santa Fe, Parroquia de San Francisco de Asis, Vol. II, 15 August 1796 to 30 December 1822.* (Albuquerque: New Mexico Genealogical Society, 2002), p. 113.

[98]1850 United States Federal Census, Territory of New Mexico. Roll M432-469; San Miguel County, San Miguel, p. 67A. Ancestry, www.ancestry.com, Provo, UT.

[99]Anderson, *Ribera, San Miguel del Bado, Burials, 1847-1955*: p. 38,

[100]Find A Grave, online http://www.findagrave.com, http://www.findagrave.com/cgi-bin/fg.cgi?page=gr&GRid=120987154&ref=acom.

v. Maria Agreda de Jesus Aragon was baptized on October 3, 1800, in Cochiti, Spanish, age five days and godparents were Bernardino de Sena Montaño and Maria Soledad Armijo.[101]

Maria Agreda de Jesus married Pedro Antonio Gallegos, son of Pablo Gallegos and Micaela Aragon, on January 28, 1816, in San Miguel del Bado. Pedro was originally from San Ysidro. Agueda was given as Gamboa, daughter of Antonio Estevan Gamboa and Maria Reyes Lucero.[102]

vi. Antonio Lucas de Jesus Aragon married Juana Maria Dolores Roybal, daughter of Miguel Roybal and Maria Ygnacia Herrera, on February 12, 1838, in San Miguel del Bado, both from here.[103]

Lucas and family were enumerated in the 1850 San Miguel census. He was age 30 and a laborer. His wife, Juana, was 29. Others in the home, all Aragons, were: Quirna, 12; Manuel, 10; Donaciano, 8; Benito, 5; Cruz, 4; Pedro, 3 and Faustio, just born.[104]

In 1860 Pecos census, Lucas was 40 and his wife, Jesusita, was 30. Others in the home, all Aragons, were: Manuel, 18; Cruz, 10; Faustin, 6; Dominga, 4; Maria, 3 and Josefa, 1.[105]

vii. Ysidora de Jesus Aragon married Jose Antonio Leyba, son of Juan Leyba and Maria Soledad Chavez, on December 2, 1837, in San Miguel del Bado, both single.[106]

viii. Maria Ysidora Aragon married (1st) Jose Claudio Gallegos, son of Jose Maria Gallegos and Juana Hurtado.

Maria Ysidora married (2nd) Jesus Maria Romero, son of Jesus Romero and Guadalupe Moya, on December 20, 1840, in San Miguel del Bado. Jesus Maria was single and Maria Ysidora was the widow of Jose Claudio Gallegos.[107]

The census taker in 1850 listed Jesus Maria Romero in the house number just before Isidora. Jesus Maria was 40, a laborer with real estate valued at $50.

---

[101]Dressen and Baca, *New Mexico Baptisms, San Buenaventura de Cochiti Church, 1736-1873*, p. 115.

[102]Padilla y Baca, *New Mexico Marriages & Marriage Investigations; San Miguel del Vado, 1802-1865*, p. 66.

[103]Arellanes, Windham and Baca, *San Miguel del Bado Church, 12 November 1829 to 10 November 1878,* p. 17.

[104]1850 United States Federal Census, Territory of New Mexico. Roll M432-469; Lucas Aragon; San Miguel County, San Miguel, p. 71B. Ancestry, www.ancestry.com, Provo, UT.

[105]1860 United States Federal Census, Territory of New Mexico. Roll M653-713; Lucas Aragon; San Miguel County, Pecos, p. 168. Ancestry, www.ancestry.com, Provo, UT.

[106]Arellanes, Windham and Baca, *San Miguel del Bado Marriages, 1829-1878*, p. 16.

[107]Arellanes, Windham and Baca, *San Miguel del Bado Marriages, 1829-1878*, p. 28.

Maria Isidora was 39. Others in the home were: Bibiana, 7; Jose J, 2 and Matias, just born.[108]

In the 1870 El Macho, San Miguel County, census, Jesus Maria was 50, a farm laborer with real estate valued at $200 and personal estate valued at $100. Isidora was 50. Others in the home were: Biviana, 28; Matias, 19 and Noberto Romero 15; Teodoro, 8 and Benigno, 5. It is possible the last two were children of Biviana.[109]

When the 1880 Pecos census was taken, Jesus Maria was not listed. Isidora was given as head of house, age 65; son Matias was 29 and Noberto was 25.[110]

(This census combines Pecos, El Macho and San Jose in one precinct)

---

[108] 1850 United States Federal Census, Territory of New Mexico. Roll M432-469; Jesus Romero; San Miguel County, San Miguel, p. 70B. Ancestry, www.ancestry.com, Provo, UT.

[109] 1870 United States Federal Census, Territory of New Mexico. Roll M593-895; Jesus Ma Romero; San Miguel County, El Macho, p. 35B. Ancestry, www.ancestry.com, Provo, UT.

[110] 1880 United States Federal Census, Territory of New Mexico. Roll 803; Isidora Romero; San Miguel County, Pecos; family #94, p. 410B, ED 036. Ancestry, www.ancestry.com, Provo, UT.

Benito de Jesus Aragon

1. Benito de Jesus Aragon, son of Vicente Aragon and Maria Rosa Gutierrez, was baptized on July 7, 1780, in Cochiti, born on the 2nd and parents were Spanish. Godparents were Gabriel Gonzales and Maria Francisca Aragon.[111]

In 1803, Benito was named as one of the San Jose del Bado settlementees and was allotted 100 *varas* of land.[112]

Benito de Jesus married Maria Dolores Sandoval on January 6, 1805, in Santa Fe. Benito was from el Bado and Maria Dolores was from Santa Fe. Godparents were Bartolo Duran and Maria Josefa Abeyta.[113]

On the 5th of August 1805, Benito de Jesus Aragon, son of Vicente Aragon and Rosa Gutierrez of La Cañada de Cochiti, enlisted at the Presidio of Santa Fe. He was from the Plaza of San Jose del Vado and was a farmer. He was 5'5" tall, age 23, married. He had black hair and eyebrows, dark eyes, short broad nose, thin beard and dark swarthy skin. He signed by his mark.[114]

Benito was shown as a soldier of the Santa Fe Presidio in 1823. He served 17 years, 4 months and 14 days.[115]

Known children of Benito de Jesus Aragon and Maria Dolores Sandoval were as follows:

i. Juana Maria Aragon was baptized on October 3, 1805, in Santa Fe, age two days and her father was a soldier. Godparents were Bartolome Maese and Rita Alari.[116]

ii. Jose de la Cruz Aragon was baptized on September 19, 1807, in Santa Fe, age two days and his father was a soldier. Godparents were Ysidro Gutierrez and Maria Manuela Leyba.[117]

---

[111]Dressen and Baca, *San Buenaventura de Cochiti Church, 1736-1873*, p. 51.

[112] Spanish Archives of New Mexico, Series 1: *San Jose Land Grant*; TW #887; Roll 5, frames 244-249.

[113]Marie J. Roybal and Lila Armijo Pfeufer, extractors, Margaret Leonard Windham and Evelyn Lujan Baca, compilers, *New Mexico Marriages, Santa Fe - St. Francis Parish and Military Chapel of Our Lady of Light (La Castrense), 1728-1857.* (Albuquerque: New Mexico Genealogical Society, 1997), p. 124.

[114]Virginia L. Olmsted, "Spanish Enlistment Papers of New Mexico, 1732-1820," *National Genealogical Society Quarterly*, (Arlington, VA: National Genealogical Society, September 1979), Vol 67:3, p. 230.

[115]Virginia L. Olmsted, *New Mexico Spanish & Mexican Colonial Censuses, 1790 * 1823 * 1845.* (Albuquerque, NM: New Mexico Genealogical Society, 1975), p. 175.

[116]May, Olmsted, Windham and Baca, *New Mexico Baptisms of Santa Fe, Parish of Saint Francis of Assisi, Vol. III, 1 January 1823 to 26 June 1833; Castrense Register, June 1798 to 26 June 1833*, p. 19.

[117]May and Olmsted, Windham and Baca, *Santa Fe Baptisms, Vol. III*, p. 22.

iii. Maria Ygnacia Aragon was baptized on December 30, 1809, in Santa Fe, age two days and godparents were Jose Roybal and Maria Roybal.[118]

Maria Ygnacia married Pablo Martinez on April 30, 1845, in Santa Fe. Pablo was the widower of Nepomocena Garcia.[119]

iv. Jose Antonio Aragon was baptized on July 11, 1813, in Santa Fe, age four days and his father was still a soldier. Godparents were Manuel Sena and Maria Jaramillo.[120]

v. Manuela Aragon was born circa 1818 and married Ygnacio Montoya, son of Antonio Montoya and Soledad Armijo.

Ygnacio was enumerated in the 1860 census living in Cienega, Santa Fe County. He was 45 and his wife, Manuela, was 42.[121]

vi. Maria Andrea Aragon was baptized on November 30, 1818, in Santa Fe, parents unknown and placed in the home of Benito Aragon. Godparents were Manuel Sena and Maria Dolores Sandoval.[122]

She died December 4, 1818, in Santa Fe, a child placed in the home of soldier Benito Aragon.[123]

---

[118]May and Olmsted, Windham and Baca, *Santa Fe Baptisms, Vol. III*, p. 29.

[119]Roybal and Pfeufer, Windham and Baca, *Santa Fe Marriages, 1728-1857*, p. 217.

[120]May and Olmsted, Windham and Baca, *Santa Fe Baptisms, Vol. III*, p. 35.

[121]1860 United States Federal Census, Territory of New Mexico. Roll M653-714; Santa Fe County, Cienega, p. 368. Ancestry, www.ancestry.com, Provo, UT.

[122]May and Olmsted, Windham and Baca, *Santa Fe Baptisms, Vol. III*, p. 47.

[123] Henrietta M. Christmas, Jeanette Gallegos and Patricia S. Rau, compiler, *New Mexico Burials, Santa Fe - St. Francis Parish and Military Chapel of Our Lady of Light (La Castrense), 1726-1834.* (Albuquerque, NM: New Mexico Genealogical Society, 2007), p. 258.

Maria Francisca Armijo

1. Maria Francisca Armijo, daughter of Manuel Armijo and Alfonsa Lucero, married Ascencio Antonio Ulibarri, son of Captain Antonio de Ulibarri and Antonia Teresa Rael de Aguilar on June 24, 1771, in Santa Fe, and witnesses were Nerio Montoya and Francisca Abeyta.[124]

Enumerated in the 1790 Santa Fe census, Asencio was Spanish, age 50 and a farmer. His wife, Maria Francisca Armijo, was Spanish and age 36. They had three sons: 13, 12 and 7; and three daughters: 5, 3 and 1. There was one male orphan, nursing, age 3.[125]

He died on February 6, 1796, in Santa Fe, Acencio 'Urribali', adult, married to Maria Armijo.[126]

In 1803, Maria Francisca was named as one of the grantees of the San Jose del Bado settlement and was allotted 60 *varas* of land.[127]

Known children of Maria Francisca Armijo and Ascencio Antonio Ulibarri were as follows:

i. Maria Getrudes Ulibarri was baptized on April 2, 1774, in Santa Fe, Spanish and godparents were Domingo Santiestevan and Maria Manuela Gomez.[128]

Maria Getrudes married Joseph Manuel Baca, son of Juan Antonio Baca and Maria Romero, circa 1787.

Joseph Manuel Baca was baptized on January 3, 1767, in Santa Fe and godparents were Antonio Urban and Maria Francisca Garcia.[129]

Enumerated as household #475 in Santa Fe in 1790, Manuel Baca was Spanish, age 22 and a farmer. His wife, Gertrudis Ulibarri, was also Spanish, and age 16. They had one son, age 1.[130]

ii. Jose Antonio Ulibarri was baptized on November 26, 1776, in Santa Fe, Spanish, born on the 21st and godparents were Domingo Romero and Lugarda Montoya.[131]

---

[124]Roybal, Pfeufer, Windham and Baca, *New Mexico Marriages, Santa Fe - St. Francis Parish and Military Chapel of Our Lady of Light (La Castrense), 1728-1857,* p. 40.

[125] Olmsted, *New Mexico Spanish & Mexican Colonial Censuses, 1790 * 1823 * 1845*, p. 72, #462.

[126] Christmas, Gallegos and Rau, *New Mexico Burials, Santa Fe - St. Francis Parish and Military Chapel of Our Lady of Light (La Castrense), 1726-1834,* p. 137.

[127]Spanish Archives of New Mexico, Series I: *San Jose Land Grant*; TW #887; Roll 5, frames 244-249;

[128]Windham and Baca, *Baptisms of Santa Fe, Parroquia de San Francisco de Asis, Vol. 1, 5 September 1747 to 17 July 1791,* p. 177.

[129]Windham and Baca, *Santa Fe Baptisms, Vol. 1, 1747-1791*, p. 115.

[130]Olmsted, *NM Spanish & Mexican Colonial Censuses, 1790 * 1823 * 1845*, p. 73.

[131]Windham and Baca, *Santa Fe Baptisms, Vol. 1, 1747-1791*, p. 204.

(See chapter on Jose Antonio Ulibarri, also a grantee of the San Jose del Bado settlement.)

iii. Jose de Jesus Ulibarri was baptized on February 10, 1778, in Santa Fe, age one day and godparents were Antonio Jose Sandoval and Getrudis Tafoya.[132]

(See chapter on Jose de Jesus Ulibarri, also a grantee of the San Jose del Bado settlement.)

iv. Jose Vicente Ulibarri was baptized on February 13, 1780, in Santa Fe, Spanish, age two days and godparents were Antonio Armijo and his wife, Maria Josefa Dominguez.[133]

He died on January 14, 1781, in Santa Fe, Spanish, son of Antonio Ascencio Ulibarri and Maria Francisca Armijo.[134]

v. Jose Santiago Ulibarri was baptized on November 20, 1782, in Santo Domingo, Spanish, born on the 27th of October and godmother was Ana Maria Ulibarri.[135]

Jose Santiago was one of the grantees of San Jose del Bado settlement and was allotted 50 *varas*.[136]

(See chapter on Jose Santiago Ulibarri, also a grantee of the San Jose del Bado settlement.)

vi. Maria Teresa Ulibarri was baptized on October 26, 1787, in Santa Fe, age three days and godparents were Jose Miguel de la Pena and Maria Rael.[137]

Maria Teresa married Juan Estevan Lopez, son of Jose Santiago Lopez and Antonia Damiana Ortega, on October 4, 1802, in Pecos. Juan Esteban was from El Bado and Maria Teresa was from Santa Fe.[138] She died before December 1821.

(See chapter on Juan Estevan Lopez, also a grantee of the San Jose del Bado settlement.)

---

[132]Windham and Baca, *Santa Fe Baptisms, Vol. 1, 1747-1791*, p. 216.

[133]Windham and Baca, *Santa Fe Baptisms, Vol. 1, 1747-1791*, p. 230.

[134]Christmas, Gallegos and Rau, *Santa Fe Burials, 1726-1834*, p. 92.

[135] Padilla y Baca, compiler, *New Mexico Baptisms, Pueblo Missions, San Felipe, Santa Ana, Santo Domingo, Cochiti, Jemez*, p. 43.

[136]Spanish Archives of New Mexico: Series I., *San Miguel del Bado Land Grant*, TW 887, Roll 5, frame 244-247.

[137]Windham and Baca, *Santa Fe Baptisms, Vol. 1, 1747-1791*, p. 290.

[138]Padilla y Baca, *San Miguel Marriages, 1802-1865*, p. 111.

vii. Maria Francisca Ulibarri married Manuel de Jesus Duran, son of Ygnacio Duran and Maria Feliciana Sandoval, on May 10, 1805, in San Miguel del Bado. Godparents were Tedoroa Vigil and Jose Vigil.[139]

(See chapter on Manuel de Jesus Duran, also a grantee of the San Jose del Bado settlement.)

viii. Juana Maria Ulibarri was baptized on June 11, 1790, in Santa Fe, age two days and godparents were Xavier Ortiz and Josefa Tenorio.[140]

ix. Maria Marta Ulibarri was born circa 1792 and married Toribio Antonio Baca, son of Joseph 'Jose Antonio' Baca and Maria Francisca Lucero, on April 28, 1813, in Santa Fe. Godparents were Ygnacio Lucero and Maria Estefana Martin.[141]

Toribio Antonio Baca was baptized on April 17, 1786, in Santa Fe, age 2 days and godparents were Miguel Gonzales and Loreta Madrid.[142]

On the 3rd of November 1833, Toribio Baca sold 50 *varas* of land at *Ancon de Sarracino* on the *acequia madre* to his brother-in-law, Santiago Ulibarri. Nicolas Tapia and Antonio Nieto signed.[143]

In the 1850 census, the census taker messed up the numbering of the families. Toribio was shown in the family of Pablo Antonio Sena, family #1239; yet Marta Baca was shown as family #1240. Toribio was 64 and a farmer with real estate valued at $800. His wife, Marta, was age 58 and they had Fernandez, age 20 and Demasia, age 13.[144]

Toribio died on June 25, 1855, in San Miguel del Bado at age 69.[145]

In 1860, Maria Marta was living next door to one of her sons, Victorinio, when the San Jose Census was taken. She was 60 and a farmer. She had a real estate value of $800 and a personal value of $600. Also in the home was Juana Baca, age 19.[146]

---

[139] Christmas, *Galisteo Marriages, 1776 - 1828*, AASF Roll 27, frame 237.

[140] Windham and Baca, *Santa Fe Baptisms, Vol. 1, 1747-1791*, p. 317.

[141] Roybal and Pfeufer, Windham and Baca, *Santa Fe Marriages, 1728-1857*, p. 135.

[142] Windham and Baca, *Santa Fe Baptisms, Vol. 1, 1747-1791*, p. 275.

[143] Henrietta M. Christmas, *Joe & Diane Stein Collection*, Accession 1983-062; Box 1, folder 13. New Mexico State Archives, 1205 Camino Carlos Rey, Santa Fe, New Mexico 87505.

[144] 1850 United States Federal Census, Territory of New Mexico. Roll M432-469; Toribio Baca; San Miguel County, San Miguel, p. 63B, Household #1240. Ancestry, www.ancestry.com, Provo, UT.

[145] Anderson, *Ribera Burials, 1848-1956*, Roll LDS #16879.

[146] 1860 United States Federal Census, Territory of New Mexico. Roll M653-713, Marta Ulibari, San Miguel County, San Jose, p. 321. Ancestry, www.ancestry.com, Provo, UT.

Maria Marta signed a will in San Miguel County on August 17, 1860.

In the name of God all powerful...
Know ye all that I Maria Marta Ulibarri am ill in bed but of sound mind and hereby make my final will and testament.
*I was married and veiled in the Holy Catholic Church to the deceased Toribio Baca, for the time of 41 years, and in said matrimony we had ten children are - 1. Maria Juana Baca, 2. Maria Sabina Baca, 3. Jose Victorino Baca, 4. Jose Victoriano Baca, 5. Jose Tomas Baca, 6. Maria Tomasa Baca, 7. Jose Fernandes Baca, 8. Maria Francisca Baca, 9. Maria de la Cruz Baca, 10. Maria Damasia Baca; these are the legitimate children of my deceased husband Toribio Baca and myself.
*My good consist of a piece of land and house composed of a *sala*, two rooms and said *sala* one quarter; I order that it is my wish to maintain that for my daughter Maria Juana Baca.
*I declare to leave my son Victorino Baca, more of my quarter share I so declare.
*I declare to have another share in a house that they monumentally call the '*serca*' it is made up of three rooms, two are in my power and one of *latas*, and said rooms, I order that they be given to my son Fernando Baca.
*I declare to have four mattresses; I order that they be given to Maria Juana Baca. I declare that I have four bedcoverings, three milled and my woven American spreads, a *serape* I also order and give the four spreads to my daughter Maria Juana Baca and the *serape*. I also declare to have five pillows, and I order they be given to my daughter, Maria Juana Baca.
I have two large rugs used, a spoon, one iron pot used, some copper pots medium, said copper pots I give to Maria Juana Baca. I declare to have four cups and plates of china, a *metate*, one___________________________, two bottles of crystal, one large of china, three *saints de retablos* and the Holy Sacrament I leave as my goods.
*I declare to have one____, one large box without iron, some axes, one table, one small saddle, one shooter? of six caliber, one white silk, a new knife, one trashcan, two spoons of pottery, some small pans, one bath of china, a roaster of iron.
*Declare to have a piece of land without fencing, but with the documents and they call it the *Ancon de Sarrasino de Yutas*, I also declare another 50 *varas* of land, and the same piece of land, I leave.
*I declare for my daughter, Maria Juana Baca, 25 *varas* of land in the land they name in the documents- the lands of Narbais, I declare. I declare to have in the same lands of the *Serca*.
*I declare a corral made of *latas* that continues onto the house, near the fence. I declare to have three oxen, four large cows, two calves of one year, abandoned, three small lambs just born, one burro, four she goats, and I order that they return to Maria Nieves Tafoya, that of which is owed.
*I declare to have two chickens and nine chicks, one pig of three years.
*I declare to have promised with my husband and my *compadre*, Maria

Ygnacia Segura, the grinding of__, the mill below the house, and said purchase was made by some new rocks of the mill who was given to me with the consideration that I mill the overage from her house; that said mill rocks is what I order my sons to comply - I order.
*I declare to leave the good of my soul, and for that of my husband, Toribio Baca, one ox, one pig and said pig I order my executors that they use for the burial of my soul and body.
*I declare that I leave to my daughter, Maria Juana Baca, one pair of cows.
*I declare that Maria Gonsales 300 sheep that I gave her as *partido*, 81 goats *al partido* in arears.
*I declare that I owe Teodoro Baca, 20 *reales* I order they be paid. I declare I owe D. Prudencio Lopes, some four *pesos*, I order they be paid as is written in a ledger box, I declare.
*I declare that I owe Santa Rita de Bernal one visit with novenas, four candles, and I order my children that they comply.
*I declare that I owe San Antonio del Pueblo, one visit upon my death? Each one of my children who wants to take.
*I declare to leave and name as my executors and administrators Victorino Baca, second Santos Esquibel, who have the full power and faculties that they understand what my good consist of. After my debts are paid, I leave in equal parts to each of my children.
*I declare to have products of the land in the *serca*, I order that they are aggregated and divided equally amongst my children. I owe my son Fernando Baca, one cow *partida* I do declare.

This I declare is my final will with the force of my conscience and in front of witnesses. 17 August 1860. Maria Marta Ulibarri, twit/ Vicente Segura, Elauterio Martin. Territory of New Mexico, county of San Miguel, presented in the office 3 December 1860. Prudencio Lopez, Probate Judge.[147]

She died November 10, 1860, wife of deceased Jose Toribio Baca, in La Cuesta.[148]

[147]*San Miguel County, New Mexico Wills, Book A*: Maria Marta Ulibarri; New Mexico Record and Archives; Accession #1974-026; Box 16996, p. 58-64; Santa Fe, NM. Translation by Henrietta Martinez Christmas.

[148]Anderson, *Ribera & San Miguel Burials 1847-1955*, p. 75.

Toribio Candelaria Crespin

Toribio's children used either Candelaria or Crespin when baptized. But the surname of Candelaria is not found in the San Miguel del Bado Baptismal book of 1829-1844 so all the children were using the surname of Crespin.[149]

A George Antonio Toribio Crespin was baptized on the 24th of April, 1774, in Albuquerque. His parents were unknown and his godfather was Juan Antonio Crespin.[150] This <u>may be</u> Toribio Candelaria Crespin.

1. Toribio Candelaria married Maria de la Cruz Archuleta on June 18, 1793, in Albuquerque; both were coyotes and godparents were Phelipe Sanchez and his wife, not named.[151]

Toribio was a grantee of the San Jose del Bado settlement. He received 75 *varas*.[152]

Known children of Toribio Candelaria and Maria de la Cruz Archuleta were as follows:

i. Juan Christoval Candelaria (Crespin) married Maria Dominga Garcia, daughter of Juan Rafael Garcia and Cruz Duran, on November 5, 1817, in San Miguel del Bado. Maria Dominga was the widow of Jose Francisco Ulibarri. Cristoval gave his surname as Candelaria.[153]

In the 1845 Las Vegas census, Juan Crespin was given as 33 and his wife, Dominga Garcia, was 30. Children still at home were Catarina, 13 and Benito, 7. The ages are incorrect for Juan and Dominga as they have their first child by1817.[154]

ii. Maria Teodora Crespin was baptized on January 8, 1804, in Pecos; and godparents were Jose Antonio Ulibarri and Maria Rosa Garcia.[155]

149Arellanes, Lila Armijo Pfeufer and Virginia L. Olmsted, extractors, Margaret Leonard Windham and Evelyn Lujan Baca, compilers, *New Mexico Baptisms, San Miguel del Bado Church, Vol. I, 1 January 1829 ~ 12 May 1844* (Albuquerque, NM: New Mexico Genealogical Society, 1997).

150New Mexico Genealogical Society, compiler, *Albuquerque Baptisms, Archdiocese of Santa Fe, 1706 - 1850* (Albuquerque, NM: New Mexico Genealogical Society, 1983), p. 156.

151Donald Dressen and Consuelo Gooch, extractors; Margaret L. Windham and Evelyn L. Baca, compilers, *New Mexico Marriages, San Felipe de Neri Church in Albuquerque, 16 June 1726 ~ 16 January 1855* (Albuquerque, NM: New Mexico Genealogical Society, 2005), p. 55.

152Spanish Archives of New Mexico, Series I, *San Miguel del Bado Land Grant*; TW #887, frames 244-247.

153Padilla y Baca, New Mexico Marriages & Marriage Investigations; San Miguel del Vado, 1802-1865, p. 49.

154 Olmsted, *New Mexico Spanish & Mexican Colonial Censuses, 1790 * 1823 * 1845*, p. 237.

155Luis Gilberto Padilla y Baca, compiler, *New Mexico Baptisms, San Miguel del Vado, Pecos Mission, 1799 - 1829* (Albuquerque, NM: Hispanic Genealogical Research Center of New Mexico, 1999), p. 29. *Pecos, San Antonio Church Baptisms, 1726-1829*, AASF Roll 6, frame 356.

Maria Teodora married Jose Juaquin Gaurista. His name was spelled several ways when they were godparents in San Miguel del Bado between July 1833 and March 1834.

iii. Maria Manuela Crespin married Antonio Garcia, son of Juan Jose Garcia and Josefa Trujillo, on November 29, 1827, in San Miguel del Bado.[156]

Enumerated in Tecolote in 1845 were Antonio Garcia, 37; Manuela Crespin, 24; Juan Jesus Garcia, 11; Silverio, 9; Barbara, 7 and Rodrigo, 5.[157]

Antonio and Manuela were living in Las Vegas when the 1870 census was enumerated. Antonio was 65 and a farm worker with no real estate or personal estate values given. Manuela was 55.[158]

Antonio and Manuela were listed in the 1880 Las Vegas census where he was age 72 and a farmer and she was age 62.[159]

Only Manuela Crespin was listed when the 1885 New Mexico Territorial census was taken. She was age 70 and a widow living with her son-in-law, Jose Sandoval and daughter, Placida Garcia.[160]

iv. Jose Laureano Candelaria (Crespin) was baptized on July 6, 1811, in San Miguel del Bado; Spanish and godparents were Jose Antonio Flores and his wife, Maria Rosa Padilla.[161]

Jose Laureano married Maria Juana Duran, daughter of Sebastian Duran and Ysidora Gonzales, on November 12, 1833, in San Miguel del Bado, no other information given.[162]

Maria Juana Duran was baptized on May 29, 1816, in San Miguel del Bado. Godparents were Salvador Ulibarri and Maria Michela Ulibarri. [163]

---

[156]Padilla y Baca, *San Miguel Marriages, 1802-1865*, p. 74.

[157]Olmsted, *NM Spanish & Mexican Colonial Censuses, 1790 * 1823 * 1845*, p. 241.

[158] 1870 United States Federal Census, Territory of New Mexico. Roll M593-895; Antonio Garcia; San Miguel County, Las Vegas; p. 130A. Ancestry, www.ancestry.com, Provo, UT.

[159] 1880 United States Federal Census, Territory of New Mexico. Roll 803; Antonio Garcia; San Miguel County, Las Vegas; ED 032, p. 299A. Ancestry, www.ancestry.com, Provo, UT.

[160] Schedules of the New Mexico Territory Census of 1885. National Archives Microfilm, National Archives & Records Administration (NARA), Washington, DC. Series M846, Roll 4; Manuela Crespin; San Miguel County, Precinct #18; ED 26, p. 20.

[161]Padilla y Baca, *Pecos Mission Baptisms, 1799 - 1829*, p. 24.

[162]Arellanes, Windham and Baca, *San Miguel del Bado Church, 12 November 1829 to 10 November 1878*, p. 7.

[163]Padilla y Baca, *Pecos Mission Baptisms, 1799 - 1829*, p. 31.

Enumerated in the 1850 San Miguel census, Jose Crespin was 25 and a servant. His wife, Juana, was 21. Children at home were Marta, 5; Polonario, 4 and Manuel Antonio, 1.[164]

In the 1870 census, Jose Crespin is shown in the family #509. He was 48 and a servant of Jose Gonzales. His wife, Juana Duran, was shown just below in family dwelling #510. She was 30 and also a servant as was their son Polinario, age 10. Other children were Marta, age 15 and Evaristo, age 5.[165]

The ages given in the above census records are off by a number of years.

[164]1850 United States Federal Census, Territory of New Mexico. Roll M432-469; Jose Crispin; San Miguel County, San Miguel; family #1222, p. 62B. Ancestry, www.ancestry.com, Provo, UT.

[165] 1860 United States Federal Census, Territory of New Mexico. Roll M653-713; Jose Crespin; San Miguel County, Upper Vegas; family #509/510, p. 147. Ancestry, www.ancestry.com, Provo, UT.

Juan Jose Duran

1. Juan Jose Duran, son of Ygnacio Duran and Maria Feliciana Sandoval, was born circa 1771 and married Getrudis Alire, daughter of Jose Alire and Maria Polonia Baca, on December 8, 1791, in Santa Fe and godparents were Salvador Tenorio and Ana Maria Rael.[166]

Juan Jose was a grantee of the San Jose del Bado settlement and he received 100 *varas* of land.[167]

Known children of Juan Jose Duran and Getrudis Alire were as follows:

i. Jose Santiago Duran was baptized on August 1, 1802 in Pecos and godparents were Marcos Martin and Maria Manuela Moran. (Mother is given as Gertrudes Arias.).[168]

ii. Juana Josefa Duran was baptized on May 29, 1812 in Pecos and godparents were Jose Francisco Ulibarri and his wife, Maria Dominga Garcia.[169]

iii. Ana Gertrudes Duran was baptized on October 15, 1814, in San Miguel del Bado, seven days old, Spanish, and godparents were Jose Maria Trujillo and Maria Andrea Montoya.[170]

iv. Jose Francisco de Jesus Duran was baptized on May 22, 1820, in San Miguel del Bado, of San Jose, and godparents were Diego Romero and Leonarda Gonzales.[171]

v. Jose Ygnacio Duran was baptized on September 6, 1824, in San Miguel del Bado, and godparents were Jose Rafael (surname missing) and Maria Dolores Chavez.[172]

No marriages or burials were found for the children of Juan Jose Duran or Getrudis Alire in San Miguel del Bado church records.

---

[166]Roybal, Pfeufer, Windham and Baca, *New Mexico Marriages, Santa Fe - St. Francis Parish and Military Chapel of Our Lady of Light (La Castrense), 1728-1857*, p. 72.

[167]Spanish Archives of New Mexico, Series I, *San Miguel del Bado Land Grant*; TW #887, frames 244-247

[168]Padilla y Baca, *New Mexico Baptisms, San Miguel del Vado, Pecos Mission, 1799 - 1829*, p. 31. *Pecos, San Antonio Church Baptisms, 1726-1829*, AASF Roll 6, frame 463.

[169]Padilla y Baca, *Pecos Mission Baptisms, 1799 - 1829*, p. 31; *Pecos, San Antonio Church Baptisms, 1726-1829*, AASF Roll 6, frame 383.

[170]Padilla y Baca, *Pecos Mission Baptisms, 1799 - 1829*, p. 31.

[171]Padilla y Baca, *Pecos Mission Baptisms, 1799 - 1829*, p. 32.

[172]Padilla y Baca, *Pecos Mission Baptisms, 1799 - 1829*, p. 32.

Manuel de Jesus Duran

1. Manuel de Jesus Duran, son of Ygnacio Duran and Maria Feliciana Sandoval, was born circa 1783.

Manuel Duran was named in the list of grantees for the San Jose del Bado settlement and he received 170 *varas*.[173]

Manuel de Jesus married (1st) Maria Francisca Ulibarri, daughter of Ascencio Antonio Ulibarri and Maria Francisca Armijo, on May 10, 1805, in San Miguel del Bado and godparents were Teodora Vigil and Jose Vigil.[174]

On the 20th of May 1805, before the alcalde Juan Antonio Anaya Almazan, Manuel Duran sold land to Santiago Ulibarri.[175]

Manuel died on January 16, 1842, in San Miguel del Bado; adult.[176]

Known children of Manuel de Jesus Duran and Maria Francisca Ulibarri were as follows:

i. Jose Maria Duran was born circa 1806 and married (1st) Peregrina Ortiz circa 1832.

Jose Maria married (2nd) Maria Juana del Refugio Rivera, daughter of Jose Vicente Rivera and Maria Paula Padilla, on October 3, 1873, in Las Vegas, residents of Las Vegas. Both were widowed.[177]

Maria Juana del Refugio Rivera was baptized on June 12, 1836, in San Miguel del Bado, of Pueblo and godparents were Juan de Dios Maese and Maria Josefa Baca.[178]

ii. Tomasa Duran was born circa 1808 and married Rafael Castillo, son of Antonio Castillo and Micaela Esquibel, on March 9, 1824, in San Miguel del Bado. Rafael was Spanish, single and originally from Santa Fe. Both were residents.[179]

---

[173]Spanish Archives of New Mexico, Series I, *San Miguel del Bado Land Grant*; TW #887, frames 244-247.

[174]Christmas, *New Mexico Baptisms, Galisteo Marriages, 1776 - 1828*, AASF Roll 27, frame 237.

[175]Christmas, *Joe & Diane Stein Collection*, Accession 1983-062; Box 1, Folder 3.

[176]NMGS Volunteers, *Pecos, San Miguel del Bado & Ribera Burials, 1796 - 1850*, p. 90.

[177]Luis Gilberto Padilla y Baca, compiler, *New Mexico Marriages, Las Vegas, Nuestra Señora de los Dolores, January 1853 - December 1882* (Albuquerque: Hispanic Genealogical Research Center of New Mexico, 2002), p. 93.

[178]Arellanes, Pfeufer, Olmsted, Windham and Baca, *New Mexico Baptisms, San Miguel del Bado Church, Vol. I, 1 January 1829 ~ 12 May 1844*, p. 85.

[179]Padilla y Baca, *San Miguel Marriages, 1802-1865*, p. 42.

In the 1845 Las Vegas census, Rafael was 45 and his wife, Tomasa Duran, was 40. Children at home were: Juan, 15; Benina, 12; Maria Socorro, 10 and Maria Luisa, 3.[180]

Manuel de Jesus married (2nd) Maria Soledad Vigil, daughter of Antonio de los Reyes Vigil and Barbara Josefa Madrid, on December 22, 1814, in San Miguel del Bado, all residents of this jurisdiction.[181]

Known children of Manuel de Jesus Duran and Maria Soledad Vigil were as follows:

i. Jose de Jesus Duran was baptized on December 2, 1816, in San Miguel del Bado and godparents were Antonio Reyes Vigil and Barbara Madrid.[182]

Jose de Jesus married Maria Reyes Gonzales, daughter of Jose Antonio Gonzales and Josefa Trujillo, on September 5, 1840, in San Miguel del Bado; both were single.[183]

ii. Maria Dolores Duran was baptized on December 12, 1817, in San Miguel del Bado, three days old and godparents were Rafael Garcia and Josefa Vigil.[184]

iii. Candido Antonio Duran was baptized on December 14, 1818, in San Miguel del Bado and godparents were Tomas Padilla and Maria Gertrudes Vigil.[185]

iv. Maria Filomena Duran was baptized on July 13, 1821, in San Miguel del Bado, of San Jose and godparents were Juan Lucero and Estefana Martin. (The record gives the mother as Maria Mercedes Vigil).[186]

v. Jose Polonio de los Dolores Duran was baptized on April 12, 1825, in San Miguel del Bado, of San Jose and godparents were Tomas Baca and Micaela Ulibarri.[187]

Jose Polonio de los Dolores married Maria Tomasa Baca, daughter of Juan Andres Baca and Maria Gertrudes Martin, on October 30, 1849, in San Miguel del Bado; both were single.[188]

---

[180]Olmsted, *New Mexico Spanish & Mexican Colonial Censuses, 1790 * 1823 * 1845*, p. 237.

[181] Padilla y Baca, *New Mexico Marriages & Marriage Investigations; San Miguel del Vado, 1802-1865*, p. 52.

[182]Padilla y Baca, *Pecos Mission Baptisms, 1799 - 1829*, p. 31.

[183]Arellanes, Windham and Baca, *San Miguel del Bado Marriages, 1829-1878*, p. 26.

[184]Padilla y Baca, *Pecos Mission Baptisms, 1799 - 1829*, p. 31.

[185]Padilla y Baca, *Pecos Mission Baptisms, 1799 - 1829*, p. 32.

[186]Padilla y Baca, *Pecos Mission Baptisms, 1799 - 1829*, p. 32.

[187]Padilla y Baca, *Pecos Mission Baptisms, 1799 - 1829*, p. 32.

[188]Arellanes, Windham and Baca, *San Miguel del Bado Marriages, 1829-1878*, p. 79.

Maria Tomasa Baca was baptized on March 11, 1836, in San Miguel del Bado, of La Cuesta and godparents were Francisco Garcia and Maria Francisca Rael.[189]

vi. Maria Josefa de la Encarnacion Duran was baptized on October 21, 1827, in San Miguel del Bado, three days old, of San Jose and godparents were Fernando Vigil and Maria Ysabel Gallegos.[190]

Maria Josefa de la Encarnacion married Francisco Gonzales, son of Jose Maria Gonzales and Maria Francisca Trujillo, on May 26, 1847, in San Miguel del Bado, both single.[191]

vii. Jose Dolores de Jesus Duran was baptized on September 26, 1830, in San Miguel del Bado, born on the 19th and godparents were Francisco Ulibarri and Luciana Ulibarri.[192]

Manuel de Jesus married (3rd) Maria Simona Gallegos, daughter of Jose Toribio Gallegos and Maria Bernarda Baca, on August 28, 1834, in San Miguel del Bado. Manuel was age 50, widower of his 1st marriage to Francisca Ulibarri and 2nd marriage to Maria Soledad Vigil. Simona was age 39, the widow of Jose Antonio Ulibarri.[193]

Maria Simona married (1st) Jose Antonio Ulibarri, son of Ascencio Antonio Ulibarri and Maria Francisca Armijo, on December 28, 1814, in San Miguel del Bado. Jose Antonio was the widower of Maria Manuela Montoya. Both were from Santa Fe.[194]

In the 1845 Las Vegas census, Simona was 40 and a widow. Children at home were Jesus Felix Ulibarri, 18; Juan de Jesus, 12 and Francisco, 5. Juan de Jesus was probably the son of Manuel and Soledad Vigil, born 1830. Francisco, at age 5, would have been a Duran, son of Manuel.[195]

Known children of Manuel de Jesus Duran and Maria Simona Gallegos were as follows:

i. Maria Juana Duran died on April 24, 1837, in San Miguel del Bado, daughter of Manuel Duran and Simona Gallegos of San Jose.[196]

ii. Jose Francisco Duran was baptized on February 1, 1842, in San Miguel del Bado; born on the 28th of January and godparents were Felis Chaves and Filomena Duran. (The record gives the mother as Soledad Vigil, but Soledad

---

[189]Arellanes, Pfeufer and Olmsted, Windham and Baca, *San Miguel del Bado Baptisms, Vol. I, 1829-1844*, p. 79.

[190]Padilla y Baca, *Pecos Mission Baptisms, 1799 - 1829*, p. 34.

[191]Arellanes, Windham and Baca, *San Miguel del Bado Marriages, 1829-1878*, p. 60.

[192]Arellanes, Pfeufer and Olmsted, Windham and Baca, *San Miguel del Bado Baptisms, Vol. I, 1829-1844*, p. 11.

[193]Arellanes, Windham and Baca, *San Miguel del Bado Church, 12 November 1829 to 10 November 1878*, p. 5. Chavez, *New Mexico Roots Ltd., (1678-1869) of the Archives of the Archdiocese of Santa Fe*, p. 459.

[194]Padilla y Baca, *San Miguel Marriages, 1802-1865*, p. 225.

[195]Olmsted, *NM Spanish & Mexican Colonial Censuses, 1790 * 1823 * 1845*, p. 236.

[196]NMGS Volunteers, *Pecos, San Miguel del Bado, Ribera Burials, 1796-1850*, p. 62.

died before 1834. Manuel died on the 16th of January 1842. The mother should be Simona Gallegos. Simona was shown with a son named Francisco in the 1845 census that was approximately the correct age.)[197]

Part of the San Jose valley – acequia is shown as the white spots[198]

[197]Arellanes, Pfeufer and Olmsted, Windham and Baca, *San Miguel del Bado Baptisms, Vol. I, 1829-1844*, p. 178.

[198]Google Maps, https://www.google.com/maps/, San Jose, NM, north of frontage road

Ygnacio Duran

1. Ygnacio Duran, son of Juan Duran and Felipa Trujillo, was born between 1738 and 1740.

Ygnacio enlisted in the Presidio of Santa Fe on the 19th of December 1764 in place of Xavier Rodriguez. He was the son of Juan Duran and Phelipa Trujillo of Abiquiu. He was a farmer, 5'4" tall, black hair, eyebrows and beard, with swarthy skin and moles on the right side of his face and on his chin. He was 24 and signed with a mark. He was placed on the invalid roster on the 1st of March 1792.[199]

Direct descendants of Ygnacio are eligible for DAR (Daughters of the American Revolution) and SAR (Sons of the American Revolution) because of his monetary contributions to the cause.

Ygnacio married Maria Feliciana Sandoval, daughter of Andres Sandoval Martinez and Maria Marquez, on October 21, 1767 in Santa Fe and witnesses were Miguel Sandoval and Maria Guadalupe Armijo.[200]

Maria Feliciana Sandoval was baptized on September 21, 1748, in Santa Fe and godparents were *el teniente general* Bernardo Antonio Bustamante and *doña* Feliciana Coca.[201]

In the 1790 Presidio of Santa Fe census, Ygnacio was called "Tomasio" and was Spanish, born in New Mexico and age 52. His wife, Feliciana Sandoval, was 34. They had three sons: 19, 17 and 7, plus four daughters: 15, 13, 5 and 3.[202]

Ygnacio was named as a grantee of San Jose del Bado settlement and he received 100 *varas* of land.

"In the summer of 1805, Manuel Baca, interim deputy justice of the district, ordered Ignacio Duran, in charge at San Jose, to beat the drum for the people to come work on the church. Another San Jose grantee, Reyes Vigil, and his sons, refused. Words were exchanged with Reyes telling Ignacio that he could "eat shit, eat a bucket of shit"!" Ignacio paid a call on Reyes and in his corral they got into a "name-calling, rock-throwing, hair-pulling brawl." This record is incomplete and does not tell what happened afterwards.[203]

Ygnacio died after May of 1811 in San Jose.

---

[199]Virginia L. Olmsted, "Spanish Enlistment Papers of New Mexico, 1732-1820," *National Genealogical Society Quarterly* Vol 67:3 (September 1979): p. 234.

[200]Roybal, Pfeufer, Windham and Baca, *New Mexico Marriages, Santa Fe - St. Francis Parish and Military Chapel of Our Lady of Light (La Castrense), 1728-1857*, p. 37.

[201]Windham and Baca, *Baptisms of Santa Fe, Parroquia de San Francisco de Asis, Vol. 1, 5 September 1747 to 17 July 1791*, p. 6.

[202]Olmsted, compiler, *Spanish and Mexican Censuses of New Mexico, 1750 to 1830*, p. 103, #27.

[203]Kessell, *Kiva, Cross and Crown*, p. 424.

Maria Feliciana died on May 26, 1811, in Pecos at age 62, both residents of the plaza of San Jose.[204]

Known children of Ygnacio Duran and Maria Feliciana Sandoval were as follows:

i. Juan Jose Duran married Getrudis Alire, daughter of Jose Alire and Maria Polonia Baca, on December 8, 1791, in Santa Fe and godparents were Salvador Tenorio and Ana Maria Rael.[205]

(See the chapter for Juan Jose Duran, also a grantee of the San Jose del Bado settlement.)

ii. Maria Manuela Duran was baptized on November 28, 1775, in Santa Fe, born on the 23rd and godparents were Joseph Mariano Martin and Maria Josepha Sandoval.[206] (See note at end of document)

iii. Antonio Encarnacion Duran was a grantee of the San Miguel del Bado settlement.[207] (See list of San Miguel del Bado land grantees in Addendum.)[208]

Antonio Encarnacion married Maria Gertrudes Lopez on December 6, 1797, in Santa Fe. Witnesses were the sacristans, not named.[209]

He died on September 2, 1807, in Pecos, son of Ygnacio Duran and married to Gertrudis Lopez, residents of the plaza de San Miguel.[210]

Maria Gertrudes married (2nd) Jose Antonio Padilla on January 2, 1811, in San Miguel del Bado. Jose Antonio was originally from the plaza of Los Padillas. Maria Gertrudes was the widow of Antonio Duran and originally from Santa Fe.[211]

iv. Maria Ygnacia Duran was baptized on November 5, 1778, in Santa Fe, age three days and godparents were Juan Miguel Tafoya and Maria Dolores Tafoya, siblings.[212]

v. Manuel Duran married (1st) Maria Francisca Ulibarri.

---

204 Christmas, *New Mexico Burials, Pecos Mission, 1798 - 1829*, AASF Roll 35, frame 708.

205 Roybal and Pfeufer, Windham and Baca, *Santa Fe Marriages, 1728-1857*, p. 72.

206 Windham and Baca, *Santa Fe Baptisms, Vol. 1, 1747-1791*, p. 190.

207 Spanish Archives of New Mexico, Series I, Roll 24, Surveyor General 119, *Land Grant Records for San Miguel del Bado*, frame 595-741.

208 Henrietta Martinez Christmas and Nancy Anderson, *The San Miguel del Bado del Rio de Pecos - The 1803 Land Grantees* (Albuquerque, NM: New Mexico Genealogical Society, 2015), p. 101.

209 Roybal and Pfeufer, Windham and Baca, *Santa Fe Marriages, 1728-1857*, p. 115.

210 Christmas, *New Mexico Burials, Pecos Mission, 1798 - 1829*, frame 704, p. 17.

211 Padilla y Baca, *New Mexico Marriages & Marriage Investigations; San Miguel del Vado, 1802-1865*, p. 169.

212 Windham and Baca, *Santa Fe Baptisms, Vol. 1, 1747-1791*, p. 224.

(See the chapter on Manuel de Jesus Duran, also a grantee of the San Jose del Bado settlement.).

vi. Juan de Jesus Duran died on January 6, 1788, in Santa Fe, child of Ygnacio Duran and Feliciana Sandoval.[213]

vii. Sebastian Duran was born circa 1795 and married Ysidora Gonzales, daughter of Juan Miguel Gonzales and Maria Manuela Gomez.

In the 1845 Plaza de Ariva (San Miguel) census, Sebastian Duran was 50 and his wife, Ysidora 'Garcia,' was 30. Children at home were Manuel, 20; Francisca, 18; Ysidro, 10 and Maria Soledad, 8.[214]

NOTE: Child #2 - Maria Manuela Duran was given as a mother in one baptismal record in San Miguel del Bado. The record of September 21, 1834, shows Jose Guadalupe Archuleta married to Manuela Duran and names the paternal grandparents as Jose de la Cruz Archuleta and Maria Soledad Segura and maternal grandparents as Ygnacio Duran and Feliciana Sandoval.[215]

Yet a further study of records for Jose Guadalupe Archuleta shows he married Maria Soledad Segura and had 7 children with her from 1825 to 1837. Maria Soledad Segura died in San Miguel del Bado April 19, 1837, wife of Guadalupe Archuleta of San Jose.[216]

Jose Guadalupe's parents were Jose de la Cruz Archuleta and Maria Manuela Angel (Moya).

Jose Guadalupe Archuleta, widower of Soledad Segura, married Maria de la Asencion Ortiz in Santa Fe on March 20, 1842.[217]

There was no other Guadalupe Archuleta in the San Miguel del Bado Baptismal records and no further records with Manuela Duran from 1829 to 1844. The record of 1834 was a mistake listing Manuela Duran as the mother. The mother have been Soledad Segura and paternal grandmother, Manuela Angel or Moya.

---

[213]Christmas, Gallegos and Rau, *New Mexico Burials, Santa Fe - St. Francis Parish and Military Chapel of Our Lady of Light (La Castrense), 1726-1834*, p. 229.

[214]Olmsted, *NM Spanish & Mexican Colonial Censuses, 1790 * 1823 * 1845*, p. 239.

[215] Windham; Baca; Arellanes; Pfeufer and Olmsted, *San Miguel Baptisms, Vol. 1*, (Albuquerque, NM: New Mexico Genealogical Society, 1997), p. 57

[216] New Mexico Volunteers; *Pecos, San Miguel del Bado, Ribera Burials, 1796-1850,* p. 61.

[217] Roybal and Pfeufer, Windham and Baca, *Santa Fe Marriages, 1728-1857*, p. 205.

Ysidro Duran

1. Ysidro Duran was born circa 1756 and married Maria Manuela Quintana on July 28, 1782, in Santa Fe. The bride was called "Ana Maria" and godparents were Ysidro Sandoval and Josefa Ortiz.[218]

In the 1790 Santa Fe census, living in household #402, Ysidro was Spanish, age 34 and a laborer. His wife, Manuela Quintana, was Spanish and age 22. They had two sons: 15 and 4; and one daughter, 6.[219]

In 1803, Ysidro was named as a grantee of the San Jose del Bado settlement and was allotted 50 *varas* of land.[220]

Known children of Ysidro Duran and Maria Manuela Quintana were as follows:

i. Maria Feliciana Duran was baptized on January 10, 1784, in Santa Fe, born on the 8th and godparents were the soldier Bartolo Martinez and his wife, Maria Josefa Trujillo.[221]

ii. Maria Josefa de Jesus Duran was baptized on February 20, 1788, in Santa Fe, born "last night" and godparents were Jose Sandoval and Maria Barbara Velarde.[222]

Maria Josefa died on January 5, 1789, in Santa Fe.[223]

iii. Jose Rafael Duran was baptized on December 3, 1790, in Santa Fe and godparents were Salvador Tenorio and Ana Maria Rael.[224]

Rafael married Maria Dolores Ulibarri, daughter of Francisco Ulibarri and Maria Antonia Vigil.

---

[218]Roybal, Pfeufer, Windham and Baca, *New Mexico Marriages, Santa Fe - St. Francis Parish and Military Chapel of Our Lady of Light (La Castrense), 1728-1857*, p. 57.

[219]Olmsted, *New Mexico Spanish & Mexican Colonial Censuses, 1790 * 1823 * 1845*, p. 69, #410.

[220]Spanish Archives of New Mexico, Series I, *San Miguel del Bado Land Grant*; TW #887; Roll 5, frames 244-249.

[221]Windham and Baca, *Baptisms of Santa Fe, Parroquia de San Francisco de Asis, Vol. 1, 5 September 1747 to 17 July 1791,* p. 253.

[222]Windham and Baca, *Santa Fe Baptisms, Vol. 1, 1747-1791*, p. 292.

[223]Christmas, Gallegos and Rau, compiler, *New Mexico Burials, Santa Fe - St. Francis Parish and Military Chapel of Our Lady of Light (La Castrense), 1726-1834*, p. 114.

[224]Windham and Baca, *Santa Fe Baptisms, Vol. 1, 1747-1791*, p. 319.

In the 1845 Las Vegas census, Rafael Duran was 55 and his wife, Dolores Ulibarri, was 45. Children at home were: Gregoria, 15; Jesus Guadalupe, 12; Juan Jose, 10 and Manuel Antonio, 5.[225]

Rafael was back in La Cuesta when the 1850 census was taken. He was age 50; and no occupation given. His wife, 'D', was also 50. Children at home were: Jose G., 18; Juan, 14; and Jose Serapio, 12.[226]

iv. Sebastian Duran married (1st) Maria Rosa Aragon, daughter of Santiago de Jesus Aragon and Maria Matiana Salas.

Maria Rosa Aragon was baptized on July 9, 1807, in San Miguel del Bado and godparents were Antonio Apodaca and Rosa Padilla.[227]

In the 1841 San Miguel census, Sebastian was 50 and his wife, Maria Rosa Aragon, was 30. Children were: Catarina, 16; Juan Rafael, 10; Juan Antonio, 8; Jose Casimiro, 5 and Jose Lino, 3.[228]

In the 1850 La Cuesta census, Sebastian was shown as age 50, a laborer with real estate valued at $50. Three of his sons were living with him: Rafael, 20; Juan Antonio, 16 and Jose Lino, 12.[229]

Sebastian married (2nd) Maria Victoria Padilla, daughter of Santiago Padilla and Andrea Herrera, on August 31, 1864, in San Miguel del Bado. Sebastian was the widower of Rosa Aragon. Victoria was the widow of Manuel Garduño. Both the groom and the bride were from La Cuesta.[230]

Maria Victoria Padilla was baptized on March 31, 1802, in Santa Fe, born on the 22nd and godparents were Jose Pablo Brito and Maria Dolores Gauna, all Spanish.[231]

v. Maria Teodora Duran married (1st) Jose Antonio Mares, son of Estevan Mares and Maria Paula Garcia, on April 20, 1816, in San Miguel del Bado. Jose

---

[225]Olmsted, *NM Spanish & Mexican Colonial Censuses, 1790 * 1823 * 1845*, p. 236.

[226] 1850 United States Federal Census, Territory of New Mexico. Roll M432-469; Rafel Duran; San Miguel County, La Cuesta; family #616, p. 31B. Ancestry, www.ancestry.com, Provo, UT.

[227]Padilla y Baca, compiler, *New Mexico Baptisms, San Miguel del Vado, Pecos Mission, 1799 – 1829,* p. 6.

[228]Christmas, Tafoya and Olguin, *New Mexico Censuses, 1790, 1793, 1803, 1823, 1829, 1841*, p. 118.

[229]1850 United States Federal Census, Territory of New Mexico. Roll: M432-469; Juan S. Duran; San Miguel County, La Cuesta; family #855, p. 44A. Ancestry, www.ancestry.com, Provo, UT.

[230]Arellanes, Windham and Baca, *San Miguel del Bado Church, 12 November 1829 to 10 November 1878*, p. 135.

[231]May, Windham and Baca, *New Mexico Baptisms of Santa Fe, Parroquia de San Francisco de Asis, Vol. II, 15 August 1796 to 30 December 1822*, p. 65.

Antonio was the widower of Maria Teodora Martin and originally from Santa Fe. Teodora Duran was originally from the Mission of Tesuque.[232]

Jose Antonio died on June 7, 1830, in San Miguel del Bado.[233]

Maria Teodora married (2nd) Juan Pedro Archuleta, son of Jose Pedro Archuleta and Maria de la Encarnacion Sanchez, on March 16, 1835, in San Miguel del Bado. Juan Pedro was the widower of (1st) Maria Antonia Manzanares; (2nd) Soledad Tafoya; and (3rd) Maria Diega Blea. Maria Teodora was the widow of Jose Antonio Mares.[234]

In the 1845 Las Vegas census, Juan Pedro was 60 and his wife, Teodora Duran, was 55. The children at home were: Benito (Mares), 20; Antonio Aban (Mares), 18; Luciano (Archuleta), 14; Jesus de la Cruz (Archuleta), 12 and Maria del Socorro (Archuleta), 5.[235] Benito and Antonio Aban were children of Teodora's first marriage to Jose Antonio Mares. Luciano and Jose de la Cruz were children of Juan Pedro's marriage to Maria Diega Blea.

[232]Padilla y Baca, *New Mexico Marriages & Marriage Investigations; San Miguel del Vado, 1802-1865,* p. 126.

[233]Christmas, *San Miguel del Bado Burials, 1829-1833*, AASF/FHL Film 0017002, frame 178.

[234]Arellanes, Windham and Baca, *San Miguel del Bado Marriages, 1829-1878*, p. 11.

[235]Olmsted, *NM Spanish & Mexican Colonial Censuses, 1790 * 1823 * 1845*, p. 237.

Antonio Maria Estrada

1. Antonio Maria Estrada, son of Pedro Antonio Estrada and Maria Guadalupe Coriz, was born circa 1771 and married Maria de la Encarnacion Garduño, daughter of Cristobal Garduño and Maria Ignacia Trujillo, on February 3, 1791, in Cochiti, both Spanish and from this jurisdiction.[236]

Antonio was one of the grantees of the San Jose del Bado settlement and was allotted 60 *varas* of land.[237]

On the 19th of October 1825, in San Jose del Bado, Antonio sold land to Santiago Ulibarri at *Ancon de Sarracino*, land from a land grant, for a pair of hoop earrings made of solid silver, five *varas* each of *sabania* (woven yardage), a *quartilla* of wheat. Signed by Tomas Sena, alcalde.[238]

He died on October 26, 1826, in San Miguel del Bado, widower of Maria Garduño of Cuesta.[239]

Maria de la Encarnacion Garduño died before January 1830.

Known children of Antonio Maria Estrada and Maria de la Encarnacion Garduño were as follows:

i. Juan Andres Estrada was baptized on January 6, 1796, in Cochiti, age four days, of Rancho and godparents were Tomas Manuel Montoya and Maria Barbara Montoya.[240]

Juan Andres married (1st) Maria Guadalupe Mondragon, daughter of Antonio Mondragon and Maria Micaela Sanchez, on April 28, 1817, in San Miguel del Bado. Juan Andres was originally from La Peña Blanca and Maria Guadalupe was originally from Santa Fe.[241]

In the 1841 San Miguel census, Juan Andres was 41 and his wife, Guadalupe Mondragon, was 26. Children were Pascuala, 18; Maria Josefa, 15; Rita, 11; Pedro, 8 and Jose Lauriano, 4.[242]

---

236 Padilla y Baca, *New Mexico Marriages - Pueblo Missions: San Felipe, Santa Ana, Santo Domingo y vecindario, Cochiti, Jemez*, p. 26.

237 Spanish Archives of New Mexico, Series I, *San Miguel del Bado Land Grant*; TW #887; Roll 45, frame 244-249.

238 Christmas, *Joe & Diane Stein Collection*, Accession 1983-062; Box 1, folder 7.

239 NMGS Volunteers, *Pecos, San Miguel del Bado & Ribera Burials, 1796 - 1850*, p. 32.

240 Dressen and Baca, *San Buenaventura de Cochiti Church Baptisms, 1736-1873*, p. 94.

241 Padilla y Baca, *New Mexico Marriages & Marriage Investigations; San Miguel del Vado, 1802-1865*, p. 61.

242 Christmas, Tafoya and Olguin, *New Mexico Censuses, 1790, 1793, 1803, 1823, 1829, 1841*, p. 120.

In the 1850 La Cuesta, San Miguel County census, Andres was 51 and a farmer with real estate valued at $100. His wife, Guadalupe, was 40. There were two children in the home: Maria, age 9 and Laureano, age 14.[243]

Juan Andres married (2nd) Maria Ramona Lucero, daughter of Jose Miguel Lucero and Maria Angela Gonzales, on March 13, 1853, in San Miguel del Bado: Juan Andres, about 54, widower of Guadalupe Mondragon with Maria Ramona Lucero, widow of Juan Baca.[244]

Maria Ramona married (1st) Juan de Jesus Baca, son of Ramon Baca and Maria Alfonsa Martin, on April 29, 1826, in San Miguel del Bado; both single.[245]

ii. Maria de Loreto Estrada was baptized on March 13, 1805, in San Miguel del Bado, Spanish and godparents were Tomas Padilla and Maria Rosa (no surname).[246]

iii. Miguel Estrada was born circa 1810 and married (1st) Barbara Anaya, daughter of Pedro Anaya and Barbara Garcia, on January 13, 1830, in San Miguel del Bado, both single.[247]

Barbara Anaya died on November 17, 1839, in San Miguel del Bado; (The record gave husband as Miguel Encinias.).[248]

Miguel married (2nd) Maria Anastacia Muñiz on February 6, 1842, in San Miguel del Bado. Miguel was the widower of Barbara Anaya and Maria Anastacia was the widow of her 1st marriage to Rafael Carabajal and her 2nd marriage to Juan Domingo Ortiz.[249]

In the 1841 San Miguel census, Anastasia was a widow, age 31.[250]

In the 1850 La Cuesta, San Miguel County, census, Miguel was 45 and a laborer with real estate valued at $50. His daughter, Josefa, was 22.[251]

He died on October 5, 1863, in Anton Chico.

---

[243] 1850 United States Federal Census, Territory of New Mexico. Roll M432-469; Andres Estrada; San Miguel County, La Cuesta, p. 27A. Ancestry, www.ancestry.com. Provo, UT.

[244] Arellanes, Windham and Baca, *San Miguel del Bado Church, 12 November 1829 to 10 November 1878*, p. 99.

[245] Padilla y Baca, *San Miguel Marriages, 1802-1865*, p. 23.

[246] Padilla y Baca, *New Mexico Baptisms, San Miguel del Vado, Pecos Mission, 1799 - 1829*, p. 37.

[247] Arellanes, Windham and Baca, *San Miguel del Bado Marriages, 1829-1878*, p. 1.

[248] NMGS Volunteers, *Pecos, San Miguel del Bado, Ribera Burials, 1796-1850*, p. 75.

[249] Arellanes, Windham and Baca, *San Miguel del Bado Marriages, 1829-1878*, p. 33.

[250] Christmas, Tafoya and Olguin, *NM Census, 1790, 1793, 1803, 1823, 1829, 1841*, p. 106.

[251] 1850 United States Federal Census, Territory of New Mexico. Roll M432-469; San Miguel County, La Cuesta, p. 20B. Ancestry, www.ancestry.com, Provo, UT.

iv. Maria Eulogia Estrada was baptized on February 16, 1812, in San Miguel del Bado and godmother was Teodora Marquez.[252]

San Jose Cemetery – east of San Jose on County Road B41C[253]

[252]Padilla y Baca, *Pecos Mission Baptisms, 1799 - 1829*, p. 38.

[253]Google Maps. Http//www.google.com/maps/. San Jose, NM

Jose Antonio Flores

1. Jose Antonio Flores was born circa 1760 and married Maria Rosa Padilla circa 1780.

In 1803, Jose Antonio was named as a grantee of the San Jose del Bado settlement and was allotted 75 *varas* of land.[254]

Maria Rosa Padilla died on March 17, 1835, in San Miguel del Bado, married to Antonio 'Torres (Flores).'[255]

Antonio was enumerated in the 1841 San Miguel census. He was a widower and age 75.[256]

He died on July 26, 1842, in San Miguel del Bado.[257]

Known children of Jose Antonio Flores and Maria Rosa Padilla were as follows:

i. Jose Candelario Flores was born circa 1782 and married Maria Luisa Padilla, daughter of Santiago Padilla and Andrea Herrera, on November 14, 1818, in San Miguel del Bado. Jose Candelario was 26 and Maria Luisa was 18.[258]

Maria Luisa Padilla was baptized on March 4, 1800, in Santa Fe, born on the 2nd and godparents were Francisco Sarracino and Ana Maria Garcia.[259]

In the 1841 San Miguel census, Candelario was a farmer and age 49. His wife, Maria Luisa Padilla, was 36. Children were Manuel, 17; Maria Alberta, 14; Facundo, 10 and Jose Guadalupe, 6.[260]

Candelario died on April 8, 1851, in San Miguel del Bado, married to Luisa Padilla.[261]

ii. Jose Antonio Flores was born circa 1789 and married Maria Rosalia Montaño, daughter of Antonio Jose Montaño and Maria Francisca Jirón, on May 16, 1809, in San Miguel del Bado, both residents of San Jose.[262]

---

[254]Spanish Archives of New Mexico, Series I, *San Jose Land Grant*; TW #887; Roll 5, frames 244-249.

[255]NMGS Volunteers, *Pecos, San Miguel del Bado, Ribera Burials, 1796-1850*, p. 54.

[256]Christmas, Tafoya and Olguin, *New Mexico Censuses, 1790, 1793, 1803, 1823, 1829, 1841*, p. 110.

[257]NMGS Volunteers, *Pecos, San Miguel del Bado & Ribera Burials, 1796 - 1850*, p. 92.

[258]Padilla y Baca, *New Mexico Marriages & Marriage Investigations; San Miguel del Vado, 1802-1865*, p. 62.

[259]May, Windham and Baca, *New Mexico Baptisms of Santa Fe, Parroquia de San Francisco de Asis, Vol. II, 15 August 1796 to 30 December 1822*, p. 41.

[260]Christmas, Tafoya and Olguin, *New Mexico Censuses, 1790, 1793, 1803, 1823, 1829, 1841*, p. 109.

[261]Anderson, *Ribera, San Miguel del Bado, Burials, 1848-1956,* AASF/FHL Film 0016879: p. 31,

[262]Padilla y Baca, *San Miguel Marriages, 1802-1865*, p. 62.

In the 1841 San Miguel census, Jose Antonio Flores was 42 and a farmer. His wife, Rosa Montaño, was 45. Children at home were Rumaldo, a farmer, 20; Jose Antonio, a farmer, 16 and Juliana, 12.[263]

Jose Antonio was enumerated in the 1850 La Cuesta census. He was 70 years old, a farmer with real estate valued at $1000. His wife, Rosa, was age 60. Also in the home was Juana Otero, age 20, no occupation or relationship given.[264]

Jose Antonio married (2nd) Maria Rosa Gallegos, daughter of Jose Antonio Gallegos and Maria Antonia Esquibel, on May 19, 1852, in San Miguel del Bado. Jose Antonio was 60 and the widower of Rosa Montaño. Maria Rosa was 28 and the widow of Justo Lopez.[265]

Jose Antonio died on February 19, 1865, in San Miguel del Bado; 80 years old, husband of Rosa Gallegos.[266]

iii. Maria Francisca Flores was born circa 1796 and married Matias Chavez, son of Jose Antonio Chavez and Maria Antonia Marquez, on August 18, 1812, in San Miguel del Bado. Matias was originally from the Villa of La Santa Cruz and Maria Francisca was originally from Santa Fe.[267]

iv. Maria Tomasa Flores was baptized on February 28, 1798, in Santa Fe, age 3 days and godparents were Jose de Jesus Romero and Maria Moya.[268]

Maria Tomasa married Juan Ygnacio Aragon, son of Santiago de Jesus Aragon and Maria Matiana Salas.

Juan Ygnacio Aragon was baptized on June 27, 1792, in Cochiti and godparents were Juan Ygnacio Salas and Maria Manuela Sandoval.[269]

Maria Tomasa died on November 27, 1838, in San Miguel del Bado at age 40, the wife of Juan Ygnacio Aragon of La Cuesta.[270]

Juan Ygnacio married (2nd) Maria Petra Valencia, daughter of Felipe Valencia and Juana Maria Montaño, on November 6, 1839, in San Miguel del Bado.

---

[263]Christmas, Tafoya and Olguin, *New Mexico Censuses, 1790, 1793, 1803, 1823, 1829, 1841*, p. 110.

[264] 1850 United States Federal Census, Territory of New Mexico. Roll M432-469; Jose Anto Flores; San Miguel County, La Cuesta; family #641, p. 32B. Ancestry, www.ancestry.com, Provo, UT.

[265]Arellanes, Windham and Baca, *San Miguel del Bado Church, 12 November 1829 to 10 November 1878,* p. 96.

[266]Anderson, *Ribera/San Miguel del Bado Burials, 1848-1955*, AASF/FHL Film 0016879.

[267]Padilla y Baca, *San Miguel Marriages, 1802-1865*, p. 43.

[268]May, Windham and Baca, *Santa Fe Baptisms, Vol. 2*, p. 18.

[269]Dressen and Baca, *San Buenaventura de Cochiti Church Baptisms, 1736-1873*, p. 80.

[270]NMGS Volunteers, *Pecos, San Miguel del Bado, Ribera Burials, 1796-1850*, p. 67.

Ygnacio was a widower of his first marriage with Tomasa Flores and Maria Petra was single.[271]

In the 1841 San Miguel census, Ygnacio Aragon was a farmer and age 50. His wife, Petra Valencia, was 35. Others in the home were Rumaldo, farmer, 23, Jose Maria, 9; Maria Getrudes, 6 and Dolores, 4.[272]

v. Francisco Estevan Flores was baptized on February 15, 1800, in Santa Fe, born on the 11th and godparents were Jose Miguel Flores and Rosa Martin, all Spanish.[273]

Francisco died on September 18, 1803, in Pecos at age 3.[274]

vi. Francisco Antonio Flores was baptized on February 27, 1802, in Santa Fe and godparents were Jose Ysidro Silva and Apolonia Silva, all Spanish.[275]

vii. Ysidro Antonio Flores was born circa 1806.

On the 26th of May 1824, Isidro was counted among landholding heads of households in El Cerrito.[276]

Ysidro Antonio married Maria Nepomucena Garcia, daughter of Juan Bautista Garcia and Maria Francisca Rael, on September 2, 1826, in San Miguel del Bado, both single.[277]

In the 1850 La Cuesta census, 'Isidoro' was age 42 and a laborer with real estate valued at $50. His wife, 'Pomesena,' was 30. Also in the home were Ramon Flores, 28; Manuel Flores, 22; Alvera Flores, 18 and Josefa Flores, 13. The record does not show relationship to Ysidro, but the last three were his known children.[278]

viii. Juana Apolonia Flores was born circa 1808 and married Jose Maria Ortega, son of Santiago Aba Ortega and Maria Clara Roybal.

In the 1841 San Miguel census, Jose Maria was a farmer and age 40. His wife, Polonia Flores, was 30. Children at home were Jose Lugardo, 20; Jose de Jesus,

---

[271]Padilla y Baca, *San Miguel Marriages, 1802-1865*, p. 10.

[272]Christmas, Tafoya and Olguin, *New Mexico Censuses, 1790, 1793, 1803, 1823, 1829, 1841*, p. 109.

[273]May, Windham and Baca, *Santa Fe Baptisms, Vol. 2*, p. 40.

[274]Christmas, *New Mexico Burials, Pecos Mission, 1798 - 1829*, AASF Roll 35, frame 699.

[275]May, Windham and Baca, *Santa Fe Baptisms, Vol. 2*, p. 64.

[276] Nostrand, *El Cerrito, New Mexico - Eight Generations In A Spanish Village*, p. 22.

[277]Padilla y Baca, *San Miguel Marriages, 1802-1865*, p. 63.

[278]1850 United States Federal Census, Territory of New Mexico. Roll M432-469; Isidro Flores; San Miguel County, La Cuesta, p. 40B; dwelling/family #787. Ancestry, www.ancestry.com, Provo, UT.

18; Andrea, 16; Maximo, 12; Juana, 10; Manuela, 8; Jose de la Ascencion, 5; Manuel, 3 and Jose Maria, 1.[279]

San Jose Cemetery

[279]Christmas, Tafoya and Olguin, *New Mexico Censuses, 1790, 1793, 1803, 1823, 1829, 1841*, p. 110.

Antonio Gallegos

1. Antonio Gallegos, adoptive son of Martin Gallegos and Maria Lucero de Godoy, was baptized on July 4, 1751, in Cochiti, son of unknown parents. The godparents were his adopted parents, Martin Gallego and Maria Lucero.[280]

Antonio married Maria Josefa Montaño, daughter of Jose Antonio Urbano Montaño and Juana Maria Ortega, on March 2, 1778, in Cochiti. The groom, Antonio, was called a *Mestizo, huerfano*, and Maria Josefa was Spanish.[281]

Antonio was named as a grantee of the San Jose del Bado settlement and was allotted 60 *varas* of land.[282]

Maria Josefa Montaño was baptized on March 24, 1759, in Santa Fe and godparents were Cristoval Baca and Maria Cristerna Armijo.[283]

Maria Josefa died on March 26, 1836, in San Miguel del Bado at age 77, wife of Jose Antonio Gallego of Las Mulas.[284]

Known children of Antonio Gallegos and Maria Josefa Montaño were as follows:

i. Maria Antonia Gallegos was baptized on February 16, 1778, in Cochiti, *Mulata*, age three days and godfather was Antonio Lucero.[285]

ii. Maria de Cruz Gallegos was baptized on September 11, 1780, in Cochiti, age three days, both parents given as Spanish and godparents were Gregorio Jose Apodaca and Diega Antonia Griego.[286]

iii. Bernardo Gallegos died February 13, 1781, in Cochiti, son of Jose Antonio Gallego and Maria Josefa Montaño, Spanish, of La Cañada (Cochiti).[287]

---

280 Dressen and Baca, *San Buenaventura de Cochiti Church Baptisms, 1736-1873,* p. 11.

281 Padilla y Baca, *New Mexico Marriages - Pueblo Missions: San Felipe, Santa Ana, Santo Domingo y vecindario, Cochiti, Jemez,* p. 21.

282 Spanish Archives of New Mexico, Series I, *San Miguel del Bado Land Grant*, TW #887; Roll 5, frames 244-247.

283 Windham and Baca, *Baptisms of Santa Fe, Parroquia de San Francisco de Asis, Vol. 1, 5 September 1747 to 17 July 1791,* p. 63.

284 NMGS Volunteers, *Pecos, San Miguel del Bado & Ribera Burials, 1796 – 1850,* p. 58.

285 Dressen and Baca, New Mexico Baptisms, San Buenaventura de Cochiti Church, 1736-1873, p. 43.

286 Dressen and Baca, New Mexico Baptisms, San Buenaventura de Cochiti Church, 1736-1873, p. 51.

287 Christmas, *Cochiti Burials, 1776 - 1873*. AASF 35, frame 391.

iv. Juan Antonio Gallegos was baptized on June 20, 1783, in Cochiti, age five days, Spanish and godparents were Jose Miguel Gallegos and Maria Luisa Gallegos.[288]

Antonio married Marta Griego, daughter of Tomas Griego and Rafaela Contreras Martin on October 5, 1828, in San Miguel del Bado.[289] He died before July 1858.

Marta married (2nd) Jose Tomas Dominguez, son of Bernabe Dominguez and Tomasa Garduño, on July 25, 1858, in San Miguel del Bado. Tomas was the widower of Candelaria Esquibel of Tres Hermanos and Marta was the widow of Antonio Gallegos of Entrañosa. The record gives Tomas's mother as Tomasa Garviso.[290]

v. Manuel Vicente Gallegos was baptized on July 2, 1790, in Cochiti, age five days and both parents given as Spanish. Godparents were Vicente Urban Montaño and Maria Josefa Valenzuela.[291]

Manuel died May 22, 1792, in Cochiti, son of Antonio Gallegos and Maria Josefa Montaño, Spanish, residents of La Cañada (Cochiti).[292]

vi. Jose Miguel Gallegos was baptized on February 28, 1796, in Cochiti, age five days and godparents were Luis Maria Baca and Maria Josefa Lopez.[293]

Jose Miguel married Maria Francisca Gonzales.

vii. Juan Lorenzo Gallegos was baptized on August 11, 1799, in Cochiti, age two days and godparents were Juan Ynocencio Archuleta and Maria Antonia Martin.[294]

Juan Lorenzo died April 12, 1800, in Cochiti, son of Jose Antonio Gallegos and Maria Josefa Montaño, Spanish, residents of La Cañada (Cochiti).[295]

viii. Jose Domingo Gallegos was born circa 1819 and married Maria Nestora Lucero, daughter of Gaspar Lucero and Lugarda Maldonado, on January 16, 1839, in San Miguel del Bado, both single.[296]

---

[288]Dressen and Baca, New Mexico Baptisms, San Buenaventura de Cochiti Church, 1736-1873, p. 56.

[289]Anderson, *New Mexico Baptisms, Galisteo Marriages, 1776 - 1828*, AASF Roll 27, frames 329/330.

[290]Arellanes, Windham and Baca, *San Miguel del Bado Church, 12 November 1829 to 10 November 1878,* p. 121.

[291]Dressen and Baca, New Mexico Baptisms, San Buenaventura de Cochiti Church, 1736-1873, p. 74.

[292]Christmas, *Cochiti Burials, 1776 - 1873.* AASF 35, frame 434.

[293]Dressen and Baca, New Mexico Baptisms, San Buenaventura de Cochiti Church, 1736-1873, p. 95.

[294]Dressen and Baca, New Mexico Baptisms, San Buenaventura de Cochiti Church, 1736-1873, p. 110.

[295]Christmas, *Cochiti Burials, 1776 - 1873.* AASF 35, frame 482/83.

[296]Arellanes, Windham and Baca, *San Miguel del Bado Marriages, 1829-1878*, p. 19.

Jose Toribio Gallegos

1. Jose Toribio Gallegos, son of Cristobal Chaves Gallegos and Prudencia Antonia (Gomez) del Castillo, was born circa 1753, in Bernalillo, according to his military enlistment.

Jose Toribio married Maria Bernarda Baca, daughter of Pablo Antonio Baca and Maria Lorenza Juana de Rivera, on November 28, 1784, in Santa Fe and godparents were Jose Miguel Tafoya, soldier of this royal presidio, and his wife, Manuela Olgin (Olgiin).[297]

Toribio was named as a grantee of the San Jose del Bado settlement and was allotted 125 *varas* of land.[298]

Toribio enlisted in the military in Santa Fe on the 15th of September 1808. He was 45, a farmer from Bernalillo. He was 5'2" tall, with black hair and fair skin.[299] On the 1st of April 1815, Toribio was promoted to 1st *Cavo.*[300]

Toribio died March 30, 1855, in San Miguel del Bado, widower of Bernardina Baca.[301]

Maria Bernarda Baca was baptized on May 21, 1767, in Santa Fe and godparents were Pablo Sandoval and Manuela Dominguez.[302] She died before 1855.

Known children of Jose Toribio Gallegos and Maria Bernarda Baca were as follows:

i. Juan Gallegos died on August 27, 1785, in Santa Fe; child of Toribio Gallegos and Barbara Baca.[303]

ii. Maria Apolonia Gallegos was baptized on February 14, 1787, in Santa Fe, age 2 days and godparents were Francisco Baca and Petrona Baca.[304]

Maria Apolonia married (1st) Diego Antonio Tapia, son of Salvador Tapia and Maria Manuela Gonzales, on October 30, 1803, in the Pecos mission.[305]

297Roybal, Pfeufer, Windham and Baca, compilers, *New Mexico Marriages, Santa Fe - St. Francis Parish and Military Chapel of Our Lady of Light (La Castrense), 1728-1857*, p. 93.

298Spanish Archives of New Mexico, Series I, *San Miguel del Bado Land Grant*; TW #887; frames 244-247.

299Baca, Spanish Enlistment Papers, 1770-1816 ~ Filiaciones Español, 2000, www.nmgs.org/filiciones.htm.

300Christmas. *Military Records ~ Colonial New Mexico ~ Notas y Revistas,* p. 37.

301Christmas, *Ribera, San Miguel del Bado, Burials, 1847-1955*: 1855, p. 51,

302Windham and Baca, *Baptisms of Santa Fe, Parroquia de San Francisco de Asis, Vol. 1, 5 September 1747 to 17 July 1791*, p. 118.

303Christmas, Gallegos and Rau, *New Mexico Burials, Santa Fe - St. Francis Parish and Military Chapel of Our Lady of Light (La Castrense), 1726-1834*, p. 107.

304Windham and Baca, *Santa Fe Baptisms, Vol. 1, 1747-1791*, p. 284.

305Padilla y Baca, *New Mexico Marriages & Marriage Investigations; San Miguel del Vado, 1802-1865*, p. 216.

Diego Antonio Tapia was born circa 1783 and died circa 1820 in San Miguel del Vado.

Diego Antonio was one of the petitioners for the Anton Chico land grant in 1822.

Maria Apolonia married (2nd) Francisco Antonio Sanchez, son of Cristoval Sanchez and Pasquala de la Luz Vigil, after October 16, 1823, in Santa Cruz. The marriage investigation began on the 16th of October 1823 for Francisco Antonio Sanchez, 25, *mexicano* of El Rancho de Guadalupe, son of Cristoval Sanchez, deceased, and Pascuala Vigil, with Apolonia Gallegos, widow of Diego Tapia, 3 years dead, residents of El Vado.[306]

Francisco Antonio Sanchez was baptized on April 4, 1796, in Santa Cruz, age seven days and godparents were Bernardo Madrid and Teresa Madrid, wife of Felipe Gonzales.[307]

Maria Apolonia died on March 27, 1825, in San Miguel del Bado at age 38; married to Francisco 'Sanitreo' (Sanchez).[308]

Francisco Antonio married (2nd) Maria Ysabel Tafoya, daughter of Manuel Tafoya and Maria Rosa Olona, circa 1826.

iii. Maria Victoria "Bitaria" Gallegos was born circa 1792 and married Bernardo Ulibarri, son of Jose Antonio Ulibarri and Maria Rosa Garcia, on November 10, 1810, in San Miguel del Bado.[309]

Bernardo was a petitioner of the Anton Chico land grant on the 24th of January 1822.

He died before January 1848.

iv. Maria Simona Gallegos was born circa 1795 and married (1st) Jose Antonio Ulibarri, son of Ascencio Antonio Ulibarri and Maria Francisca Armijo, on December 28, 1814, in San Miguel del Bado. Jose Antonio was the widower of Maria Manuela Montoya. Both were from Santa Fe.[310]

(See the Chapter for Jose Antonio Ulibarri, also a grantee of the San Jose del Bado settlement.)

Maria Simona married (2nd) Manuel Duran, son of Ygnacio Duran and Maria Feliciana Sandoval, on August 28, 1834, in San Miguel del Bado. Manuel was

---

306Chavez, *New Mexico Roots Ltd.*, p. 1717.

307Olmsted, Windham and Baca, compilers, *New Mexico Baptisms, Santa Cruz de la Cañada Church, Vol. II, 1795-1827*, p. 4.

308NMGS Volunteers, *Pecos, San Miguel del Bado & Ribera Burials, 1796 – 1850*, p. 19.

309Padilla y Baca, *San Miguel Marriages, 1802-1865*, p. 225.

310Padilla y Baca, *San Miguel Marriages, 1802-1865*, p. 225.

a widower of his first marriage to Francisca Ulibarri and 2nd marriage to Maria Soledad Vigil. Simona was the widow of Jose Antonio Ulibarri.[311]

(See the Chapter for Manuel de Jesus Duran, also a grantee of the San Jose del Bado settlement.)

When the 1845 Las Vegas census was enumerated, Simona was 40 and a widow. Children at home were Jesus Felix Ulibarri, 18; Juan de Jesus, 12 and Francisco, 5. Francisco, at age 5, would have been a Duran, son of Manuel.[312]

v. Jose Julian Gallegos was born on February 16, 1798, in Santa Fe, age two days and godparents were Alejandro Martin and Teodora Marquez.[313]

Julian married Maria Ygnacia Rael, daughter of Alonzo Rael and Maria Manuela de Jesus Armijo, on January 7, 1817, in San Miguel.[314]

Maria Ygnacia Rael was baptized on July 2, 1801, in Santa Fe, Spanish, age three days and godparents were Salvador Armijo and Maria Manuela Garcia.[315]

After the death of Julian, Maria Ygnacia married (2nd) Salvador Antonio Montoya, son of Paulin Montoya and Josefa Ortiz, circa 1825/1826.

vi. Maria Ysabel Gallegos was born circa 1799 and married Jose Maria Vigil, son of Ygnacio Vigil and Ygnacia Lopez, on December 20, 1815, in San Miguel del Bado.[316]

vii. Jose Loreto Gallegos was baptized on June 8, 1800, in Santa Fe, Spanish, born on the 3rd and godparents were Juan Domingo Maldonado and Maria Francisca Lovato.[317]

viii. Rosalia Gallegos was born circa 1801 and married Juan Esquibel, son of Ramon Esquibel and Maria de la Luz Trebol, on July 9, 1817, in San Miguel del Bado; both originally from Santa Fe.[318]

She died on November 14, 1847, in San Miguel del Bado, adult and married to Juan Esquibel.[319]

---

[311] Arellanes, Windham, and Baca, *San Miguel del Bado Church, 12 November 1829 to 10 November 1878*, p. 5.

[312] Olmsted, *New Mexico Spanish & Mexican Colonial Censuses, 1790 * 1823 * 1845*, p. 236.

[313] May, Windham and Baca, *New Mexico Baptisms of Santa Fe, Parroquia de San Francisco de Asis, Vol. II, 15 August 1796 to 30 December 1822,* p. 17.

[314] Padilla y Baca, *San Miguel Marriages, 1802-1865*, p. 66.

[315] May, Windham and Baca, *Santa Fe Baptisms, Vol. 2*, p. 57.

[316] Padilla y Baca, *San Miguel Marriages, 1802-1865*, p. 236.

[317] May, Windham and Baca, *Santa Fe Baptisms, Vol. 2*, p. 44.

[318] Padilla y Baca, *San Miguel Marriages, 1802-1865*, p. 59.

[319] NMGS Volunteers, *Pecos, San Miguel del Bado, Ribera Burials, 1796-1850*, p. 112.

ix. Maria Soledad Gallegos was baptized on July 11, 1802, in Pecos, of el Bado and godparents were Juan de Jesus Blea and Matiana Moya.[320]

She died on September 5, 1803, in Pecos at age 1, child of Toribio Gallegos and Bernardina Baca.[321]

x. Jose Antonio Gallegos was baptized on July 12, 1804, in Pecos, of el Bado, Spanish, and godparents were Estevan Lopez and Maria Manuela Montoya.[322]

Jose Antonio married Maria Ygnacia Ulibarri, daughter of Jose Antonio Ulibarri and Maria Manuela de la Ascencion Montoya.

He died on March 17, 1840, in San Miguel del Bado at age 35, married to Ygnacia Ulibarri.[323]

Maria Ygnacia Ulibarri was baptized on October 6, 1805, in Pecos, Spanish and godparents were Alexandro Martin and Teodora Marquez.[324]

Maria Ygnacia married (2nd) Jose Rafael de Jesus Martin, son of Manuel Martin and Maria Rosa Sena, on February 8, 1841, in San Miguel del Bado. Rafael was single and Ygnacia Ulibarri was the widow of Antonio Gallegos.[325]

Ygnacia died before March 1852.

xi. Fernando de Jesus Gallegos was baptized on June 1, 1806, in Pecos, of el Bado, Spanish and godparents were Salvador Tapia and Rafaela Tapia.[326]

Fernando de Jesus married Juliana Padilla, daughter of Diego Padilla and Maria Nicolasa Lopez, on April 28, 1824, in San Miguel del Bado, both from San Miguel.[327]

Juliana Padilla was baptized on March 2, 1811, in Pecos, of el Bado and godparents were Juan Esteban Lopez and Maria Teresa Ulibarri.[328]

---

320 Padilla y Baca, compiler, *New Mexico Baptisms, San Miguel del Vado, Pecos Mission, 1799 - 1829*, p. 40. *Pecos, San Antonio Church Baptisms*, 1726-1829, AASF Roll 6, frame 354,

321 Christmas, *New Mexico Burials, Pecos Mission, 1798 - 1829*, AASF Roll 35, frame 699.

322 Padilla y Baca, *Pecos Mission Baptisms, 1799 - 1829*, p. 40.

323 NMGS Volunteers, *Pecos, San Miguel del Bado, Ribera Burials, 1796-1850*, p. 77.

324 Padilla y Baca, *Pecos Mission Baptisms, 1799 - 1829*, p. 117.

325 Arellanes, Windham and Baca, *San Miguel del Bado Marriages, 1829-1878*, p. 29.

326 Padilla y Baca, *Pecos Mission Baptisms, 1799 - 1829*, p. 40.

327 Padilla y Baca, *San Miguel Marriages, 1802-1865*, p. 67.

328 Padilla y Baca, *Pecos Mission Baptisms, 1799 - 1829*, p. 90.

In the 1841 San Miguel census, Fernando Gallegos was 34 and a soldier. His wife, Maria Juliana Padilla, was 28. Children were Guadalupe, 12; Alta Gracia, 9; Estefana, 7; Antonio Jose, 2 and Miguel, 1.[329]

Juan F Gallegos was enumerated in the 1850 La Cuesta census. He was 46 years old, a farmer with real estate valued at $700. His wife, Juliana, was 29. Children were Antonio Jose, 11 and Atanacia, 1. Also in the home was Francisco Archuleta, age 18.[330]

In 1860, Fernando was living in El Pueblo, San Miguel County, and was 54 years old. He was a farmer with real estate valued at $2,000 and personal estate valued at $12,000. His wife, Juliana, was 48 and daughter, Atanacia, was 11.[331]

Fernando was back in San Jose by 1870 and was farming. His real estate was worth $1,000 and personal estate worth $1,647. His wife was not listed on the census, but his daughter, Altagracia was his housekeeper. Her husband, Jesus Rivera, appears to be deceased. Her children, Somasa, 6 and Josefa, 3, were also in the home. A domestic servant, Jose Gallego, was 14 and Eulogia Gallego, 16, was the seamstress.[332]

Juliana died before June 1870.

Fernando de Jesus married (2nd) Maria Encarnacion Lucero on March 4, 1872, in San Miguel del Bado. Fernando was the widower of Juliana Padilla and was from las Colonias (Anton Chico parish). Maria Encarnacion was the widow of Francisco Salazar.[333]

Maria Encarnacion Lucero was born circa 1824 and married (1st) Francisco Antonio Salazar, son of Juan Manuel Salazar and Antonia Josefa Quintana, on January 19, 1840, in San Miguel del Bado. Francisco was the widower of Maria Dolores Silva and Maria Encarnacion was single.[334]

xii. Agustina Leonicia Gallegos was baptized on August 28, 1810, in Pecos, parents unknown and godparents were Toribio Gallegos and Bernarda Baca of the Plaza of San Jose.[335]

---

[329] Christmas, Tafoya and Olguin, *New Mexico Censuses, 1790, 1793, 1803, 1823, 1829, 1841*, p. 112.

[330] 1850 United States Federal Census, Territory of New Mexico. Roll M432-469; Juan F Gallegos; San Miguel County, La Cuesta; family #748, p. 38B. Ancestry, www.ancestry.com, Provo, UT.

[331] 1860 United States Federal Census, Territory of New Mexico. Roll M653-713; Jose Bernardo Gallego; San Miguel County, El Pueblo; family #2109, p. 49. Ancestry, www.ancestry.com, Provo, UT.

[332] 1870 United States Federal Census, Territory of New Mexico. Roll M593-895; J Fernando Gallegos; San Miguel County, San Jose; p. 14A. Ancestry, www.ancestry.com, Provo, UT.

[333] Arellanes, Windham and Baca, *San Miguel del Bado Marriages, 1829-1878*, p. 154.

[334] Arellanes, Windham and Baca, *San Miguel del Bado Marriages, 1829-1878*, p. 23.

[335] Christmas, *New Mexico Baptisms, San Miguel del Vado, Pecos Mission, 1799 - 1829*, Roll 6, frame 370.

xiii. Maria Gertrudes Gallegos was baptized on June 2, 1811, in Pecos, of el Bado, three days old and godparents were Tomas Padilla and Maria Gertrudes (no surname).[336]

San Jose Cemetery

[336]Padilla y Baca, *Pecos Mission Baptisms, 1799 - 1829*, p. 40.

Diego Gonzales

1. Diego Gonzales married Ana Maria Hurtado.

Diego was named as a grantee for the San Jose del Bado settlement and was allotted 50 *varas* of land.[337]

Ana Maria Hurtado died on May 9, 1796, in Cochiti, married to Diego Gonzales, residents of Rancho.[338]

Known children of Diego Gonzales and Ana Maria Hurtado were as follows:

i. Maria Ignacia Gonzales was born circa 1763 and married Juan Cristobal Lopez, son of Laureano Lopez and Juana Getrudes Ulibarri, on December 3, 1781, in Albuquerque. The marriage investigation began in Albuquerque on October 13, 1781, for Juan Cristobal Lopez, age 23, son of Laureano Lopez and Juana Ulibarri, with Maria Ignacia Gonzales, age 18, daughter of Diego Gonzales and Ana Maria Hurtado. Godparents at the wedding were Lazaro Garcia and Maria Luisa Carbajal.[339]

A baptismal record was found in Albuquerque for Juan Cristobal Lopez, of unknown parents and godparents were Laureano Lopez and Josepha Lopez, dated February 15, 1752.[340]

ii. Maria Zaragoza Gonzales married Juan Armijo, son of Antonio Jose Armijo and Rosalia Aragon on June 24, 1789, in Cochiti. Witnesses were Santiago Aragon and Santiago Crespin.[341]

iii. Maria Andrea Gonzales married Manuel Armijo, son of Antonio Jose Armijo and Rosalia Aragon, on August 4, 1789, in Cochiti. Both were Spanish and witnesses were Bartolome Padilla and Visente Montaño.[342]

---

337 Spanish Archives of New Mexico, Series I: *San Miguel del Bado Land Grant*; TW 877; Roll 5, frames 244-247.

338 Christmas, *Cochiti Burials, 1776 - 1873*. AASF 35: frame 453.

339 Chavez, *New Mexico Roots Ltd.*, p. 925. Dressen, Gooch, Windham and Baca, *New Mexico Marriages, San Felipe de Neri Church in Albuquerque*, p. 40.

340 New Mexico Genealogical Society, *Albuquerque Baptisms, Archdiocese of Santa Fe, 1706 - 1850*, p. 351.

341 Padilla y Baca, *New Mexico Marriages - Pueblo Missions: San Felipe, Santa Ana, Santo Domingo y vecindario, Cochiti, Jemez*, p. 25.

342 Padilla y Baca, *New Mexico Marriages - Pueblo Missions: San Felipe, Santa Ana, Santo Domingo y vecindario, Cochiti, Jemez*, p. 25

iv. Rafael Bernardo Gonzales was baptized on August 21, 1775, in Albuquerque, Spanish and godparents were Juan Joseph Candelaria and Barbara Garcia,[343]

v. Diego Antonio Gonzales was born circa 1776 and married Maria Olaya (Eulalia) de Jesus Montaño.[344]

(See chapter on Diego Antonio Gonzales, also a grantee of the San Jose del Bado settlement.)

vi. Juan Manuel Gonzales was born circa 1777 and married Maria Manuela Valencia, daughter of Jose Valencia and Maria Manuela Gonzales.

(See chapter on Manuel Gonzales, also a grantee of the San Jose del Bado settlement.)

---

[343]New Mexico Genealogical Society, *Albuquerque Baptisms, Archdiocese of Santa Fe, 1706 – 1850,* p. 270.

[344] Padilla y Baca, *New Mexico Marriages - Pueblo Missions: San Felipe, Santa Ana, Santo Domingo y vecindario, Cochiti, Jemez,* p. 29.

Diego Antonio Gonzales

1. Diego Antonio Gonzales, son of Diego Gonzales and Ana Maria Hurtado, married Maria Olaya (Eulalia) de Jesus Montaño, daughter of Vicente Urban Montaño and Maria Candelaria Montoya, on January 7, 1796, in Cochiti. Both were Spanish.[345]

Diego Antonio was a grantee of the San Jose del Bado settlement and was allotted 300 *varas* of land.[346]

Diego died on March 11, 1814, in Pecos.[347]

Maria Olaya (Eulalia) de Jesus Montaño was baptized on March 13, 1782, in Cochiti, born on the 9th, Spanish and residents of la Cañada. Godparents were Juan Mathias Barela and Juana Paula Romero.[348]

Known children of Diego Antonio Gonzales and Maria Eulalia (Olaya) de Jesus Montaño were as follows:

i. Luis Maria Gonzales was baptized on October 23, 1796, in Cochiti, seven days old and godparents were Diego Antonio Montoya and Maria Manuela Martin.[349]

Luis Maria married (1st) Maria Magdalena Maes.

Maria Magdalena Maes died on October 13, 1849. Magdalena "Salas" left a widower, Luis Maria Gonzales.[350]

Luis Maria married (2nd) Maria Teodocia Duran, daughter of Juan Bautista de Jesus Duran and Maria Anastacia Martin, on January 18, 1850, in San Miguel del Bado. Luis was the widower of Magdalena Maes and Maria Teodocia was single.[351]

In the 1860 El Cerrito census, Luis was age 70, a musician with real estate valued at $400 and personal estate valued at $650. His wife, Teodosia, was 29. Children at home were Piedad, 8; Viviana, 5 and Apolinia, 2.[352]

345Padilla y Baca, *New Mexico Marriages - Pueblo Missions: San Felipe, Santa Ana, Santo Domingo y vecindario, Cochiti, Jemez*), p. 29.

346Spanish Archives of New Mexico, Series I, *San Miguel del Bado Land Grant*; TW #887; Roll 5, frames 244-249.

347Christmas, *New Mexico Burials, Pecos Mission, 1798 - 1829*, AASF Roll 35, frame 714, p. 23.

348Dressen and Baca, *New Mexico Baptisms, San Buenaventura de Cochiti Church, 1736-1873*, p. 53.

349Dressen and Baca, *New Mexico Baptisms, San Buenaventura de Cochiti Church, 1736-1873*, p. 98.

350NMGS Volunteers, *Pecos, San Miguel del Bado & Ribera Burials, 1796 - 1850*, p. 120.

351Arellanes, Windham and Baca, *San Miguel del Bado Church, 12 November 1829 to 10 November 1878*, p. 83.

3521860 United States Federal Census, Territory of New Mexico. Roll M653-713; Luis Ma Gonzales; San Miguel County, El Cerrito, family #1806, p. 30B. Ancestry, www.ancestry.com, Provo, UT.

Luis died on July 6, 1863, in La Cuesta, 75 years old, husband of Maria Teodora Duran.[353]

Maria Teodocia married (2nd) Juan Francisco Garduño, son of Jose Manuel Garduño and Maria Juana Apodaca, on November 4, 1863, in San Miguel del Bado. Teodocia was the widow of Luis Maria Gonzales.[354]

ii. Maria Salome Gonzales was baptized on March 19, 1799, in Santo Domingo; eight days old and godparents were Ysidro Antonio Lovato and Juana Barbara Gaona.[355]

She died on April 2, 1803, in Pecos at age 4.[356]

iii. Miguel Albino Gonzales was baptized on June 4, 1804, in Pecos, Spanish and godparents were Toribio Candelaria and Ularia de la Cruz.[357]

Miguel Albino married Maria Fabiana Blea, daughter of Jose Rafael Manuel Blea and Maria de la Luz Maese, on September 7, 1833, in San Miguel del Bado.[358]

In the 1841 San Miguel del Bado census, Miguel Alvino was 27, and his wife, Faviana Blea, was 25 and children were: Pelegrina, 7; Maria Perfecta, 6; Tomasa, 3 and Lauriano, 2.

In the 1845 Reyes de San Agustin, San Miguel County census, Miguel Albino was 35 and his wife, Altagracia (Fabiana), was 26. Children were Perfeta, 10; Tomasa, 8; Juan Francisco, 5; Mariano, 3 and Matiana, 1.[359]

In the 1850 Las Vegas census, Miguel Albino 'Gonzalez' gave his age as 42, a farmer with real estate valued at $200. His wife, Fabina, was 32 and children were: Pelegrena, (f), 16; Perfecta, 13; Tomasa, 11, Jose Lauriano, 10; Marcos, 9; Antonia, 4 and Nicolasa, 2.[360]

In the 1860 San Miguel County census, living in San Agustin, Miguel Albino (M. A.) was 54 and a laborer. His real estate was valued at $600 and personal estate was $3500. His wife, Fabiana, was 36 and children at home were:

---

[353]Anderson, *Ribera/San Miguel del Bado Burials, 1848-1955*, AASF/FHL Film 0016879.

[354]Arellanes, Windham and Baca, *San Miguel del Bado Marriages, 1829-1878*, p. 132.

[355]Padilla y Baca, compiler, *New Mexico Baptisms, Pueblo Missions, San Felipe, Santa Ana, Santo Domingo, Cochiti, Jemez*, p. 45.

[356]Christmas, *New Mexico Burials, Pecos Mission, 1798 - 1829*, frame 699.

[357]Padilla y Baca, compiler, *New Mexico Baptisms, San Miguel del Vado, Pecos Mission, 1799 - 1829*, p. 46.

[358]Arellanes, Windham and Baca, *San Miguel del Bado Marriages, 1829-1878*, p. 7.

[359]Olmsted, *New Mexico Spanish & Mexican Colonial Censuses, 1790 * 1823 * 1845*, p. 248.

[360]1850 United States Federal Census, Territory of New Mexico. Roll M432-469, Miguel Albino Gonzalez; San Miguel County, Las Vegas, p. 17A. Ancestry, www.ancestry.com, Provo, UT.

Marcos, 18; Perfecta, 16; Ambrosio, (f), 13; Nicolasa, 12; Victor, 9; Luciano, 7; Casimiro, 6 and Carmen, 3.[361]

Miguel Albino died after 1860; he was buried in the church at Los Valles de San Agustin, NM.

In the 1870 San Miguel County census, living in San Agustin, Fabiana gave her age as 50 with real estate valued at $200. Children at home were: Perfecta, 20; Ambrosia, 16; Luciano, 13; Nicolasa, 11; Casimiro, 9; Carmen, 10; Epitacio, 9 and Margarita, 6.[362]

iv. Jose Serapio 'Serafin' Gonzales was baptized on September 12, 1812, in Pecos, four days old and godparents were Juan Estevan Gonzales and his wife, Maria Soledad Aragon. This record records the surname as Bustos and father as Diego Bustos and mother as Maria Olaya Montaño. He was known as Gonzales in all later records.[363]

Jose Serapio 'Serafin' married Francisca Rael, daughter of Antonio Jose Rael and Francisca Aragon, on November 3, 1836, in San Miguel del Bado, both from this jurisdiction.[364]

In the 1841 San Miguel census, Serafin was 25 and his wife, Francisca Rael, was 22. They show no children, but their daughter Maria may be with Francisca's parents next door, age 3.[365]

Serafin was enumerated in the 1850 La Cuesta census as 30 years old and a servant. His wife, Francisca, was 27. Children at home were Veranda, 11; Juan B., 5 and Jesusita, 1.[366]

In the 1870 La Cuesta census, Serafin was age 45, a farm worker with real estate valued at $100. His wife, Francisca, was 40. Children at home were Juan, 25, farm worker; Cecilia, 18, seamstress; and Abran, age 6.[367]

---

361 1860 United States Federal Census, Territory of New Mexico. Roll M653-713, M A Gonzales; San Miguel County, San Agustin, p. 199. Ancestry, www.ancestry.com, Provo, UT.

362 1870 United States Federal Census, Territory of New Mexico. Roll M593-895, Faviana Blea; San Miguel County, San Agustin, p. 115B. Ancestry, www.ancestry.com, Provo, UT.

363 Padilla y Baca, *Pecos Mission Baptisms, 1799 - 1829*, p. 24.

364 Arellanes, Windham and Baca, *San Miguel del Bado Marriages, 1829-1878*, p. 14.

365 Christmas, Tafoya and Olguin, *New Mexico Censuses, 1790, 1793, 1803, 1823, 1829, 1841*, p. 118.

366 1850 United States Federal Census, Territory of New Mexico. Roll M432-469; Serafin Gonzales; San Miguel County, La Cuesta, family #883, p. 45B. Ancestry, www.ancestry.com, Provo, UT.

367 1900 United States Federal Census, Territory of New Mexico. Roll M593-895; Serafin Gonzales; San Miguel County, La Cuesta, family #62, p. 69A. Ancestry, www.ancestry.com, Provo, UT.

Juan Manuel Gonzales

1. Juan Manuel Gonzales, son of Diego Gonzales and Ana Maria Hurtado, was born circa 1777 and married Maria Manuela Valencia, daughter of Jose Valencia and Maria Manuela Gonzales, on November 3, 1797, in Cochiti, both Spanish.[368]

Juan was named as a grantee of the San Jose del Bado settlement. He received 50 *varas* of land.[369]

Maria Manuela Valencia married (2nd) Jose Francisco Chaves, son of Jose Vicente Chavez and Maria Casilda Jaramillo, on November 7, 1817, in San Miguel del Bado.[370]

Known children of Juan Manuel Gonzales and Maria Manuela Valencia were as follows:

i. Maria Guadalupe Bustos (Gonzales) died on August 14, 1802, in Pecos, child of Juan Bustos and Maria Balencia.[371]

ii. Maria Manuela Bustos (Gonzales) was baptized on July 9, 1803, in San Miguel del Bado and godmother was Francisca Garcia. [372]

It is not known why the surname Bustos was used instead of Gonzales.

---

[368]Padilla y Baca, *New Mexico Marriages - Pueblo Missions: San Felipe, Santa Ana, Santo Domingo y vecindario, Cochiti, Jemez,* p. 30.

[369]Spanish Archives of New Mexico, Series I: *San Miguel del Bado Land Grant*; TW 877; Roll 5, frames 244-247. Albuquerque Genealogy Center, Albuquerque.

[370]Padilla y Baca, *New Mexico Marriages & Marriage Investigations; San Miguel del Vado, 1802-1865*, p. 43.

[371]Christmas, *New Mexico Burials, Pecos Mission, 1798 - 1829*, AASF Roll 35, frame 698, p. 14.

[372] Padilla y Baca, New *Mexico Baptisms, San Miguel del Vado, Pecos Mission, 1799 - 1829*, p. 24.

Juan Estevan Lopez

1. Juan Estevan Lopez, son of Santiago Lopez and Antonia Damiana Ortega,was baptized on January 7, 1778, in Santa Fe, age one day and godparents were Andres Martin and his wife, Maria Antonia Lovato. The record shows they were color quebrado[373].[374]

Juan Estevan married (1st) Maria Teresa Ulibarri, daughter of Ascencio Antonio Ulibarri and Maria Francisca Armijo, on October 4, 1802, in Pecos. Juan Esteban was from el Bado and Maria Teresa was from Santa Fe.[375]

Maria Teresa Ulibarri was baptized on October 26, 1787, in Santa Fe, age three days and godparents were Jose Miguel de la Peña and Maria Rael.[376]

She died before December 1821.

As a grantee of the San Jose del Bado settlement, Juan Estevan received 50 varas of land.[377]

Known children of Juan Estevan Lopez and Maria Teresa Ulibarri, all born in San Miguel del Bado, were as follows:

i. Jose Maria de Jesus Lopez was baptized on January 2, 1806, Spanish and godparents were Toribio Gallegos and Vernarda Baca.[378]

ii. Luisa Maria Lopez was baptized on August 22, 1808, Spanish, of the Plaza de San Miguel and godparents were Juan Urvan and Rosa de Herrera.[379]

She died on January 18, 1809, in San Miguel del Bado. The record gives her name as Luis instead of Luisa.[380]

iii. Maria Manuela Lopez was baptized on January 7, 1810, Spanish, of San Jose and godparents were Jose Ygnacio Lucero and Maria Geronima Chavez.[381]

---

[373]*color quebrado* denotes a racial mixture, possibly of white, Indian and black or any combination of the three.

[374]Windham and Baca, *Baptisms of Santa Fe, Parroquia de San Francisco de Asis, Vol. 1, 5 September 1747 to 17 July 1791,* p. 215.

[375]Padilla y Baca, *New Mexico Marriages & Marriage Investigations; San Miguel del Vado, 1802-1865*, p. 111.

[376]Windham and Baca, *Santa Fe Baptisms, Vol. 1, 1747-1791*, p. 290.

[377]Spanish Archives of New Mexico, Series I, *San Miguel del Bado Land Grant*; TW #887; Roll 5, frames 244-247.

[378]Padilla y Baca, N*ew Mexico Baptisms, San Miguel del Vado, Pecos Mission, 1799 - 1829*, p. 57.

[379]Padilla y Baca, *Pecos Mission Baptisms, 1799 - 1829*, p. 58.

[380]Christmas, *New Mexico Burials, Pecos Mission, 1798 - 1829*, AASF Roll 35, frame 705.

[381]Padilla y Baca, *Pecos Mission Baptisms, 1799 - 1829*, p. 58.

Maria Manuela married Jose Miguel Aragon, son of Juan de la Cruz Aragon and Teodora de Jesus Baca.

Jose Miguel enlisted in the military on the 18th of September 1808 in Santa Fe. He was 14 years old and son of Juan Jose Aragon and Teodora Baca. He was 4' tall. He was an *El Tambor*. His hair was red and his complexion was white.[382]

In the 1841 San Miguel del Bado census, 2nd District, Miguel was a farmer and age 46. His wife, Manuela Lopez, was 28 and children at home were: Maria Pelaxia (Pelagia), 12; Serafina, 10; Maria Josefa, 8; Luis, 5 and Maria Leonor, 1.[383]

iv. Jose Ramon Lopez died on July 5, 1813, in San Miguel del Bado, one day old.[384]

v. Maria Ysabel Lopez was baptized on July 17, 1814, Spanish, three days old, of el Vado and godparents were Santiago Ulibarri and Maria Josefa Duran.[385]

Maria Ysabel married (1st) Juan Antonio Gallegos on January 2, 1831, in San Miguel del Bado. Juan Antonio was the widower of Maria Polonia Esquibel.[386]

Maria Ysabel married (2nd) Jose Maria Martin, son of Juan Rafael Martin and Juana Manuela Sandoval, on October 30, 1857, in San Miguel del Bado. Jose Maria was the widower of Gregoria Baca and his parents were from San Francisco, jurisdiction of Galisteo. Ysabel was the widow of Juan Antonio Gallegos.[387]

In the 1850 San Miguel census, Antonio was 53 years old, a farmer with real estate valued at $800. His wife, Isabel, was 30.[388]

Antonio died before October 1857 in San Miguel del Bado.

vi. Juana Maria Lopez was baptized on July 27, 1818, three days old and godfather was Felix Xaramillo.[389]

382Evelyn Lujan Baca, Enlistment Rolls for Santa Fe Presidio, 2000, www.nmgs.org/filiciones.htm. p. 1.

383Christmas, Tafoya and Olguin, *New Mexico Censuses, 1790, 1793, 1803, 1823, 1829, 1841*, p. 103.

384NMGS Volunteers, compiler, *Pecos, San Miguel del Bado & Ribera Burials, 1796 - 1850* (Albuquerque, NM: New Mexico Genealogical Society, 2014), p. 11.

385Padilla y Baca, *Pecos Mission Baptisms, 1799 - 1829*, p. 58.

386Arellanes, Windham and Baca, *New Mexico Marriages, San Miguel del Bado Church, 12 November 1829 to 10 November 1878,* p. 3.

387Arellanes, Windham and Baca, *San Miguel del Bado Marriages, 1829-1878*, p. 117.

3881850 United States Federal Census, Territory of New Mexico. Roll M432-467; Antonio Gallego; San Miguel County, San Miguel, p. 58A, dwelling/household #1135. Ancestry, www.ancestry.com, Provo, UT

389Padilla y Baca, *Pecos Mission Baptisms*, 1799 - 1829, p. 58.

Juana Maria married Francisco Antonio Lucero, son of Jose Lucero and Geronima Sandoval, on January 14, 1836, in San Miguel del Bado, both single.[390]

In the 1845 Las Vegas census, Francisco was 28, his wife, Juana Lopez, was 22. Children at home were: Maria Julia, 7; Remedios, 6; Juan Jose, 2 and Lupina, 1.[391]

Enumerated in the 1870 Las Vegas census, Francisco was 61 and a farmer. He had real estate valued at $300 and personal estate valued at $3130. His wife, Juana, was 53 and a seamstress. Children at home were Leandro, 21, farm laborer; Esmejildo (Meregildo), 24, farm laborer; Tomasa, 18 (Duran), seamstress (wife of Meregildo); and their two children, Eugenio, 3 and Antonia, 2.

Also in the home was Juana and Francisco's daughter, Daria, and husband, Antonio Portello, and their son, Victoriano.[392]

vii. Jose Justo Lopez was baptized on July 20, 1821, of the Plaza of San Jose and godparents were Jose Antonio Ulibarri and Maria Simona Gallegos.[393]

Jose Justo married Maria Rosa Gallegos, daughter of Jose Antonio Gallegos and Maria Antonia Esquibel, on September 7, 1840, in San Miguel del Bado.[394]

He died on October 10, 1848, in San Miguel del Bado at age 27, adult, and left a widow, Maria Rosa Gallego.[395]

Maria Rosa was a widow when the 1850 San Miguel census was enumerated. She was 23 years old. Children at home were Antonio Jose, 7; Pablo, 5 and Maria Justa, 2.[396]

Maria Rosa married (2nd) Jose Antonio Flores, son of Jose Antonio Flores and Maria Rosa Padilla, on May 19, 1852, in San Miguel del Bado. Jose Antonio was 60 and widower of Rosa Montaño. Maria Rosa was 28 and the widow of Justo Lopez.[397]

---

[390]Arellanes, Windham and Baca, *San Miguel del Bado Marriages*, 1829-1878, p. 13.

[391]Olmsted, *New Mexico Spanish & Mexican Colonial Censuses, 1790 * 1823 * 1845*, p. 238.

[392]1870 United States Federal Census, Territory of New Mexico. Roll M593-895; Francisco Lucero; San Miguel County, Las Vegas, p. 142A. Ancestry, www.ancestry.com, Provo, UT.

[393]Padilla y Baca, *Pecos Mission Baptisms*, 1799 - 1829, p. 59.

[394]Padilla y Baca, *San Miguel Marriages*, 1802-1865, p. 112.

[395]NMGS Volunteers, *Pecos, San Miguel del Bado, Ribera Burials*, 1796-1850, p. 116.

[396]1850 United States Federal Census, Territory of New Mexico. Roll M432-467; Ma Rosa Gallego; San Miguel County, San Miguel, p. 58A, dwelling/household #1136. Ancestry, www.ancestry.com, Provo, UT.

[397]Arellanes, Windham and Baca, *San Miguel del Bado Marriages, 1829-1878*, p. 96.

Juan Estevan married (2nd) Maria Dolores Baca, daughter of Tomas Antonio Baca and Maria Leonicia 'Dionciana' Lucero, on December 22, 1821, in Santa Fe. Estevan was the widower of Maria Teresa Ulibarri of el Vado. Maria Dolores was single and from la Sienega. They were veiled on the 4th of February 1822 in the parish of del Vado and Ribera. Witnesses were *don* Rafael Sena of Santa Fe and Lorenzo Marques of el Vado.[398]

Maria Dolores Baca was baptized on April 11, 1797, in Santa Fe, age four days and godparents were Juan Estevan Baca and Josefa Madrid.[399]

She died on June 5, 1866, in San Miguel del Bado, 60 years old and wife of deceased Juan Estevan Lopez of San Jose.[400]

Known children of Juan Estevan Lopez and Maria Dolores Baca were as follows:

i. Juan Estevan Lopez died on January 4, 1826 in San Miguel del Bado.[401]

ii. Prudencio Lopez married Maria Ygnacia Vigil, daughter of Antonio Alejandro Vigil and Dolores Olivas.

In the 1860 San Jose census, Prudencio was 35 and a merchant. He had real estate worth $2500 and personal estate of $7095. His wife, Ygnacia, was 30. Children at home were: Maria Teodora, 16; Roman, 13; Rita, 9; Benigno, 7; Florencia, 3 and Faustino, 5. There were three servants: Cleto Olivas, 21; Ygnacio Garcia, 22 and Juan Lopez, 23.[402]

In the 1870 San Jose census, Prudencio was 45 and a farmer. His real estate was worth $4400 and his personal estate was worth $4550. Ygnacia was a seamstress and age 41. Children still at home were: Benigno, 15; Faustin, 13; Florencia, 11 and Escolastica, 7. Also in the home was Jose Lopez, age 15.[403]

Maria Ygnacia Vigil was baptized on July 30, 1827, in Santa Cruz, born on the 29th and godparents were Bartolo Quintana and Vicenta Lucero.[404]

---

398 Roybal, Pfeufer, Windham and Baca, *New Mexico Marriages, Santa Fe - St. Francis Parish and Military Chapel of Our Lady of Light (La Castrense), 1728-1857,* p. 153.

399 May, Windham and Baca, *New Mexico Baptisms of Santa Fe, Parroquia de San Francisco de Asis, Vol. II, 15 August 1796 to 30 December 1822*, p. 5.

400 Anderson, *Ribera, San Miguel del Bado, Burials, 1847-1955*: p. 100.

401 NMGS Volunteers, *Pecos, San Miguel del Bado, Ribera Burials, 1796-1850*, p. 24.

402 1860 United States Federal Census, Territory of New Mexico. Roll M653-713, Prudencio Lopez; San Miguel County, Lower Sapeyo (San Jose), p. 317. Ancestry, www.ancestry.com, Provo, UT

403 1870 United States Federal Census, Territory of New Mexico. Roll M593-895, Prudencio Lopez; San Miguel County, San Jose, p. 205. Ancestry, www.ancestry.com, Provo, UT

404 Virginia Langham Olmsted, Margaret Leonard Windham and Evelyn Lujan Baca, *New Mexico Baptisms, Santa Cruz de la Cañada Church, Vol. 3, 1827-1856* (Albuquerque, NM: New Mexico Genealogical Society, 1997), p. 1.

iii. Maria Petra Lopez was baptized on October 28, 1825, in San Miguel del Bado, of San Jose and godparents were Salvador Jaramillo and Dolores Baca.[405]

Maria Petra married Juan Bautista Atencio, son of Juan Agustin Atencio and Maria del Rosario Duran, on January 22, 1847, in San Miguel del Bado, both single.[406]

She died on October 24, 1861, in La Cuesta, twenty seven years old.

Petra signed her will on the 14th of October 1861. She named her husband, Juan Bautista Atencio and her son, Luisano Atencio. She also named her brothers: D. Prudencio Lopez and D. Antonio Lopez. Executors were Faustino Lopez and Juan Bautista Atencio and they were issued Letters of Administration on the 11th of November 1861. Sureties were Crestino Romero and Pablo Ulibarri.[407]

Juan Bautista Atencio was baptized on February 18, 1825, in Pecos Mission, of La Cuesta and godparents were Lorenzo Marquez and Josefa Anaya.[408]

In the 1850 La Cuesta census, Juan B. was 25, a farmer with real estate valued at $75. His wife, Petra, was 20.[409]

In the 1860 census, still living in La Cuesta, Juan 'Hortensio' was 30 and a laborer with no real estate or personal estate given. His wife, Petra, was 31. They had one son, Severo, who was 12. Also in the home were three servants: Gertrudis Gonzales, 18; Marcos Valencia, 21 and Juan Antonio Duran, 28.[410]

Juan Bautista married (2nd) Maria Juana Sedillo on February 8, 1878, in San Miguel del Bado. Juan was the widower of Maria Petra Lopez and Maria Juana was the widow of Martin Saenz. Witnesses included Jose Atencio and Soledad Lopez.[411]

---

[405]Padilla y Baca, *Pecos Mission Baptisms, 1799 - 1829*, p. 59.

[406]Arellanes, Windham and Baca, *San Miguel del Bado Marriages, 1829-1878*, p. 56.

[407]Anderson, *Ribera/San Miguel del Bado Burials, 1848-1955*, AASF/FHL Film No. 0016879; *The New Mexico Genealogist*, New Mexico Genealogical Society: Vol. XIII, No. 4, December 1974, "San Miguel County Wills," extracted by Amelia Garcia and Virginia L. Olmsted. San Miguel County Probate Book No. 3, p. 119; 1859-1862 at the New Mexico Archives.

[408]Padilla y Baca, *Pecos Mission Baptisms, 1799 - 1829*, p. 13.

[409]1850 United States Federal Census, Territory of New Mexico. Roll M432-469; Juan B Atencio; San Miguel County, La Cuesta; family #785, p. 40B. Ancestry, www.ancestry.com, Provo, UT

[410]1860 United States Federal Census, Territory of New Mexico. Roll M653-713; Juan Hortensio; San Miguel County, La Cuesta; family #1866, p. 246. Ancestry, www.ancestry.com, Provo, UT

[411]Arellanes, Windham and Baca, *San Miguel del Bado Marriages, 1829-1878*, p. 171.

iv. Maria Dolores Lopez was baptized on April 23, 1827, in San Miguel del Bado, age two days, of San Jose and godparents were Albino Ulibarri and Maria Soledad Baca.[412]

v. Jose Faustino Lopez was baptized on February 17, 1831, in San Miguel del Bado, born on the 14th and godparents were Ascencio Baca and Petra Baca.[413]

Jose Faustino married Rosita Pacheco, daughter of Jose Ygnacio Pacheco and Maria Juana Vigil, on November 15, 1851, in San Miguel del Bado. Faustin was 18 and Maria Rosa was 14. Both were single.[414]

In the 1860 San Jose census, Faustino was 27, a clerk, with real estate valued of $200 and personal estate valued at $860. His wife, Rosa Pacheco, was 22. Children at home were Margarita, 7; Petra, 5; Pedro, 3 and Dorotea, two months.[415]

The Upper Las Vegas 1870 census shows that Faustin was deceased. His widow, Rosa was 35, with real estate valued at $300 and personal estate valued at $250. Children at home were: Petra, 12; Pedro, 10; Bacilio, 8; Faustina, 6; Guillermo, 5 and Tomas, 2, all with Lopez surnames.[416]

vi. Maria Soledad Lopez was born circa 1832 and married Jose Pedro Delfin Atencio, son of Juan Agustin Atencio and Maria del Rosario Duran, on January 9, 1848, in San Miguel del Bado, both single.[417]

Jose Pedro Delfin Atencio was baptized on December 3, 1826, in Pecos Mission, born two days ago in La Cuesta and godparents were Jose Manuel Tenorio and Maria de Jesus Tenorio.[418]

Pedro was enumerated in the 1850 census living in La Cuesta. He was 20, a laborer with real estate valued at $50. His wife, Soledad, was 18 and they had one son, Jose Conciscion, age 1.[419]

---

[412]Padilla y Baca, *Pecos Mission Baptisms, 1799 - 1829*, p. 59.

[413]Arellanes, Pfeufer, Olmsted, Windham and Baca, *New Mexico Baptisms, San Miguel del Bado Church, Vol. I, 1 January 1829 ~ 12 May 1844*, p. 14.

[414]Arellanes, Windham and Baca, *San Miguel del Bado Marriages, 1829-1878*, p. 94.

[415]1860 United States Federal Census, Territory of New Mexico. Roll M653-713; Faustino Lopez; San Miguel County, San Jose, family #3024, p. 97. Ancestry, www.ancestry.com, Provo, UT

[416]1870 United States Federal Census, Territory of New Mexico. Roll M593-895; Rosa Pacheco; San Miguel County, Upper Las Vegas, p. 255A. Ancestry, www.ancestry.com, Provo, UT.

[417]Arellanes, Windham and Baca, *San Miguel del Bado Marriages, 1829-1878*, p. 64.

[418]Padilla y Baca, *Pecos Mission Baptisms, 1799 - 1829*, p. 13.

[419]1850 United States Federal Census, Territory of New Mexico. Roll M432-469; Petro Atercio; San Miguel County, La Cuesta; family #781, p. 40A. Ancestry, www.ancestry.com, Provo, UT.

Jose Atencio was living in Arroyo del Conchas when the 1870 census was enumerated. He was 42, a farm worker with real estate and personal estate valued at $300. His wife, Soledad, was 40. Children at home were: Concepcion (m), 20; Catarino (m), 18; Teresa, 16; Nieves, 13; Ricarda, 10; Francisco, 7; Dorotea, 5 and Placido, six months.[420]

vii. Maria Efigenia Lopez married Jose de Jesus Garcia, son of Juan Garcia and Francisca Rael, on August 23, 1848, in San Miguel del Bado, both single.[421]

Jose de Jesus was enumerated in the 1850 La Cuesta census. He was a laborer with real estate valued at $50. His wife, Efigenia, was 18. No children were shown.[422]

Jose de Jesus and Efigenia were enumerated in the 1860 La Cuesta census. He was 33, a laborer with real estate valued at $250 and personal estate valued at $1000. Efigenia was 29. Also in the home were Juana Valverde, 33, servant; Concencion, 14, servant; and Ricardo Ortega, age 7, shepherd.[423]

viii. Maria Donaciana Lopez was baptized on April 24, 1833, in San Miguel del Bado and godparents were Jose Antonio Gallegos and Maria Ygnacia Ulibarri.[424]

Maria Donaciana married Jose Guadalupe Garcia, son of Juan Garcia and Francisca Rael, on January 9, 1848, in San Miguel del Bado, both single.[425]

In the 1850 La Cuesta census, Jose G. was 24, a laborer and had real estate valued at $50. His wife, Donaciana, was 16. They had one daughter, Emiliana, age 2.[426]

Guadalupe had moved his family to Arroyo de Conchas when the 1870 census was enumerated. He was 44, a farm worker with real estate valued at $300 and personal estate valued at $200. His wife, Donaciana, was 33. Children at home

---

[420]1870 United States Federal Census, Territory of New Mexico. Roll M593-895; Jose Atencio; San Miguel County; Arroyo de Conchas, p. 6B. Ancestry, www.ancestry.com, Provo, UT.

[421]Arellanes, Windham and Baca, *San Miguel del Bado Marriages, 1829-1878*, p. 68.

[422]1850 United States Federal Census, Territory of New Mexico. Roll M432-469; Jose Jesus Garcia; San Miguel County, La Cuesta, family #803, p. 41B. Ancestry, www.ancestry.com, Provo, UT.

[423]1860 United States Federal Census, Territory of New Mexico. Roll M653-713; Jose de Jesus Garcia; San Miguel County, La Cuesta; family #1899, p. 249. Ancestry, www.ancestry.com, Provo, UT.

[424]Arellanes, Pfeufer and Olmsted, Windham and Baca, *San Miguel del Bado Baptisms, Vol. I, 1829-1844*, p. 38.

[425]Arellanes, Windham and Baca, *San Miguel del Bado Marriages, 1829-1878*, p. 64.

[426]1850 United States Federal Census, Territory of New Mexico. Roll M432-469; Jose G Garcia; San Miguel County, La Cuesta; family #789, p. 40B. Ancestry, www.ancestry.com, Provo, UT.

were: Emeliana, 17; Hilario, 15; Juana, 12; Jose de la Cruz, 9 and Juliana, age 3.[427]

Guadalupe was serving as the Justice of Peace when the 1880 La Cuesta census was enumerated. He was 53; his wife, Donaciana, was 46 and children at home were Hilario, 22; Jose de la Cruz, 18 and Juliana Garcia, 13.[428]

ix. Maria Cesaria Lopez was baptized on November 14, 1835, in San Miguel del Bado, of San Jose and godparents were Santiago Ortega and Manuela Baca.[429]

Maria Cesaria married Jose Agapito Vigil, son of Antonio Alejandro Vigil and Dolores Olivas, on February 9, 1850, in San Miguel del Bado, both single.[430]

Cesaria died before July 1870.

Jose Agapito Vigil was baptized on March 17, 1830, in Santa Cruz, age one day, of Puebla and godparents were Francisco Sanchez and Maria Ysabel Tafoya.[431]

In the 1860 San Jose census, Agapito was age 28 and a merchant with real estate valued at $200 and personal estate valued at $1000. His wife, Cesaria, was 23 and children at home were: Ramon, 10; Doroteo, 8; Francisco, 5 and Albina, 2.[432]

Jose Agapito married (2nd) Maria Francisca Antonia Blea, daughter of Jose Desiderio Blea and Josefa Lucero, on July 20, 1870, in Las Vegas. Agapito was the widower of Cesaria Lopez and Francisca was the widow of Cruz Crespin. Godparents were Domingo Peña and Monica Gallegos.[433]

Agapito was living in Las Vegas when the 1870 census was enumerated. He had also just remarried. He was 39 and a farm worker with real estate valued at $275 and personal estate valued at $468. His second wife was Francisca, age 38. Vigil children at home were: Doroteo, 14; Francisco, 12; Albina, 10; Maria,

---

[427] 1870 United States Federal Census, Territory of New Mexico. Roll M593-895; Guadalupe Garcia; San Miguel County; Arroyo de Conchas, p. 6B. Ancestry, www.ancestry.com, Provo, UT.

[428] 1880 United States Federal Census, Territory of New Mexico. Roll 803; Guadalupe Garcia; San Miguel County, La Cuesta, ED 030, p. 263C. Ancestry, www.ancestry.com, Provo, UT.

[429] Arellanes, Pfeufer and Olmsted, Windham and Baca, *San Miguel del Bado Baptisms, Vol. I, 1829-1844*, p. 75.

[430] Arellanes, Windham and Baca, *San Miguel del Bado Marriages, 1829-1878*, p. 84.

[431] Olmsted, Windham and Baca, *Santa Cruz Baptisms, Vol. 3, 1827-1856*, p. 26.

[432] 1860 United States Federal Census, Territory of New Mexico. Roll M653-713; Agapito Vigil; San Miguel County, San Jose; family #3101, p. 105. Ancestry, www.ancestry.com, Provo, UT.

[433] Padilla y Baca, *New Mexico Marriages, Las Vegas, Nuestra Señora de los Dolores, January 1853 - December 1882*, p. 78.

8; Candelaria, 6 and Manuel, 4. Francisca had a son, Venancio Crespin, age 12, living with them.[434]

x. Jose Santiago Lopez was baptized on November 1, 1837, in San Miguel del Bado, age 3 days, born in San Jose and godparents were Francisco Lopez and Petra Baca.[435]

Jose Santiago married Estefana Aragon, daughter of Antonio de los Reyes Aragon and Maria Estefana de Altagracia Gonzales, on September 21, 1856, in San Miguel del Bado. Santiago was from San Jose and Estefana was from La Cuesta. Godparents were Jose de Jesus Garcia and Efigenia Lopez.[436]

Santiago signed his will on the 8th of December 1860. He named his wife, Estefanita Aragon, and one daughter, Maria Luscita Lopez. He also named his two brothers: Prudencio Lopez and Juan Atencio, (brother in law). Her father was Antonio Reyes Aragon. Witnesses were Antonio Tafoya, Fernando Villanueva and Ignacio Aragon. His executor, Antonio Reyes Aragon, probated the will on the 14th of December 1860.[437]

Estefana Aragon was baptized on January 5, 1842, in San Miguel del Bado, born on the 27th of December and godparents were Juan Andres Aragon and Juana Maria de los Reyes Aragon.[438]

Estefana married (2nd) Jose Albino Garcia, son of Miguel Garcia and Maria Rosalia Varela, on December 14, 1861, in San Miguel del Bado. Estefana was the widow of Santiago Lopez.[439]

---

[434]1870 United States Federal Census, Territory of New Mexico. Roll M593-895; Agapito Vigil; San Miguel County, Upper Las Vegas, p. 255A. Ancestry, www.ancestry.com, Provo, UT.

[435]Arellanes, Pfeufer and Olmsted, Windham and Baca, *San Miguel del Bado Baptisms, Vol. I, 1829-1844*, p. 103.

[436]Arellanes, Windham and Baca, *San Miguel del Bado Marriages, 1829-1878*, p. 112.

[437]*The New Mexico Genealogist*, Vol. XIII, No. 3, September 1974, "San Miguel County Wills," extracted by Amelia Garcia and Virginia L. Olmsted. San Miguel County Probate Book No. 3, p. 75; 1859-1862 at the New Mexico Archives.

[438]Arellanes, Pfeufer and Olmsted, Windham and Baca, *San Miguel del Bado Baptisms, Vol. I, 1829-1844*, p. 176.

[439]Arellanes, Windham and Baca, *San Miguel del Bado Marriages, 1829-1878*, p. 129.

Jose Francisco Lucero

1. Jose Francisco Lucero married Maria de la Luz Apodaca. Francisco was from Cochiti.

Francisco was a grantee of the San Jose del Bado settlement and was allotted 150 *varas* of land.[440]

He died on December 22, 1834, in San Miguel del Bado; married to Maria de la Luz Apodaca of San Miguel.[441]

Maria de la Luz Apodaca died on January 22, 1839, in San Miguel del Bado; wife of Jose Francisco Lucero of San Jose.[442]

Known children of Jose Francisco Lucero and Maria de la Luz Apodaca were as follows:

i. Maria Dolores Lucero married Antonio Jose Gallegos, son of Jose Eleuterio Gallegos and Josefa Aragon, on January 20, 1816, in San Miguel del Bado. Antonio Jose was originally from San Ildefonso and Maria Dolores was originally from Cochiti.[443]

ii. Juan Francisco Lucero married Maria Josefa Gallegos on January 8, 1799, in Cochiti, both Spanish.[444]

(See chapter for Juan Francisco Lucero, also a grantee of the San Jose del Bado settlement.)

iii. Jose Eusebio Lucero married (1st) Maria Geronima Sandoval of Cochiti.

He married (2nd) Maria Andrea Sena, daughter of Jose Ygnacio Sena and Rafaela Martin, on April 5, 1817, in San Miguel del Bado. Jose Eusebio was the widower of Maria Geronima Sandoval of Cochiti. Maria Andrea was originally from Santa Fe.[445]

Jose Eusebio married (3rd) Maria Catarina Gutierrez, daughter of Manuel Miguel Gutierrez and Maria Francisca Torres, on July 31, 1844, in San Miguel

---

[440]Spanish Archives of New Mexico, Series I, *San Miguel del Bado Land Grant*; TW #887; Roll 5, frame 244-147.

[441]NMGS Volunteers, compiler, *Pecos, San Miguel del Bado & Ribera Burials, 1796 - 1850* (Albuquerque, NM: New Mexico Genealogical Society, 2014), p. 53.

[442]NMGS Volunteers, *Pecos, San Miguel del Bado, Ribera Burials, 1796-1850*, p. 68.

[443]Anderson, *Galisteo/Pecos Marriages, 1776-1828*; AASF Roll 27; frame 262.

[444]Christmas, *Cochiti Marriages, 1776 - 1827*, AASF Roll 27: frame 111.

[445]Padilla y Baca, *New Mexico Marriages & Marriage Investigations; San Miguel del Vado, 1802-1865*, p. 115.

del Bado. Jose was the widower of Maria Andrea Sena and Maria Catarina was single.[446]

Maria Catarina Gutierrez was baptized on May 11, 1827, in San Miguel del Bado, ten days old, of El Pueblo and godparents were Antonio Gonzales and Juana Leyba.[447]

In the 1845 Las Vegas census, Jose was 67 and his wife, Catalina Gutierrez, was 19. (Jose was younger than 67).[448]

iv. Francisco Antonio de Jesus Lucero was baptized on December 12, 1779, in Cochiti, born on the 8th and godparents were Francisco Antonio Lucero and Juana Gonzales.[449]

Francisco died on December 12, 1781, in Cochiti, one year old.

v. Maria Ynes Lucero was baptized on January 14, 1784, in Cochiti, born on the 8th and godparents were Juan Jose Montoya and Maria Antonia Maese.[450]

vi. Juan Ygnacio Lucero married Maria Ysabel Martin, daughter of Alexandro Martin and Maria Teodora Marquez, on June 27, 1809, in San Miguel del Bado.[451]

Juan "J" Lucero was enumerated in the 1850 San Miguel census. He was age 70, a laborer with real estate valued at $50. His wife, "Is", was 60. Daughter, Ilaria (Hilaria,) was 25. They were living next door to daughter Maria Vidal.[452]

Juan Ygnacio died September 18, 1851, in San Miguel del Bado, adult, married to Maria Ysabel Martin.[453]

Maria Ysabel died at Las Mulas on the 31st of May 1868. She was from Rio de las Bacas, 57 years old and widow of the late Juan Ignacio Lucero.[454]

---

446 Arellanes, Windham and Baca, *New Mexico Marriages, San Miguel del Bado Church, 12 November 1829 to 10 November 1878,* p. 43.

447 Padilla y Baca, *New Mexico Baptisms, San Miguel del Vado, Pecos Mission, 1799 - 1829*, p. 54.

448 Olmsted, *New Mexico Spanish & Mexican Colonial Censuses, 1790 * 1823 * 1845*, p. 238.

449 Dressen and Baca, *New Mexico Baptisms, San Buenaventura de Cochiti Church, 1736-1873*, p. 50.

450 Dressen and Baca, *New Mexico Baptisms, San Buenaventura de Cochiti Church, 1736-1873*, p. 57.

451 Padilla y Baca, *San Miguel Marriages, 1802-1865*, p. 115.

452 1850 United States Federal Census, Territory of New Mexico. Roll M432-469; Juan J Lucero; San Miguel County, San Miguel, p. 66A, family #1287. Ancestry, www.ancestry.com, Provo, UT.

453 Anderson, *Ribera, San Miguel del Bado, Burials, 1847-1955*: AASF/FHC Film 0016879, p. 32.

454 Anderson, *Ribera, San Miguel del Bado, Burials, 1847-1955*: AASF/FHC Film 0016879, p. 106.

vii. Juana Maria Lucero was baptized on May 3, 1789, in Cochiti, age nine days, Spanish and godparents were Paulin Montoya and Maria Josefa Ortiz.[455]

viii. Juan Estevan Lucero was baptized on January 8, 1792, in Cochiti, age seven days and godparents were Juan Jose Aragon and Maria Manuela Dominguez.[456]

Juan Estevan married Maria Anastacia Martin, daughter of Dolores Martin, on November 5, 1817, in San Miguel del Bado. Maria Anastacia was the "natural" daughter of Dolores Martin and unknown father.[457]

Juan Estevan died before March 1835.

Maria Anastacia married (2nd) Juan Bautista de Jesus Duran, son of Juan de Jesus Duran and Juana Maria Gonzales, on March 16, 1835, in San Miguel del Bado. Juan Bautista was single and Maria Anastacia was the widow of Estevan Lucero.[458]

---

[455] Dressen and Baca, New Mexico Baptisms, San Buenaventura de Cochiti Church, 1736-1873, p. 67.

[456] Dressen and Baca, New Mexico Baptisms, San Buenaventura de Cochiti Church, 1736-1873, p. 78.

[457] Padilla y Baca, *San Miguel Marriages, 1802-1865*, p. 115.

[458] Arellanes, Windham and Baca, *San Miguel del Bado Marriages, 1829-1878*, p. 11.

Jose Manuel Lucero

1. Jose Manuel Lucero, son of Ygnacio Lucero and Maria Arias, was a grantee of the San Jose del Bado settlement and was allotted 300 *varas*.[459]

Manuel married Maria Manuela Armijo, daughter of Jose Manuel Armijo and Maria Andrea Gonzales, on February 3, 1803, at the Pecos Mission.[460]

Maria Manuela Armijo was baptized on October 9, 1789, in Cochiti, five days old, Spanish and godparents were Diego Felipe Borrego and Francisca Gurule.[461]

Known child of Jose Manuel Lucero and Maria Manuela Armijo was:

i. Maria Felipa Lucero married Cresencio Martinez, son of Jose Antonio Martinez and Maria Ygnacia Griego.

   In the 1845 Tecolote census, Cresencio was 34 and his wife, Felipa "Lucero," (Quinones?) was 23. Daughter, Maria Manuela, was 12.[462]

   In the 1850 Tuckelata, San Miguel County census, Cresencio was 40, a laborer with real estate valued at $50. His wife, Felipa, was 30. Children at home were Manuela, 12; Jose, 7 and Nicanora, 3.[463]

   In the 1860 Alamos census, Crecencio was given as age 55 and a laborer. His wife, Felipa, was 45 and children are Higinio, 17, a shepherd; Nicarnora, 13; Victoriano, 8; Leonicia, 2 and Salvador F. Martin (no relationship shown), 21, also a shepherd.

   But in the 1870 Alamos census, Crecencio has gotten younger - age 40, a farm laborer with real estate valued at $150. His wife, Felipa, has also gotten younger, age 30. Children at home are Victoriano, 10 and Dionicia, 5.

During this time period, most did not read and did not have calendars or Bibles so they based their ages on Saint Days. Also, anyone could have given the information, not just the family.[464]

---

[459]Spanish Archives of New Mexico, Series I, *San Miguel del Bado Land Grant*; TW 887; Roll 5, fr 244-247.

[460]Padilla y Baca, *New Mexico Marriages & Marriage Investigations; San Miguel del Vado, 1802-1865*, p. 115.

[461]Dressen and Baca, *New Mexico Baptisms, San Buenaventura de Cochiti Church, 1736-1873,* p. 70.

[462]Olmsted, *New Mexico Spanish & Mexican Colonial Censuses, 1790 * 1823 * 1845*, p. 242.

[463]1850 United States Federal Census, Territory of New Mexico. Cresencio Martinez; Roll M432-469; San Miguel County, Tuckelata, p. 75B. Ancestry, www.ancestry.com, Provo, UT.

[464]1860 United States Federal Census, Territory of New Mexico. Crencencio Martin; Roll M653-713; San Miguel County, El Monton de Alamos, p. 79. Ancestry, www.ancestry.com, Provo, UT;

1870 United States Federal 1870 Census, Territory of New Mexico. Crecencio Martinez; Roll M593-895, San Miguel County, Monton de Alamos, p. 152B. Ancestry, www.ancestry.com, Provo, UT.

Juan Francisco Lucero

1. Juan Francisco Lucero, son of Jose Francisco Lucero and Maria de la Luz Apodaca, married Maria Josefa Gallegos on January 8, 1799, in Cochiti, both Spanish.[465]

Francisco was a grantee of the San Jose del Bado settlement and was allotted 100 *varas* of land.[466]

In the 1860 San Jose census, Juan was 88 years old, a farmer with real estate valued at $180. Living in the home was his daughter, Francisca (widow of Mariano Mexias), age 40 and her children. Also in the home was a two year old, Piedad, placed in the care of Juan Lucero in 1858.[467]

Known children of Juan Francisco Lucero and Maria Josefa Gallegos were as follows:

i. Manuel Antonio Lucero died on November 12, 1803, in San Miguel del Bado, son of Francisco Lucero and Maria Gallegos.[468]

ii. Jose Antonio Lucero married Maria del Refugio Mexias, daughter of Jose Antonio "Juan" Mexias and Maria del Carmen Chavez, on November 8, 1832, in San Miguel del Bado.[469]

Jose was enumerated in the 1850 San Miguel census as 50 years old and a laborer. His wife, Refugia, was 40. Children at home were Maria d S. (Maria de Santos), age 2 and Donaciana, 2. (Maria Santos was baptized in 1844 and Donaciana was baptized in 1840).[470]

iii. Maria Lorenza Lucero married Jose Miguel Ulibarri, son of Jose Antonio Ulibarri and Maria Rosa Garcia.

Jose Miguel Ulibarri was baptized on September 27, 1801, in Santa Fe, age three days and godparents were Miguel Lovato and Rosalia Armijo.[471]

465Christmas, *Cochiti Marriages, 1776 - 1827*, AASF Roll 27: frame 111.

466Spanish Archives of New Mexico, Series I, *San Miguel del Bado Land Grant*; TW #887; Roll 5, frame 244-247. Albuquerque Genealogy Center, Albuquerque.

4671860 United States Federal Census, Territory of New Mexico. Roll M653-713; Juan Lucero; San Miguel County, San Jose; family #3063, p. 101. Ancestry, www.ancestry.com, Provo, UT.

468NMGS Volunteers, *Pecos, San Miguel del Bado & Ribera Burials, 1796 - 1850*, p. 5.

469Arellanes, Windham and Baca, *San Miguel del Bado Church, 12 November 1829 to 10 November 1878*, p. 6.

4701850 United States Federal Census, Territory of New Mexico. Roll 432-469; Jose Lucero; San Miguel County, San Miguel, p. 59B; dwelling/household #1162. Ancestry, www.ancestry.com, Provo, UT.

471May, Windham and Baca, *New Mexico Baptisms of Santa Fe, Parroquia de San Francisco de Asis, Vol. II, 15 August 1796 to 30 December 1822,* p. 59.

He died on March 18, 1864, in San Miguel del Bado, 70 years old, husband of Lorenza Lucero.[472]

iv. Juan Pablo de Jesus Lucero was baptized on May 9, 1810, in San Miguel del Bado, of San Jose and godfather was Jose Bernardo Ulibarri.[473]

v. Francisca Romana Lucero was baptized on March 14, 1819, in San Miguel del Bado and godparents were Antonio Ulibarri and Maria Beatris Lucero.[474]

Francisca Romana married Mariano Mexias, son of Jose Antonio "Juan" Mexias and Maria del Carmen Chavez, on October 6, 1839, in San Miguel del Bado, both single.[475]

Francisca was living with her father, Juan Francisco, when the 1860 San Jose census was enumerated. Juan was 50 and Francisca was 35 years old. Also in the home were her children: Filomena (Florentina); Simona, 15; Filomeno, 14 and Juan, 13.[476]

vi. Maria de la Piedad Lucero (Mexias) was baptized on July 25, 1858, in San Miguel del Bado, two days old, of San Jose. Parents were unknown and she was placed in the care of Juan Lucero. Godparents were Jose Maria Sais and Maria Lugarda Lucero.[477]

When Maria Piedad married Jose de la Cruz Anaya on January 29, 1876, in San Miguel, she was called the daughter of Mariano Mexias and Francisca Lucero.

(Francisca was #v. above and the daughter of Juan Francisco and Maria Josefa Gallegos.)

---

[472]Anderson, *Ribera/San Miguel del Bado Burials, 1848-1955*, AASF/FHL Film 0016879.

[473]Padilla y Baca, *New Mexico Baptisms, San Miguel del Vado, Pecos Mission, 1799 - 1829*, p. 60.

[474]Padilla y Baca, *Pecos Mission Baptisms, 1799 - 1829*, p. 61.

[475]Arellanes, Windham and Baca, *San Miguel del Bado Marriages, 1829-1878*, p. 20.

[476]1850 United States Federal Census, Territory of New Mexico. Roll M653-713; Juan Franco Lucero; San Miguel County, San Jose; family #3063, p. 101. Ancestry, www.ancestry.com, Provo, UT.

[477]Ernestino Tafoya and Edward J. Schoolcraft, compiler, *Bautismos, San Miguel del Vado, July 1853 - June 1868* (Albuquerque, NM: Hispanic Genealogical Research Center of New Mexico, July 1996), p. 132.

Miguel Antonio Maes

This family presented several puzzles and we have not been able to solve them so we will present the original records which we used for our research. There were no census records for Cochiti or San Juan/Ojo Caliente for the time period in question. No other Miguel Maes(e) married to a Maria Salas was found in Cochiti, San Juan, Santa Clara, Santa Cruz, Santa Fe, etc. for this time period.

~~~~~~~~~~~~~~~~~~~~~~

1. Miguel Antonio Maes married Maria Perpetua Salas.

Miguel was a grantee of the San Jose del Bado settlement and was allotted 117 *varas* of land.[478]

Miguel Maese and Ramon Maese died on April 25, 1804, in San Miguel del Bado, killed by a bear.[479] Was this the father, Miguel (though he was not noted as deceased when his daughter, Maria de la Luz, married), or were these two sons, Ramon and Miguel? No marriages were found for either of the sons.

Known children of Miguel Antonio Maes and Maria Perpetua Salas were as follows:

i. Ramon de Jesus Maes was baptized on April 18, 1789, in Cochiti, Spanish, age eight days and godparents were Antonio Lucero and Maria Antonia Duran.[480]

ii. Maria Dolores Maes was baptized on April 28, 1791, in Cochiti, age five days and godparents were Juan Armijo and Maria Manuela Gonzales.[481]

iii. Maria Manuela Maes died December 4, 1794, in Cochiti, daughter of Miguel Antonio Maes and Maria Perpetua Salas, residents of la Cañada.[482]

iv. Miguel Antonio Maes was baptized on August 20, 1794, in Cochiti; four days old and godparents were Antonio Ramon Montaño and Maria Manuela Sanchez.[483]

---

[478]Spanish Archives of New Mexico, Series I, *San Miguel del Bado Land Grant*; TW #887; Roll 5, frames 244-247.

[479]NMGS Volunteers, *Pecos, San Miguel del Bado & Ribera Burials, 1796 - 1850*, p. 6.

[480]Dressen and Baca, *New Mexico Baptisms, San Buenaventura de Cochiti Church, 1736-1873*, p. 67.

[481]Dressen and Baca, *New Mexico Baptisms, San Buenaventura de Cochiti Church, 1736-1873*, p. 76.

[482]Christmas, *Cochiti Burials, 1776 - 1873*. AASF Roll 35, frame 440.

[483]Dressen and Baca, *New Mexico Baptisms, San Buenaventura de Cochiti Church, 1736-1873*, p. 87.
~~~~~~~~~~~~~~~~~~~~~~

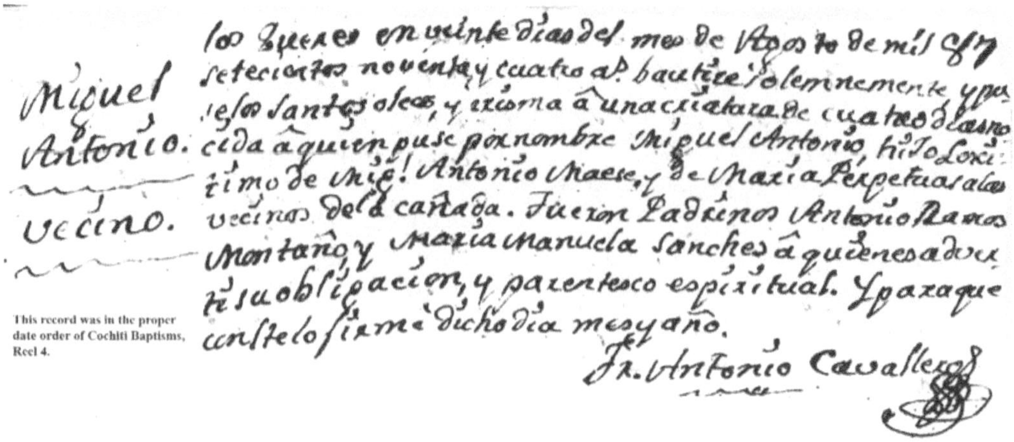

Miguel Antonio. Vecino.

los Sueres en veinte dias del mes de Agosto de mil s/
setecientos noventa y cuatro aº. bauticé solemnemente y pu
se los Santos oleos, y crisma a una criatura de cuatro dias na
cida a quien puse por nombre Miguel Antonio, hijo legí
timo de Mig! Antonio Maese, y de Maria Perpetua Salas
vecinos de la cañada. Fueron Padrinos Antonio Ramos
Montaño y Maria Manuela Sanches a quienes adver
tí su obligacion, y parentesco espiritual. Y para que
conste lo firmé dicho dia mes y año.
Fr. Antonio Caballero

This record was in the proper date order of Cochiti Baptisms, Reel 4.

v. Maria Manuela Maes was baptized on February 8, 1795, in Cochiti; age five days and godparents were Jose Antonio Gallegos and Maria Josefa Montaño.[484] (Was she adopted?)

This record was in the proper date order of Cochiti Baptisms, Reel 4.

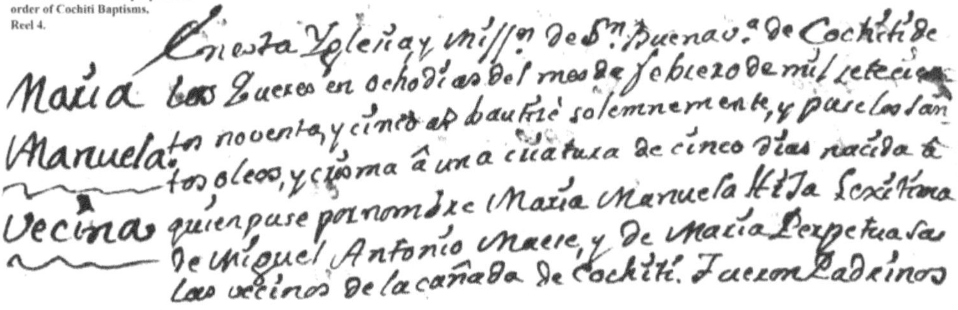

Maria Manuela. Vecina

En esta Yglesia y Mission de Sn. Buenavª de Cochiti de
los Sueres en ocho dias del mes de febrero de mil seteci
entos noventa y cinco aº bauticé solemnemente, y puse los San
tos oleos, y crisma a una criatura de cinco dias nacida a
quien puse por nombre Maria Manuela hija legítima
de Miguel Antonio Maese, y de Maria Perpetua Salas
los vecinos de la cañada de Cochiti. Fueron Padrinos

vi. Maria de la Luz Maese was baptized on May 31, 1795, in San Juan de los Caballeros, born on the 28th in Ojo Caliente and godparents were Ramon Salas and Maria Dolores Lucero.[485]

---

[484]Dressen and Baca, *New Mexico Baptisms, San Buenaventura de Cochiti Church, 1736-1873*, p. 89.

[485]Members of NMGS, compiler, *New Mexico Baptisms, Church in San Juan de los Caballeros, 1726-1798* (Albuquerque, NM: New Mexico Genealogical Society, May 2016), p. 249.

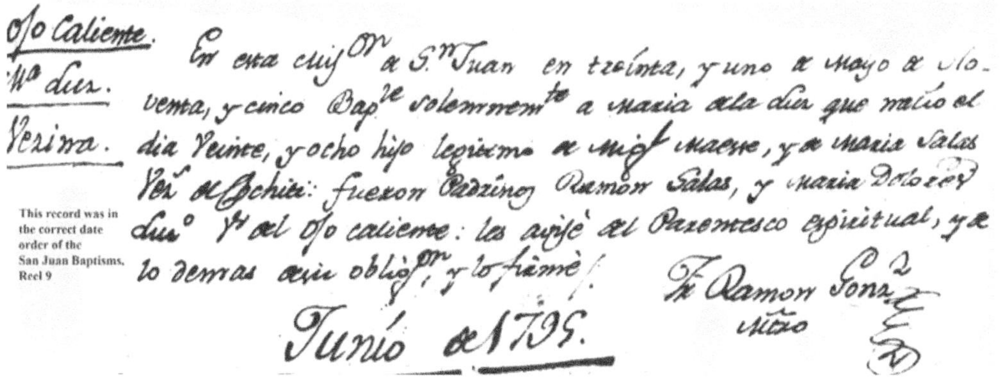

Maria de la Luz married Jose Rafael Manuel Blea, son of Juan de Jesus Blea and Maria Matiana Moya, on December 16, 1814, in Pecos. Jose Rafael was originally from Santa Fe and a resident here with Maria de la Luz Maese who was originally from Ojo Caliente.[486] All the parents are residents of this jurisdiction and none are noted as deceased.

Maria de la Luz died on January 25, 1859, in Valle de San Agustin, San Miguel County, at age 63.

In the 1841 San Miguel census, Rafael Blea was a farmer, age 37. His wife, Maria de la Luz Maes, was 34. Children at home were Tiburcia, 18; Alvina (Albino) , 9; Santiago, 7; Irinea, 4 and Juan, 10.[487]

In the 1845 Reyes de San Agustin (San Miguel) census, Jose Rafael was 54 and his wife, Lus Garcia (should be Maes), was 45. Children were Jose Albino, 17; Santiago, 15; Maria Trinidad, 10 and Juan Antonio, 7.[488]

Jose Rafael Manuel married (2nd) Maria Concepcion Villapando, daughter of Juan Jesus Villapando and Maria Paula Lujan, on March 7, 1859, in Anton Chico, both from San Agustin. Rafael was the widower of Maria de la Luz Maes and Maria Concepcion was the widow of Jose B. Barela.[489]

vii. Maria Andrea Maes was baptized on December 4, 1798, in Cochiti, age eight days and godparents were Juan Apodaca and Maria Polonia Chavez.[490]

---

[486]Padilla y Baca, *New Mexico Marriages & Marriage Investigations; San Miguel del Vado, 1802-1865,* p. 35.

[487]Christmas, Tafoya and Olguin, *New Mexico Censuses, 1790, 1793, 1803, 1823, 1829, 1841*, p. 107.

[488]Olmsted, *New Mexico Spanish & Mexican Colonial Censuses, 1790 * 1823 * 1845*, p. 248.

[489]Luis Gilberto Padilla y Baca, *New Mexico Marriages, Anton Chico, La Yglesia de San Jose, April 1857 - December 1940* (Albuquerque, NM: Hispanic Research Center of New Mexico, 2003), p. 4.

[490]Dressen and Baca, *New Mexico Baptisms, San Buenaventura de Cochiti Church, 1736-1873*, p. 107.

Alejandro Martin

1. Alejandro Martin was the young Spaniard that was 'given' to Juan de Baptista Anza, the Governor of New Mexico, by Tosapoy, a Comanche Captain on January 3, 1786. Alejandro had been a captive of the Comanche for eleven years.[491]

Alejandro was a soldier at the Santa Fe Presidio in July 31, 1787, when Jose Mares, Cristobal de los Santose and he left Santa Fe for Bexar to deal with Comanche *rancherias*.[492]

Alejandro married Maria Teodora Marquez on August 8, 1788, in Santa Fe.[493]

In the 1790 Presidio of Santa Fe census, under the soldiers retired, invalids or both, Alejandro was in household #144. He was Spanish, born in New Mexico and age 23. His wife, Teodora Marquez, was 16 and they had one daughter, age 1.[494]

In the muster roll of December 1, 1795, at the Royal Presidio of the Villa of Santa Fe, Alejandro was one of the Interpreters for Comanche and was present.[495]

Alejandro was one of the grantees of the San Jose del Bado settlement and was allotted 100 *varas* of land.[496]

Alejandro was the paid Comanche interpreter for Governor Chacon in the San Miguel/San Jose area. Alejandro replaced Jose Maria Gurule in 1804 because of "Gurulé's unruly conduct, cheating and horse thieving."[497]

He died on November 13, 1812, in Pecos; buried at the church of San Miguel del Bado.[498]

Known children of Alejandro Martin and Maria Teodora Marquez were as follows:

i. Pio Quinto Martin married (1st) Maria Leonicia Pacheco, daughter of Manuel Vicente Pacheco and Maria Concepcion Brito.

---

[491]Kessell, *Kiva, Cross and Crown*, p. 405.

[492]Thomas W. Kavanagh, *The Comanches: A History, 1706-1875* (Lincoln, NE: University of Nebraska Press, 1996), p. 138 (extracted by Henrietta M. Christmas.).

[493]Roybal, Pfeufer, Windham and Baca, *New Mexico Marriages, Santa Fe - St. Francis Parish and Military Chapel of Our Lady of Light (La Castrense), 1728-1857*, p. 99

[494]Virginia L. Olmsted, compiler, *Spanish and Mexican Censuses of New Mexico, 1750 to 1830* (Albuquerque, NM: New Mexico Genealogical Society, 1981), p. 110.

[495]Christmas, *Military Records ~ Colonial New Mexico ~ Notas y Revistas*, p. 222.

[496]Spanish Archives of New Mexico, Series I, *San Miguel del Bado Land Grant*; TW #887; Roll 5; frame 244-247. Albuquerque Genealogy Center, Albuquerque.

[497]Kessell, *Kiva, Cross & Crown*, p. 430.

[498]Christmas, *New Mexico Burials, Pecos Mission, 1798 - 1829*, AASF Roll 35, frame 710, p. 20.

Leonicia died on October 19, 1839, in San Miguel del Bado; Maria 'Dionicia,' married with Pioquinto Martin.[499]

Quinto married (2nd) Susana Roybal, daughter of Felix Roybal and Maria Cecilia Gallegos, on March 20, 1840, in San Miguel del Bado. Quinto was the widower of Leonicia Pacheco.[500]

Quinto was enumerated in the 1850 census living in Tuckelata. He was age 50, a farmer with real estate valued at $150. His wife, Susana, was 24. They had the following children: Francisco, 5; Felipa, 3 and Domingo, three months. Also in the home was Rosaria Marques, age 18.[501]

ii. Maria Gregoria Martin married Jose Domingo Romero, son of Jose Maria Romero and Maria Antonia Lain, on January 11, 1827, in San Miguel del Bado, both single.[502]

Jose Domingo Romero was baptized on July 23, 1800, in Santa Fe, born on the 20th, Spanish and godparents were Bartolome Fernandez and Luisa Tenorio.[503]

iii. Maria Ygnacia Martinez married Antonio Tapia on October 20, 1805, in San Miguel del Bado. (The bride's surname was found using baptismal records.)[504]

In the 1841 San Miguel census, Jose Antonio Tapia was a farmer and age 56. His wife, Maria Ygnacia Martin, was 50 and a daughter, Nestora, was 13.[505]

iv. Maria Paula Martin married Quito Vicente Montaño, son of Antonio Montaño and Ana Maria Aragon, on September 22, 1811, in San Miguel del Bado. Vicente was originally from Rio de Chama and Maria Paula was originally from Santa Fe.[506]

In the 1845 Plaza de Ariva (San Miguel) census, Vicente was 60 and his wife, Paula Martin, was 50.[507]

---

[499]NMGS Volunteers, *Pecos, San Miguel del Bado & Ribera Burials, 1796 - 1850*, p. 74.

[500]Arellanes, Windham and Baca, *San Miguel del Bado Church, 12 November 1829 to 10 November 1878*, p. 24.

[501]1850 United States Federal Census, Territory of New Mexico. Roll M432-469; Quinto Martin; San Miguel County, Tuckelata; family #1706, p. 88A. Ancestry, www.ancestry.com, Provo, UT.

[502]Padilla y Baca, *New Mexico Marriages & Marriage Investigations; San Miguel del Vado, 1802-1865*, p. 183.

[503]May, Windham and Baca, *New Mexico Baptisms of Santa Fe, Parroquia de San Francisco de Asis, Vol. II, 15 August 1796 to 30 December 1822*, p. 002), p. 45.

[504]Padilla y Baca, *San Miguel Marriages, 1802-1865*, p. 216.

[505]Christmas, Tafoya and Olguin, *New Mexico Censuses, 1790, 1793, 1803, 1823, 1829, 1841,* p. 110.

[506]Padilla y Baca, *San Miguel Marriages, 1802-1865*, p. 148.

[507]Olmsted, *New Mexico Spanish & Mexican Colonial Censuses, 1790 * 1823 * 1845*, p. 240 .

In the 1850 Las Vegas census, Vicente was age 50 and a laborer with real estate valued at $50. His wife, Paula, was also age 50.[508]

v. Maria Ysabel Martin married Juan Ygnacio Lucero, son of Jose Francisco Lucero and Maria de la Luz Apodaca, on June 27, 1809, in San Miguel del Bado.[509]

He died September 18, 1851 in San Miguel del Bado, adult, married to Maria Ysabel Martin.[510]

At Las Mulas on the 31st of May 1868, buried the body of Maria Ysabel Martinez, from Rio de las Bacas, 57 years old and widow of the late, Juan Ignacio Lucero.[511]

vi. Maria Josefa Petra Martin was baptized on April 20, 1799, in Santa Fe, three days old, daughter of soldier and Interpreter, Alejandro Martin and Teodora Marquez. Godparents were Tomas Sena and Josefa Quintana.[512]

Maria Josefa Petra married Antonio Jose Ulibarri, son of Francisco Ulibarri and Maria Antonia Vigil, circa 1822/1823. The marriage investigation in San Jose del Bado was started on the 29th of October and forwarded to Durango on the 27th of December 1822 for Antonio Jose Ulibarri, 28, a native of Santa Fe and resident of San Jose del Vado and Maria Josefa Petra Martin, 23, widow of her 1st husband, Cristobal Aragon, and also a resident of San Jose del Vado.

One impediment was raised by Gregorio Vigil, 36, married and from Vado who said he had a relationship with Maria Josefa Martin. The Priest, Father Bragado, stated the impediment was difficult to believe as the couple were from honorable families. On the 11th of February 1823, Vicar General Millán Rodriguez granted a dispensation from an impediment of affinity in the 3rd degree.[513]

Antonio Jose Ulibarri was baptized on January 4, 1794, in Santa Fe, born that day and godparents were Jose Maria Larrañga and Maria Paula, his sister.[514]

---

[508]1850 United States Federal Census, Territory of New Mexico. Roll M432-469; Vicinto Montano; San Miguel County, Las Vegas; family #154, p. 8B. Ancestry, www.ancestry.com, Provo, UT

[509]Padilla y Baca, *San Miguel Marriages, 1802-1865*, p. 115.

[510] *Ribera, San Miguel del Bado, Burials, 1847-1955*: AASF/FHC Film 0016879, p. 32.

[511]*Ribera, San Miguel del Bado, Burials, 1847-1955*: AASF/FHC Film 0016879, p. 106

[512]Rick Hendricks, John B. Colligan, compiler, *New Mexico Prenuptial Investigations from the Archivos Historicos del Arzobispado de Durango, 1800-1893* (Las Cruces, NM: Rio Grande Historical Collection, NMSU Library, 2000), p. 148.

[513]Hendricks, Colligan, *NM Prenuptial Investigations, Durango, 1800-1833*, p. 148.

[514]Hendricks, Colligan, *NM Prenuptial Investigations, Durango, 1800-1833*, p. 148.

In the 1845 Las Vegas census, Antonio was 45 and his wife, Juana Martin, was 40. Children at home were: Ramon, 20; Josefa, 19 and Susana, 5.[515]

vii. Jose Matias Martin died on January 1, 1803, in Santa Fe.[516]

viii. Salvador Martin was baptized on June 4, 1804, in Pecos; and godparents were Antonio Ulibarri and Maria Rosa Noriega.[517]

ix. Jose Pablo Martin was baptized on June 13, 1805, in San Miguel del Bado; Spanish and godparents were Salvador Tapia and Manuela Gonzales.[518]

x. Jose Leon Martin married Maria Paula Moya, daughter of Juan Ynocencio Moya and Maria Felipa Flores, on October 3, 1827, in San Miguel del Bado.

In the 1850 San Miguel census, Leon was given as age 40 and a farmer with real estate valued at $200. His wife, Paula, was 35. They have a boy, Juan Amado Martinez, age five months in the home, but census does not give the relationship.[519]

Maria Paula married (2nd) Miguel Lopez on November 21, 1856, in San Miguel del Bado. Miguel was the widower of Dorotea Romero and Paula was the widow of Jose Leon Martin.[520]

xi. Maria Rita Albina Martin was baptized on February 25, 1807, in Pecos, of the plaza of San Jose and godfather was Rafael Sena.[521]

Maria Rita Albina married Juan Cristoval Sena, son of Estevan Sena and Maria Ynes Moya, on November 16, 1825, in San Miguel del Bado.[522]

In the 1845 Plaza de Garcias (San Miguel) census, Juan Cristoval was 40 and his wife, Rita Martin, was 35. Children were Roque, 15; Antonio Jose, 12; Maria Ysidra, 10; Vivana, 9; Jose Felis, 7; Maria de la Cruz, 5; Albina, 3 and Dolores, 1.[523]

---

[515]Olmsted, *NM Spanish & Mexican Colonial Censuses, 1790 * 1823 * 1845*, p. 236.

[516]Christmas, *New Mexico Burials, Pecos Mission, 1798 - 1829*, frame 699.

[517]Padilla y Baca, *New Mexico Baptisms, San Miguel del Vado, Pecos Mission, 1799 - 1829*, p. 69. *Pecos, San Antonio Church Baptisms, 1726-1829*, AASF Roll 6, frame 357.

[518]Padilla y Baca, *Pecos Mission Baptisms, 1799 - 1829*, p. 69.

[519]1850 United States Federal Census, Territory of New Mexico. Roll M432-469; Leon Martinez; San Miguel County, San Miguel; family #1089, p. 56A. Ancestry, www.ancestry.com, Provo, UT

[520]Arellanes, Windham and Baca, *San Miguel del Bado Marriages, 1829-1878*, p. 113.

[521]Christmas, *New Mexico Baptisms, San Miguel del Vado, Pecos Mission, 1799 - 1829*, AASF Roll 6, frame 362.

[522]Padilla y Baca, *San Miguel Marriages, 1802-1865*, p. 208.

[523]Olmsted, *NM Spanish & Mexican Colonial Censuses, 1790 * 1823 * 1845*, p. 247.

Bernardo Martin

1. Bernardo Martin married (1st) Rosa Tafoya.

Rosa Tafoya died on May 20, 1785, in Santa Fe, married to Bernardo Martin.[524]

Bernardo was a grantee of the San Jose del Bado settlement and was allotted 100 *varas* of land.[525]

Known children of Bernardo Martin and Rosa Tafoya, all born in Santa Fe, were as follows:

i. Lugarda Martin was baptized on January 15, 1769, and godparents were Francisco Tapia and Maria Teodora de Tapia.[526]

She died on August 28, 1785, in Santa Fe at age 16, daughter of Bernardo Martin and Francisca Rosa Tafoya.[527]

ii. Antonio Joseph Martin was baptized on October 10, 1771, and godparents were Juan Rodrigues and Antonia Rodrigues.[528]

iii. Juan Nepomuceno Martin was baptized on May 16, 1774, Spanish and godparents were Juan Cristoval Gonzales and Ana Maria Segura.[529]

Juan married Maria Cristina Marquez, daughter of Justo Marquez and Maria Francisca Sanchez, April 19, 1797, in Santa Fe. Juan was called Spanish and only the given name of Juan was used.[530]

iv. Juan Pedro Martin was baptized on July 1, 1777, born yesterday and godparents were Antonio Solano and Maria Rosa Jiron. (The record shows his mother as Rosa Lovato.).[531]

524Christmas, Gallegos and Rau, *New Mexico Burials, Santa Fe - St. Francis Parish and Military Chapel of Our Lady of Light (La Castrense), 1726-1834*, p. 106.

525Spanish Archives of New Mexico, Series I, *San Miguel del Bado Land Grant*; TW 887; Roll 5, fr. 244-247. Albuquerque Genealogy Center, Albuquerque.

526Windham and Baca, *Baptisms of Santa Fe, Parroquia de San Francisco de Asis, Vol. 1, 5 September 1747 to 17 July 1791*, p. 125.

527Christmas, Gallegos and Rau, *Santa Fe Burials, 1726-1834*, p. 107.

528Windham and Baca, *Santa Fe Baptisms, Vol. 1, 1747-1791*, p. 155.

529Windham and Baca, *Santa Fe Baptisms, Vol. 1, 1747-1791*, p. 179.

530 Roybal, Pfeufer, Windham and Baca, *Santa Fe Marriages, 1728-1857*, p. 114.

531Windham and Baca, *Santa Fe Baptisms, Vol. 1, 1747-1791*, p. 212.

v. Maria Dolores Rosa Martin was baptized on February 16, 1782, age two days and godparents were Gregorio Armijo and Maria Fermina Armijo.[532]

She died on January 24, 1800, in Santa Fe at age 17, single, daughter of 'Vermando' Martin and Maria Rosa Tafoya.[533]

vi. Jose Bernardo Martin was baptized on December 3, 1784, born on the 2nd and godparents were Jose Martin and Ana Maria Marquez.[534]

He died on November 12, 1785, in Santa Fe, shown as Bernardo Pedro, son of Bernardo Martin and Maria Rosa Tafoya.[535]

Bernardo married (2nd) Juana Maria Antonia Trujillo on January 30, 1786, in Santa Fe. Bernardo was the widower of Rosa Tafoya. Witnesses included Lorenzo Marquez and Jose Gonzales.[536]

In the 1790 Santa Fe census, Bernardo was Spanish, age 34 and a farmer. His wife, Juana Antonia Trujillo, was also Spanish and age 23. They had two sons, ages 14 and 12 and one daughter, age 7.[537]

Known children of Bernardo Martin and Juana Maria Antonia Trujillo were as follows:

i. Maria Antonia Martin was baptized on May 30, 1787, in Santa Fe, age three days and godparents were Ysidro Ygnacio Rael and Maria Margarita Rael.[538]

Maria Antonia died on January 6, 1789, in Santa Fe at age 1, child of Bernardo Martinez and Juana Antonia Trujillo.[539]

ii. Maria Barbara Martin was baptized on January 13, 1790, in Santa Fe, age two days and godparents were Jose Manuel Mares and Maria Manuela Mares.[540]

Maria Barbara died on August 15, 1790, in Santa Fe; child of Bernardo Martin and Juana Antonia Trujillo.[541]

---

[532]Windham and Baca, *Santa Fe Baptisms, Vol. 1, 1747-1791*, p. 237.

[533]Christmas, Gallegos and Rau, *Santa Fe Burials, 1726-1834*, p. 147.

[534]Windham and Baca, *Santa Fe Baptisms, Vol. 1, 1747-1791*, p. 261.

[535]Christmas, Gallegos and Rau, *Santa Fe Burials, 1726-1834*, p. 108.

[536]Roybal, Pfeufer, Windham and Baca, *New Mexico Marriages, Santa Fe - St. Francis Parish and Military Chapel of Our Lady of Light (La Castrense), 1728-1857*, p.95.

[537]Olmsted, *New Mexico Spanish & Mexican Colonial Censuses, 1790 * 1823 * 1845*, p. 68; household #371.

[538]Windham and Baca, *Santa Fe Baptisms, Vol. 1, 1747-1791*, p. 287.

[539]Christmas, Gallegos and Rau, *Santa Fe Burials, 1726-1834*, p. 114.

[540]Windham and Baca, *Santa Fe Baptisms, Vol. 1, 1747-1791*, p. 313.

[541]Christmas, Gallegos and Rau, *Santa Fe Burials, 1726-1834*, p. 122.

iii. Maria del Rosario Martin was baptized on September 26, 1796, in Santa Fe, age two days and godparents were Santiago Rodriguez and Feliciana Rodriguez.[542]

iv. Maria Juana Martin was baptized on November 10, 1799, in Santa Fe, Spanish, born on the 8th and godparents were Jose Miguel Gutierres and Antonia Martin, also Spanish. (The record shows the mother as Antonia Carrillo.).[543]

v. Maria Polonia Martin was baptized on April 26, 1803, in Pecos, born in the month of May and godparents were Francisco Chavez and Geronima Sandoval.[544]

Maria Polonia died on May 25, 1803, in Pecos.[545]

542May, Windham and Baca, *New Mexico Baptisms of Santa Fe, Parroquia de San Francisco de Asis, Vol. II, 15 August 1796 to 30 December 1822*, p. 002), p. 2.

543May, Windham and Baca, *Santa Fe Baptisms, Vol. 2*, p. 38.

544Padilla y Baca, *New Mexico Baptisms, San Miguel del Vado, Pecos Mission, 1799 - 1829*, p. 69; *Pecos, San Antonio Church Baptisms, 1726-1829*, AASF Roll 6, frame 355.

545Christmas, *New Mexico Burials, Pecos Mission, 1798 - 1829*, AASF Roll 35, frame 702, p. 16.

Marcos Martin

1. Marcos Martin married Maria Manuela Moran on September 8, 1782, in Santa Fe. Godparents for the marriage were Manuel Miera and Maria Josefa Quintana. Witnesses were Lorenzo Marquez and Lucas Moya.[546]

Marcos was a grantee of the San Jose del Bado settlement and was allotted 100 *varas* of land.[547]

Maria Manuela Moran died on June 9, 1839, in San Miguel del Bado, wife of Marcos Martin of San Jose.[548]

Known children of Marcos Martin and Maria Manuela Moran were as follows:

i. Salvador Martin died on April 8, 1787, in Santa Fe; child of Marcos Martin and Manuela Moran.[549]

ii. Ana Maria Martin was born on September 24, 1788, in Santa Fe; age three days and godparents were Diego Manuel Baca and Ana Maria Esquibel. (Mother given as Manuela Tafoya.).[550]

She died on October 19, 1788, in Santa Fe; child of Marcos Martin and Manuela Moran.[551]

iii. Maria Teodora Martin died on January 3, 1794, in Santa Fe; child of 'Mateo' Martin and Manuela Moran.[552]

iv. Unnamed Martin was born on March 4, 1798 and died on March 6, 1798, in Santa Fe, two day old son of Marcos Martin and Manuela Moran.[553]

---

[546]Roybal, Pfeufer, Windham and Baca, *New Mexico Marriages, Santa Fe - St. Francis Parish and Military Chapel of Our Lady of Light (La Castrense), 1728-1857*, p. 57.

[547]Spanish Archives of New Mexico, Series I, *San Miguel del Bado Land Grant*; TW #887; Roll 5, frames 244-247.

[548]NMGS Volunteers, compiler, *Pecos, San Miguel del Bado & Ribera Burials, 1796 - 1850* (Albuquerque, NM: New Mexico Genealogical Society, 2014), p. 72.

[549]Christmas, Gallegos and Rau, *New Mexico Burials, Santa Fe - St. Francis Parish and Military Chapel of Our Lady of Light (La Castrense), 1726-1834*, p. 111.

[550]Windham and Baca, *Baptisms of Santa Fe, Parroquia de San Francisco de Asis, Vol. 1, 5 September 1747 to 17 July 1791,* p. 297.

[551]Christmas, Gallegos and Rau, *Santa Fe Burials, 1726-1834*, p. 113.

[552]Christmas, Gallegos and Rau, *Santa Fe Burials, 1726-1834*, p. 130.

[553]Christmas, Gallegos and Rau, *Santa Fe Burials, 1726-1834*, p. 142.

v. Maria Paula Martin was baptized on March 6, 1798, in Santa Fe, age three days and godparents were Jose de Ulibarri and Maria Francisca Ulibarri.[554]

vi. Maria Francisca Martin was baptized on February 1, 1799, in Santa Fe, age two days and godparents were Jose Ulibarri and Manuela Montoya.[555]

She died on August 8, 1802, in Pecos at age 3, child of Marcos Martin and 'Micaela' Moran.[556]

vii. Juan Andres Martin was baptized on November 15, 1801, in Santa Fe, age two days and godparents were Toribio Gallegos and Bernarda Baca.[557]

viii. Maria Juliana de Jesus Martin was baptized on January 11, 1803, in Santa Fe, age three days, Spanish and godparents were Francisco Baca and Maria Dolores Blea.[558]

ix. Maria Rosa Martinwas baptized on June 4, 1804, in Pecos, Spanish and godparents were Jose Montoya and Maria Teodora Vigil, also Spanish.[559]

Maria Rosamarried Manuel Luciano Montaño, son of Juan Miguel Montaño and Maria Soledad Armijo, on March 28, 1822, in San Miguel del Bado. Maria Rosalia was Spanish and single.[560]

She died on September 30, 1845, in San Miguel del Bado at age 41, widow of Manuel Urban of Las Vegas.[561]

In the 1845 Tecolote census, Manuel Montaño was 40 and his wife, Rosaria Martin, was 29. Children were: Jose Miguel, 20; Manuela, 17; Eulalio, 15; Jesus Felipe, 12; Geronimo, 10; Patrocinio, 9; Francisca, 7 and Jose Antonio, 3. Servants were Jose Eusedio, 22; Maria Josefa Lucero, 30; Manuel Antonio, 22; Maria de Jesus, 19; Manuela, 15 and Jose Ysidro, 12.[562]

---

[554]May, Windham and Baca, *New Mexico Baptisms of Santa Fe, Parroquia de San Francisco de Asis, Vol. II, 15 August 1796 to 30 December 1822,* p. 18.

[555]May, Windham and Baca, *Santa Fe Baptisms, Vol. 2*, p. 29.

[556]Christmas, *New Mexico Burials, Pecos Mission, 1798 - 1829*, AASF Roll 35, frame 698, p. 14.

[557]May, Windham and Baca, *Santa Fe Baptisms, Vol. 2*, p. 61.

[558]May, Windham and Baca, *Santa Fe Baptisms, Vol. 2*, p. 72.

[559]Christmas, *Pecos, San Antonio Church Baptisms, 1726-1829*, AASF Roll 6, frame 357.

[560]Padilla y Baca, *New Mexico Marriages & Marriage Investigations; San Miguel del Vado, 1802-1865*, p. 148.

[561]NMGS Volunteers, *Pecos, San Miguel del Bado, Ribera Burials, 1796-1850*, p. 100.

[562]Olmsted, *New Mexico Spanish & Mexican Colonial Censuses, 1790 * 1823 * 1845*, p. 242.

Pedro Antonio Martin

1. Pedro Antonio Martin married Maria Andrea Duran on January 21, 1795, in Santa Fe and godparents were Antonio Sandoval and Tomasa Rodriguez. Witnesses were Salvador Tenorio and Nicolas Apodaca.[563]

Pedro was a grantee of the San Jose del Bado settlement. He received 200 *varas* of land.[564]

He died on March 4, 1811, in San Miguel del Bado, Spanish.[565]

Known children of Pedro Antonio Martin and Maria Andrea Duran were as follows:

i. Juana Josefa Martin was baptized on February 19, 1798, in Santa Fe, age two days and godparents were Manuel Coris and Francisca Estrada.[566]

Juana Josefa married Juan Domingo Blea, son of Juan Miguel Blea and Maria Rosalia Garcia, circa 1818.

Juan Domingo Blea was baptized on August 27, 1798, in Santa Fe and godparents were Jose Maria Baca and Maria Ygnacia Quintana.[567]

He died on March 21, 1821, in San Miguel del Bado at age 22, adult, from el Vado, married to Juana Martin and he died suddenly.[568]

Juana was the head of house when the 1860 Las Vegas census was enumerated. She was age 66. Also in the home were her son-in-law, Gabriel Sanchez, age 38, daughter, Balbina, age 35 and their children: Sabina, 18; Sostena, 15 and Modesto, 12.[569]

---

[563]Roybal, Pfeufer, Windham and Baca, *New Mexico Marriages, Santa Fe - St. Francis Parish and Military Chapel of Our Lady of Light (La Castrense), 1728-1857*, p. 73.

[564]Spanish Archives of New Mexico, Series I, *San Miguel del Bado Land Grant*; TW #887; Roll 5, frame 244-247. Albuquerque Genealogy Center, Albuquerque.

[565]NMGS Volunteers, compiler, *Pecos, San Miguel del Bado & Ribera Burials, 1796 - 1850* (Albuquerque, NM: New Mexico Genealogical Society, 2014), p. 10.

[566]May, Windham and Baca, *New Mexico Baptisms of Santa Fe, Parroquia de San Francisco de Asis, Vol. II, 15 August 1796 to 30 December 1822*, p. 17.

[567]May, Windham and Baca, *Santa Fe Baptisms, Vol. 2*, p. 24.

[568]Christmas, Gallegos and Rau, *New Mexico Burials, Santa Fe - St. Francis Parish and Military Chapel of Our Lady of Light (La Castrense), 1726-1834*, p. 295.

[569]1860 United States Federal Census, Territory of New Mexico. Roll M653-713; Juana Martin; San Miguel County, Las Vegas; family #444, p. 323. Ancestry, www.ancestry.com, Provo, UT.

Juana was enumerated in the 1870 census in Las Vegas living with Gabriel Sanchez and Juana's daughter, Balbina Blea Sanchez. Juana was age 75 on this census.[570]

ii. Manuel de Jesus Martin was baptized on February 16, 1801, in Santa Fe, Spanish, age two days and godparents were Juan Jose Duran and Getrudis Alire.[571]

iii. Ana Maria Josefa Martin married Jose Simon Blea, son of Juan Miguel Blea and Maria Rosalia Garcia, on December 12, 1823, in San Miguel del Bado, both Spanish and single.[572]

She died on October 20, 1847, in San Miguel del Bado; widow of Simon Blea. (Simon was still alive.)[573]

Jose Simon Blea was baptized on January 18, 1803, Spanish, age 2 days and godparents were Jose Tomas Martin and Maria Petrona Romero.[574]

In the 1850 San Miguel del Bado census, Simon, 48, and his son, Jose Miguel, 16, were living together.[575]

Jose Simon married (2nd) Maria Miguela Sanchez, daughter of Domingo Sanchez and Maria Garcia, on November 19, 1855, in San Miguel del Bado. 'Cimon,' 54, was the widower of Maria Ana Martin. Maria Miquela was 15 and single.[576]

In the 1860 San Jose, San Miguel Co., census, Simon had remarried. He was 56 and Miquela was 25. They had two sons: Benignio, 6 and Leandro, 4.[577]

iv. Jose Toribio Martin was baptized on June 4, 1804, in Pecos and godparents were Jesus Duran and Josefa Duran.[578]

---

[570]1860 United States Federal Census, Territory of New Mexico. Roll M653-713; Juana Martin, San Miguel County, Las Vegas; p. 143A. Ancestry, www.ancestry.com, Provo, UT.

[571]May, Windham and Baca, *Santa Fe Baptisms, Vol. 2*, p. 52.

[572]Padilla y Baca, *New Mexico Marriages & Marriage Investigations; San Miguel del Vado, 1802-1865*, p. 35.

[573]NMGS Volunteers, *Pecos, San Miguel del Bado, Ribera Burials, 1796-1850*, p. 111.

[574]May, Windham and Baca, *Santa Fe Baptisms, Vol. 2*, p. 72.

[575]1850 United States Federal Census, Territory of New Mexico. Roll: M432-469; Simon Blea; San Miguel County, San Miguel, family #1199, p. 61B. Ancestry, www.ancestry.com, Provo, UT.

[576]Arellanes, Windham and Baca, *San Miguel del Bado Church, 12 November 1829 to 10 November 1878,* p. 110.

[577]1860 United States Federal Census, Territory of New Mexico. Roll: M653-713; Simon Blea; San Miguel County, San Jose; family #3087, p. 104. Ancestry, www.ancestry.com, Provo, UT.

[578]Padilla y Baca, *New Mexico Baptisms, San Miguel del Vado, Pecos Mission, 1799 - 1829*, p. 69.

v. Maria Marina Martin was baptized on February 13, 1807, in San Miguel del Bado, Spanish, of San Jose and godparents were Juan Miguel (no surname) and Maria de la Cruz (no surname).[579]

Maria Marina married Jose Ramon Benavides, son of Domingo Benavides and Maria Guadalupe Garcia, on February 3, 1828, in San Miguel del Bado, both single.[580]

In the 1850 Las Vegas census, Ramon was age 40 and a laborer with real estate valued at $50. His wife, Mariana, was 35. Daughter, Francisca, was age 15 and there was a Manuel, age 12.[581]

Jose Ramon married (2nd) Maria Nestora Tapia, daughter of Antonio Tapia and Maria Ygnacia Martinez, on October 3, 1851, in San Miguel del Bado. Ramon was 40 and the widower of Maria Marina Martin. Nestora was 21 and single.[582]

Ramon died on April 25, 1886, in La Liendre.

vi. Maria Dominga Martin was baptized on August 6, 1808, in San Miguel del Bado, Spanish, of San Jose and godmother was Maria Margarita (no surname given).[583]

---

[579]Padilla y Baca, *Pecos Mission Baptisms, 1799 - 1829*, p. 70.

[580]Padilla y Baca, *San Miguel Marriages, 1802-1865*, p. 32.

[581]1850 United States Federal Census, Territory of New Mexico. Roll: M432-469; Ramon Beniridis; San Miguel County, Las Vegas; family #219, p. 11B. Ancestry, www.ancestry.com, Provo, UT.

[582]Arellanes, Windham and Baca, *San Miguel del Bado Marriages, 1829-1878*, p. 92.

[583]Padilla y Baca, *Pecos Mission Baptisms, 1799 - 1829*, p. 70.

Juan Francisco Urban Montaño

1. Juan Francisco Urban Montaño married Rosa Herrera on July 29, 1783, in Santa Fe. Godparents were Jose Manuel Belarde and Josefa Escudero. Juan Francisco's wife was given as Rosa Nieto.[584]

Living in household #525 in Tesuque when the 1790 census was enumerated, Juan Francisco was Spanish, age 28 and a farmer. His wife, Rosa de Herrera, was also Spanish and age 22. Children at home were three sons, ages 5, 3 and 2 and one daughter, age 1.[585]

Juan was named as a grantee of the San Jose del Bado settlement as Juan Urban Montaño and was allotted 100 *varas* of land.[586]

Known children of Juan Francisco Urban Montaño and Rosa Herrera were as follows:

i. Julian Montaño married Ana Maria Herrera.

Ana Maria Herrera died on February 26, 1825, in San Miguel del Bado, shown as Ana Maria 'Perea,' married to Julian Montaño of the Plaza of San Jose.[587]

ii. Francisco Jose Montaño was baptized on October 18, 1784, in Santa Fe, age three days and godparents were Francisco Casados and his wife, Maria Sandoval.[588]

iii. Jose Antonio Montaño was baptized on April 4, 1786, in Santa Fe, age three days and godparents were Francisco Romero and Ysabel Aliri.[589]

Jose Antonio married Maria de Jesus Estrada, daughter of Pedro Antonio Estrada and Maria Guadalupe Coris, on October 19, 1807, in San Miguel del Bado. Antonio was Spanish and both were from San Jose.[590]

Maria de Jesus Estrada died on January 10, 1847, in San Miguel del Bado, adult, widow of Antonio Urban.[591]

---

[584]Roybal, Pfeufer, Windham and Baca, *New Mexico Marriages, Santa Fe - St. Francis Parish and Military Chapel of Our Lady of Light (La Castrense), 1728-1857*, p. 60.

[585]Olmsted, *New Mexico Spanish & Mexican Colonial Censuses, 1790 * 1823 * 1845*, p. 76.

[586]Spanish Archives of New Mexico, Series I, *San Miguel del Bado Land Grant*; TW #887; Roll 5, frames 244-247.

[587]NMGS Volunteers, *Pecos, San Miguel del Bado & Ribera Burials, 1796 - 1850*, p. 19.

[588]Windham and Baca, *Baptisms of Santa Fe, Parroquia de San Francisco de Asis, Vol. 1, 5 September 1747 to 17 July 1791*, p. 260.

[589]Windham and Baca, *Santa Fe Baptisms, Vol. 1, 1747-1791*, p. 275.

[590]Padilla y Baca, *New Mexico Marriages & Marriage Investigations; San Miguel del Vado, 1802-1865*, p. 148.

[591]NMGS Volunteers, *Pecos, San Miguel del Bado, Ribera Burials, 1796-1850*, p. 105.

iv. Maria Manuela Montaño was baptized on May 29, 1790, in Santa Fe, age two days and godparents were Juan Antonio Armijo and Maria de la Luz Ortiz.[592]

Maria Manuela married Juan Jose Garcia, son of Juan Garcia and Maria Luisa Martin, on July 26, 1816, in San Miguel del Bado; Juan Jose was the widower of Josefa Jaramillo and originally from Santa Fe.[593]

Juan Jose Garcia died on February 10, 1846 and was buried in the cemetery in Las Vegas, adult and widower of Manuela Montano.[594]

v. Juan Andres Montaño married Maria Efigenia Lucero, daughter of Miguel Lucero and Maria de la Luz Sandoval, on November 5, 1817, in San Miguel del Bado.[595]

He died on January 22, 1850, in San Miguel del Bado, married to Efigenia Lucero.[596]

vi. Ysidro Montaño married (1st) Maria de la Luz Duran.

Maria de la Luz Duran died on July 9, 1837, in San Miguel del Bado, wife of Ysidro "Duran" of San Jose.[597]

Ysidro married (2nd) Maria Tomasa Archuleta, daughter of Jose Miguel Archuleta and Maria Guadalupe Baca, on February 6, 1838, in San Miguel del Bado. Ysidro was the widower of Maria de la Luz Duran and Maria Tomasa was single.[598]

In the 1850 San Miguel Census, Isidro's age was given as 59, a laborer, with real estate worth $50. His wife, Tomasa, was 48 and children at home were Jose C., 11; Manuel, 9; Julian, 6 and Santiago, 4.[599]

Maria Tomasa Archuleta died on January 19, 1851, in San Miguel del Bado, married to Ysidro Montano.[600]

Ysidro married (3rd) Maria Apolonia Roybal, daughter of Julian Roybal and Maria Gertrudis Valdez, on April 2, 1851, in San Miguel del Bado.

---

592 Windham and Baca, *Santa Fe Baptisms, Vol. 1, 1747-1791*, p. 316.

593 Padilla y Baca, *San Miguel Marriages, 1802-1865*, p. 74.

594 NMGS Volunteers, *Pecos, San Miguel del Bado, Ribera Burials, 1796-1850*, p. 101.

595 Padilla y Baca, *San Miguel Marriages, 1802-1865*, p. 148.

596 Anderson, *Ribera, San Miguel del Bado, Burials, 1847-1955*: p. 23a.

597 NMGS Volunteers, *Pecos, San Miguel del Bado, Ribera Burials, 1796-1850*, p. 62.

598 Arellanes, Windham and Baca, *San Miguel del Bado Church, 12 November 1829 to 10 November 1878*, p. 17.

599 1850 United States Federal Census, Territory of New Mexico. Roll M432-469; Isidro Montana; San Miguel County, San Miguel, Family #1236, p. 63B. Ancestry, www.ancestry.com, Provo, UT.

600 Anderson, *Ribera & San Miguel Burials, 1847-1955*, p. 29.

Maria Apolonia Roybal was baptized on June 14, 1836, in San Miguel del Bado, of Pecos, age two months and godparents were Juan Estevan Aragon and Juana Maria Lucero.[601]

The 1860 San Jose census was confusing as it lists Ysidro with a Dolores Baca. Dolores (male) was listed as head of house, age 50, farmer, with real estate valued at $140 and personal estate valued at $185. Ysidro was age 58, also a farmer and with real estate valued at $200 and personal estate valued at $290. Children in the home are all Ysidro's: Apolonia, 15 (Was this Apolonia his wife and baptized in 1851?); Clemente, 21; Julian, 15; Santiago, 12; Juan, 6 and Nicanora, 2. Juan and Nicanora are children of Ysidro and Apolonia Roybal.[602]

In the 1870 San Jose census, Isidro was 78. Children at home were: Apolonia, 28; Juan, 14; Nicanora, 13 and Celsa, age 10.[603]

vii. Miguel Montaño married Maria Nieves Martin, daughter of Tomas Martin and Maria Petrona 'Petra' Romero.

Maria Nieves Martin was baptized on May 2, 1806, in Santa Fe, age three days and godparents were Juan Rafael Martin and Manuela Sandoval.[604]

In the 1841 San Miguel census, Maria de las Nieves was a widow and age 27. Children at home were: Francisca, 16; Juan, 15; Camilo, 12; Catarina, 11; Santiago, 10; Loreta, 9; Pablo, 8 and Jose Gabino, 1.[605]

Maria Nieves married (2nd) Manuel Baltasar Ribera, son of Miguel Ribera and Maria de Jesus Herrera, on January 14, 1857, in San Miguel del Bado. Baltasar was from La Cuesta and Maria Nieves was the widow of Miguel Montaño.[606]

viii. Pedro Antonio Montaño was baptized on December 31, 1799, in Santa Fe, Spanish, born on the 26th of December and godparents were Pedro Ascencio Apodaca and Maria Ysabel Moya, also Spanish.[607]

---

601 Arellanes, Pfeufer and Olmsted, Windham and Baca, *New Mexico Baptisms, San Miguel del Bado Church, Vol. I, 1 January 1829 ~ 12 May 1844*, p. 85

602 1860 United States Federal Census, Territory of New Mexico. Roll M653-713; Ysidro Montano; San Miguel County, San Jose; family #3021; p. 97. Ancestry, www.ancestry.com, Provo, UT.

603 1870 United States Federal Census, Territory of New Mexico. Roll M593-895; Isidro Montano; San Miguel County, San Jose; p. 205A. Ancestry, www.ancestry.com, Provo, UT.

604 May, Windham and Baca, *New Mexico Baptisms of Santa Fe, Parroquia de San Francisco de Asis, Vol. II, 15 August 1796 to 30 December 1822*, p. 002), p. 104.

605 Christmas, Tafoya and Olguin, *New Mexico Censuses, 1790, 1793, 1803, 1823, 1829, 1841*, p. 110.

606 Arellanes, Windham and Baca, *San Miguel del Bado Marriages, 1829-1878*, p. 114.

607 May, Windham and Baca, *Santa Fe Baptisms, Vol. 2*, p. 39.

ix. Lorenzo Eusebio Montaño was baptized on August 14, 1803, in Pecos and godparents were Antonio Gallegos and his wife, not named.[608]

x. Jose Montaño died on November 9, 1827, in San Miguel del Bado, adult son of Juan Montano and Rosa de Herrera of San Jose.[609]

xi. Martin 'Faustin' Montaño was baptized on November 15, 1807, in San Miguel del Bado, Spanish, of San Jose and godparents were (no given name) Tapia and Polonia Gallegos.[610]

Martin 'Faustin' married Juana Tomasa Marquez, daughter of Jose Francisco Marquez and Maria Antonia Rael, on February 20, 1831, in San Miguel del Bado, both from here.[611]

Martin Urban was 47 and a laborer with real estate worth $50 when he was enumerated in the 1850 La Cuesta census. His wife, Juana T., was 20 (she was born about 1817). Children were: Jose Urban, 15 and Jose de Jesus Urban, 12. (Jose de Jesus was born in 1850.).[612]

xii. Maria de la Cruz Montaño married Juan Chavez, son of Juan Domingo Chavez and Maria Francisca Martin.

She died on April 20, 1859, married to Juan Chaves.[613]

In the 1845 Tecolote census, Juan Chavis was 50 and his wife, Cruz "Urban," was 30. Children were: Maria de la Cruz, 14; Jose Eufamio, 13; Andrea, 11 and Antonia, 9.[614]

Living in 'Tuckelata' when the 1850 census was enumerated, Juan was 42, a farmer with real estate worth $400. His wife, Maria de la Cruz, was 30. Also in the home were: Jose Antonio, 18; Andrea, 14; Antonia, 11; 'Custosina', 10; Geronimo, 9; Francisca, 8; Pedro, 7 and Juan, 6.[615]

---

[608]Padilla y Baca, *New Mexico Baptisms, San Miguel del Vado, Pecos Mission, 1799 - 1829*, p. 78. *Pecos, San Antonio Church Baptisms, 1726-1829*, Roll 6, frame 356.

[609]NMGS Volunteers, *Pecos, San Miguel del Bado, Ribera Burials, 1796-1850*, p. 36.

[610]Padilla y Baca, *Pecos Mission Baptisms, 1799 - 1829*, p. 78.

[611]Arellanes, Windham and Baca, *San Miguel del Bado Marriages, 1829-1878*, p. 4.

[612]1850 United States Federal Census, Territory of New Mexico. Roll M4320469; Martin Urban; San Miguel County, La Cuesta; family #838, p. 43A. Ancestry, www.ancestry.com, Provo, UT.

[613]Anderson, *Ribera & San Miguel Burials, 1847-1955*, p. 66.

[614]Olmsted, *NM Spanish & Mexican Colonial Censuses, 1790 * 1823 * 1845*, p. 243.

[615]1850 United States Federal Census, Territory of New Mexico. Roll M4320469; Juan Chavis; San Miguel County, Tuckelata; family #1435, p. 74A. Ancestry, www.ancestry.com, Provo, UT.

Jose Antonio Montoya

1. Jose Antonio Montoya, son of Juan Manuel Montoya and Maria Chaves, married (1st) Maria Teodora Vigil on March 13, 1801, in Santa Fe, both Spanish of Santa Fe. Witnesses were not given.[616]

Antonio was a grantee of the San Jose del Bado settlement and was allotted 150 *varas* of land.[617]

Maria Teodora Vigil died on September 23, 1808, in San Miguel del Bado, Spanish, resident of Sam Miguel del Bado.[618]

Known children of Jose Antonio Montoya and Maria Teodora Vigil were as follows:

i. Pedro Ygnacio Montoya was baptized on June 4, 1804, in Pecos, Spanish and godparents were Jose Gregorio Vigil and Maria Gertrudes Vigil. (The baptismal record shows the mother as Maria Micaela Morana.).[619]

ii. Francisco Antonio Montoya died on September 29, 1808, in San Miguel del Bado, child, son of Jose Montoya.[620]

Jose Antonio married (2nd) Maria de la Encarnacion Salas, daughter of Alonzo Salas and Juana Paula Gomez, on July 29, 1812, in San Miguel del Bado. Jose Antonio was the widower of Teodora Vigil and originally from Atrisco.[621]

Maria de la Encarnacion Salas was baptized on June 15, 1785, in Cochiti, age 8 days and godparents were Ygnacio Lucero and Juana Maria de los Reyes Salas.[622]

Known children of Jose Antonio Montoya and Maria de la Encarnacion Salas, both born in San Miguel del Bado, were as follows:

i. Maria Teresa de Jesus Montoya was baptized on November 20, 1812, three days old and godparents were Santiago de Jesus Aragon and his daughter, Maria Dolores Aragon.[623]

---

[616] Roybal, Pfeufer, Windham and Baca, *New Mexico Marriages, Santa Fe - St. Francis Parish and Military Chapel of Our Lady of Light (La Castrense), 1728-1857*, p. 119.

[617] Spanish Archives of New Mexico, Series I, *San Miguel del Bado Land Grant*; TW 877, Roll 5, frame 244-247.

[618] NMGS Volunteers, compiler, *Pecos, San Miguel del Bado & Ribera Burials, 1796 - 1850* (Albuquerque, NM: New Mexico Genealogical Society, 2014), p. 8.

[619] Padilla y Baca, *New Mexico Baptisms, San Miguel del Vado, Pecos Mission, 1799 - 1829*, p. 80. *Pecos, San Antonio Church Baptisms, 1726-1829*, AASF Roll 6, frame 357.

[620] NMGS Volunteers, *Pecos, San Miguel del Bado, Ribera Burials, 1796-1850*, p. 8.

[621] Padilla y Baca, *New Mexico Marriages & Marriage Investigations; San Miguel del Vado, 1802-1865*, p. 152.

[622] Dressen and Baca, *New Mexico Baptisms, San Buenaventura de Cochiti Church, 1736-1873*, p. 59.

[623] Padilla y Baca, *Pecos Mission Baptisms, 1799 - 1829*, p. 80.

ii. Maria Feliciana Montoya was baptized on May 29, 1814, age one day and godparents were Jose Lopez and Maria Guadalupe Herrera.[624]

Maria Feliciana married Jose Mariano Barros, son of Juan Manuel Barros and Monica Rosalia 'Lapalia' Jirón.

Jose Mariano Barros was baptized on February 23, 1806, in Santa Clara and godparents were Jose Antonio Fernandez and Juana Lorenza Atencio.[625]

In the 1850 La Cuesta census, Mariano was age 37 and a farmer with real estate worth $150. His wife, Feliciana, was 25. Children at home were Juan de Dios, 18, a laborer with real estate valued at $50, and Marcelino, age 10.[626]

In the 1860 La Cuesta census, Mariano was 50, a tailor with real estate valued at $200 and personal estate worth $350. His wife, Feliciana, was 39.[627]

Jose Mariano married (2nd) Maria Josefa Aragon on November 10, 1874, in San Miguel del Bado. Mariano was the widower of Feliciana Montoya and Maria Josefa was the widow of Juan Tapia. Both were from la Cuesta.[628]

---

[624]Padilla y Baca, *Pecos Mission Baptisms, 1799 - 1829*, p. 80.

[625]Thomas D. Martinez, compiler, *Santa Clara Baptisms, 1728-1861* (California: Self Published, June 2009), p. 266.

[626]1850 United States Federal Census, Territory of New Mexico. Roll M432-469; Mariano Varas; San Miguel County, La Cuesta, p. 32B, family #637. Ancestry, www.ancestry.com, Provo, UT.

[627]1860 United States Federal Census, Territory of New Mexico. Roll M653-713; J Mariano Barrios; San Miguel County, La Cuesta, p. 249, family #1891. Ancestry, www.ancestry.com, Provo, UT.

[628]Arellanes, Windham and Baca, *San Miguel del Bado Church, 12 November 1829 to 10 November 1878*, p. 162.

Maria Ysabel Moya

1. Maria Ysabel Moya, daughter of Juan Moya and Paula Antonia Lucero, was baptized on February 15, 1762, in Santa Fe and godmother was Ana Maria Moya.[629]

Maria Ysabel married (1st) Juan Domingo Trujillo, son of Pedro 'Carrillo' Trujillo and Juliana Barbara Baca, on August 21, 1781, in Santa Fe, both of Santa Fe and godparents were Juan Cristoval Segura and Mariana Barela.[630]

Juan Domingo Trujillo was baptized on December 20, 1758, in Santa Fe and godparents were Juan Cayetano Unanue and Ana Maria Garduño.[631]

Domingo died on February 8, 1803, in Pecos at age 44, married to Ysabel Moya.[632]

Maria Ysabel was one of the women named as a grantee of the San Jose del Bado settlement and was allotted 50 *varas* of land.[633]

Known children of Maria Ysabel Moya and Juan Domingo Trujillo were as follows:

i. Maria Gregoria 'Carrillo' was baptized on March 14, 1782, in Santa Fe, age three days and godparents were Juan Joseph Martines and Maria de la Luz Martines.[634]

   She died on May 31, 1782, in Santa Fe, child of Juan Domingo Trujillo and Ysabel Moya.[635]

ii. Maria Getrudis 'Carrillo' was baptized on March 9, 1783, in Santa Fe, born on the 7th and godparents were Jose Miguel Unanue and Maria Candelaria.[636]

iii. Ysabel Trujillo died on April 13, 1785, in Santa Fe, child of Juan Domingo Trujillo and Ysabel Moya.[637]

---

[629]Windham and Baca, *Baptisms of Santa Fe, Parroquia de San Francisco de Asis, Vol. 1, 5 September 1747 to 17 July 1791*, p. 82.

[630]Roybal, Pfeufer, Windham and Baca, *New Mexico Marriages, Santa Fe - St. Francis Parish and Military Chapel of Our Lady of Light (La Castrense), 1728-1857*, p. 54.

[631]Windham and Baca, *Santa Fe Baptisms, Vol. 1, 1747-1791*, p. 61.

[632]Christmas, *New Mexico Burials, Pecos Mission, 1798 - 1829*, AASF Roll 35, frame 699.

[633]Spanish Archives of New Mexico, Series I, *San Miguel del Bado Land Grant*; TW #887; frame 244-247. Albuquerque Genealogy Center, Albuquerque.

[634]Windham and Baca, *Santa Fe Baptisms, Vol. 1, 1747-1791*, p. 238.

[635]Christmas, Gallegos and Rau, *New Mexico Burials, Santa Fe - St. Francis Parish and Military Chapel of Our Lady of Light (La Castrense), 1726-1834*, p. 99.

[636]Windham and Baca, *Santa Fe Baptisms, Vol. 1, 1747-1791*, p. 247.

[637]Christmas, Gallegos and Rau, *Santa Fe Burials, 1726-1834,* p. 104

iv. Joseph Matias Trujillo was baptized on February 25, 1785, in Santa Fe, age two days and godparents were Joseph Jasinto Perea and Paula Perea.[638]

v. Jose Francisco Trujillo was baptized on August 19, 1786, in Santa Fe, surname given as Carrillo. He was two days old and godparents were Francisco Mares and Maria Mares.[639]

vi. Jose de Jesus Trujillo was baptized on January 15, 1789, in Santa Fe, age two days and godparents were Manuel Martin and Manuela Moran.[640]

vii. Jose Maria 'Carrillo' was baptized December 14, 1790, in Santa Fe, born on the 12th and godparents were Tomas Antonio Griego and Maria de la Luz Domingues.[641]

viii. Ysidro Trujillo was baptized on May 20, 1797, in Santa Fe, age five days and godparents were Juan Francisco Montoya and Ana Maria Trujillo.[642]

Ysidro married Maria Ygnacia Suazo, daughter of Antonio Suazo and Maria Josefa Varela, circa 1825.

ix. Maria Matiana Trujillo was baptized on February 27, 1799, in Santa Fe, age two days, Spanish and godparents were Jose Maria Trujillo and Andrea Montoya.[643]

Maria Matiana married Juan Miguel Mestas, son of Pascual Mestas and Maria Rosa Molina, on February 18, 1817, in San Miguel del Bado. Juan was the widower of Maria Perfecta Salas and originally from Santa Clara mission. Matiana was originally from Santa Fe.[644]

x. Juana Maria Trujillo died on February 1, 1800, in Santa Fe, child of Juan Domingo Trujillo and Ysabel Moya, Spanish.[645]

xi. Pedro Antonio Trujillo was baptized on April 29, 1801, in Santa Fe, age two days and godparents were Jose Naranjo and Monica Ortiz.[646]

---

638 Windham and Baca, *Santa Fe Baptisms, Vol. 1, 1747-1791*, p. 264.

639 Windham and Baca, *Santa Fe Baptisms, Vol. 1, 1747-1791*, p. 279.

640 Windham and Baca, *Santa Fe Baptisms, Vol. 1, 1747-1791*, p. 300.

641 Windham and Baca, *Santa Fe Baptisms, Vol. 1, 1747-1791*, p. 320.

642 Windham and Baca, *Santa Fe Baptisms, Vol. 1, 1747-1791*, p. 7.

643 May, Windham and Baca, *New Mexico Baptisms of Santa Fe, Parroquia de San Francisco de Asis, Vol. II, 15 August 1796 to 30 December 1822*, p. 002), p. 30.

644 Padilla y Baca, *San Miguel Marriages, 1802-1865*, p. 145.

645 Christmas, Gallegos and Rau, *Santa Fe Burials, 1726-1834*, p. 148.

646 May, Windham and Baca, *Santa Fe Baptisms, Vol. 2*, p. 55.

Pedro Antonio married Maria Francisca Tafoya, daughter of Jose Antonio Tafoya and Maria Encarnacion Baca, on March 9, 1824, in San Miguel del Bado, both single.[647]

Maria Francisca Tafoya was baptized on October 12, 1807, in Santa Fe, age two days and godparents were Jose Miguel Tafoya and Maria Getrudis Lovato.[648] She died before November 1851.

Maria Ysabel married (2nd) Jose Antonio Jaramillo on September 20, 1805, in San Miguel del Bado; Maria Ysabel was the widow of Juan Domingo Trujillo.[649]

Jose Antonio Jaramillo died on August 16, 1826, in San Miguel del Bado, widower of Ysabel Moya of San Jose.[650]

Ysabel died December 29, 1831, in Santa Fe, widow of Jose Jaramillo.[651]

Known child of Maria Ysabel Moya and Jose Antonio Jaramillo was:

i. Manuel Jaramillo married Maria Ramona Lujan, daughter of Buenaventura Lujan and Maria Josefa de Jesus Gomez, on January 12, 1835, in San Miguel del Bado, both single.[652]

Maria Ramona Lujan was baptized on June 5, 1796, in Santa Cruz, age three days and godparents were Vicente Quintana and his wife, Maria de la Luz Silva.[653]

---

647 Padilla y Baca, *San Miguel Marriages, 1802-1865*, p. 221.

648 May, Windham and Baca, *Santa Fe Baptisms, Vol. 2*, p. 118.

649 Padilla y Baca, *New Mexico Marriages & Marriage Investigations; San Miguel del Vado, 1802-1865*, p. 105.

650 NMGS Volunteers, *Pecos, San Miguel del Bado, Ribera Burials, 1796-1850*, p. 30.

651 Christmas, Gallegos and Rau, *New Mexico Burials, Santa Fe - St. Francis Parish and Military Chapel of Our Lady of Light (La Castrense), 1726-1834*, p. 338.

652 Arellanes, Windham and Baca, *San Miguel del Bado Church, 12 November 1829 to 10 November 1878*, p. 10.

653 Olmsted, Windham and Baca, *New Mexico Baptisms, Santa Cruz de la Cañada Church, Vol. II, 1795-1827*, p. 6.

Juan Cristoval Tapia

1. Cristoval Tapia married Paula Romero who was also known as Paula Martin.

Cristoval was a grantee of the San Jose del Bado settlement and was allotted 126 *varas* of land.[654]

Both Cristoval and Paula died before January 1827.

Known son of Cristoval Tapia and Paula Romero was:

i. Jose Manuel Tapia was baptized on January 8, 1804, in Pecos and godparents were Diego Tapia and Maria Polonia Gallegos, his wife.[655]

Jose Manuel married Maria de la Luz Aragon, daughter of Tomas Aragon and Maria Manuela Trujillo, on January 25, 1827, in San Miguel del Bado. Jose Manuel's parents were both deceased and Maria's parents were from La Cuesta.[656]

Maria de la Luz Aragon was baptized on May 2, 1812, in San Ildefonso; from Jacona.[657]

In the 1841 San Miguel census, Jose Manuel was 24 and his wife, Maria de la Luz Aragon, was 25. Children were: Maria Agapita, 12; Biviana, 6; Juan, 4 and Paubla, 2.[658]

In the 1850 Las Vegas census, Jose Manuel was age 40, a farmer with real estate valued at $150. His wife, 'La Cruz', was 30. Children at home were: Bibiana, 16; Juan, 12 and Josepa, 9.[659]

---

[654]Spanish Archives of New Mexico, Series I, *San Miguel del Bado Land Grant*; TW #887; Roll 5, frame 244-247. Albuquerque Genealogy Center, Albuquerque.

[655]Padilla y Baca, *New Mexico Baptisms, San Miguel del Vado, Pecos Mission, 1799 - 1829*, p. 109. *Pecos, San Antonio Church Baptisms, 1726-1829*, AASF Roll 6, frame 356.

[656]Padilla y Baca, *New Mexico Marriages & Marriage Investigations; San Miguel del Vado, 1802-1865*, p. 216.

[657]Henrietta M. Christmas, *San Ildefonso Baptisms*, AASF/FHL Film #17000, p. 43.

[658]Christmas, Tafoya and Olguin, *New Mexico Censuses, 1790, 1793, 1803, 1823, 1829, 1841*, p. 119.

[659]1850 United States Federal Census, Territory of New Mexico. Roll M432-469; Jose Manuel Tapia; San Miguel County, Las Vegas, family #389, p. 19B. Ancestry, www.ancestry.com, Provo, UT.

Salvador Tapia

1. Salvador Tapia, son of Miguel Antonio Tapia and Brienda Antonia Romero, was born circa 1753 and married (1st) Maria Manuela Gonzales, daughter of Diego Gonzales, on February 12, 1775, in Belen. Salvador was age 20, Spanish, of Pajarito and son of Miguel Tapia and Brianda(?). Maria Manuela was Spanish and of the Isleta parish, daughter of Diego Gonzales and Teordora (no surname). In the actual marriage record, they are called *mulatos*.[660]

Manuela was known as Manuela Bustos in some records.

Salvador was a grantee of the San Jose del Bado settlement and was allotted 200 *varas* of land.[661]

Known children of Salvador Tapia and Maria Manuela Gonzales were as follows:

i. Diego Antonio Tapia married Maria Apolonia Gallegos, daughter of Jose Toribio Gallegos and Maria Bernarda Baca, on October 30, 1803, in the Pecos mission.[662]

Diego died circa 1820 in San Miguel del Vado.

Maria Apolonia Gallegos was baptized on February 14, 1787, in Santa Fe, age 2 days and godparents were Francisco Baca and Petrona Baca.[663]

Maria Apolonia married (2nd) Francisco Antonio Sanchez, son of Cristoval Sanchez and Pasquala de la Luz Vigil, after October 16, 1823, in Santa Cruz. On the 16th of October 1823, a marriage investigation began for Francisco Antonio Sanchez, 25, *Mexicano*, of El Rancho de Guadalupe, son of Cristoval Sanchez, deceased, and Pascuala Vigil with Apolonia Gallegos, widow of Diego Tapia, 3 years dead, both residents of El Vado.[664]

Maria Apolonia died on March 27, 1825, in San Miguel del Bado at age 38, married to Francisco 'Sanitreo' (Sanchez).[665]

ii. Jose Antonio Tapia married Maria Ygnacia Martinez, daughter of Alejandro Martin and Maria Teodora Marquez, on October 20, 1805, in San Miguel del

---

[660]Chavez, *Roots Ltd, DM's or Pre-Nuptial Investigations, (1678-1869),* p. 1880. Pfeufer, Buxton, Windham and Baca, *Marriages and Baptisms, San Augustin de la Isleta Church, Marriages: 1726-1846; Baptisms: 1730-1776; 1829-1842*, p. 20.

[661]Spanish Archives of New Mexico, Series I, *San Miguel del Bado Land Grant*; TW# 887, Roll 5, frames 244-47. Albuquerque Genealogy Center, Albuquerque, NM.

[662]Padilla y Baca, *San Miguel Marriages, 1802-1865*, p. 216.

[663]Windham and Baca, *Baptisms of Santa Fe, Parroquia de San Francisco de Asis, Vol. 1, 5 September 1747 to 17 July 1791*, p. 284.

[664]Chavez, *Roots Ltd, DM's or Pre-Nuptial Investigations, (1678-1869*, p. 1717.

[665]NMGS Volunteers, *Pecos, San Miguel del Bado, Ribera Burials, 1796-1850*, p. 19.

Bado. The bride's surname was not given in the marriage record, but was found using their children's baptismal records.[666]

In the 1841 San Miguel census, Jose Antonio Tapia was a farmer and age 56. His wife, Maria Ygnacia Martin, was 50 and a daughter, Nestora, was 13.[667]

iii. Maria Rafaela Tapia was baptized on November 5, 1787, in Cochiti, age eight days and godparents were Jose Maria Maese and Rosa Chaves.[668]

iv. Salvador Antonio Tapia was baptized on March 7, 1790, in Cochiti, 8 days old and godparents were Diego Basquez Borrego and Francisca Gurule.[669]

Salvador Antonio married (1st) Juana Maria de la Luz Estrada on December 11, 1810, in the Pecos Mission. Salvador was a resident of the plaza of San José del Bado.[670]

Juana Maria de la Luz Estrada died on December 15, 1825, in San Miguel del Bado, wife of Salvador Tapia.[671]

Salvador and his brothers, Lorenzo and Diego, plus others, petitioned for land that was called the Anton Chico Land Grant. They wanted a "small piece of land" which was 383,856 acres. They settled on the land, but were driven out by the Comanches. Two of the original settlers with twelve others moved back onto the land in 1834.[672]

Salvador Antonio married (2nd) Ynes (Maria de Nieves) Sisneros, daughter of Antonio de Jesus Sisneros and Barbara Antonia Valdez, on March 20, 1827, in San Miguel del Bado. Salvador was a widower of his 1st marriage to Maria de la Luz Estrada and Maria de Nieves was single.[673]

Ynes died on April 3, 1839, in San Miguel del Bado, adult, wife of Salvador Tapia of Anton Chico.[674]

---

[666]Padilla y Baca, *San Miguel Marriages, 1802-1865*, p. 216.

[667]Christmas, Tafoya and Olguin, *New Mexico Censuses, 1790, 1793, 1803, 1823, 1829, 1841*, p. 110.

[668]Donald Dressen and Evelyn L. Baca, *San Buenaventura de Cochiti Church, 1736-1873* (Albuquerque, NM: New Mexico Genealogical Society, 2000), p. 64.

[669]Dressen and Baca, *New Mexico Baptisms, San Buenaventura de Cochiti Church, 1736-1873*, p. 72.

[670]Padilla y Baca, *San Miguel Marriages, 1802-1865*, p. 216.

[671]NMGS Volunteers, *Pecos, San Miguel del Bado, Ribera Burials, 1796-1850*, p. 23.

[672]*Henrietta M. Christmas,* "Miguel Antonio Tapia, from Pajarito to Anton Chico," *Herencia*, V.13:4, The Quarterly Journal of the Hispanic Genealogical Research Center of New Mexico. (Albuquerque, NM, Hispanic Genealogical Research Center of New Mexico, October 2005).

[673]Padilla y Baca, *San Miguel Marriages, 1802-1865*, p. 216.

[674]NMGS Volunteers, *Pecos, San Miguel del Bado, Ribera Burials, 1796-1850*, p. 69.

Salvador Antonio married (3rd) Ana Maria Gomez, daughter of Jose Gomez and Maria Tomasa Bernal, on May 6, 1839, in San Miguel del Bado. Salvador, 46 years old, widower of both his 1st marriage to Maria Luz Estrada and 2nd marriage to Maria Ines Sisneros, married Ana Maria, age 16.[675]

Living in La Cuesta when the 1850 census was enumerated, Salvador was 78 years old, a farmer with real estate valued at $200. His wife, Anna, was 18. Children at home were: Miguel, 15; Luis, 10; Mauricio, 9; Jose de Jesus, 6; Maria Bacilia, 4 and Juliana, just born.[676]

Salvador was 89 years old and blind when the 1860 San Antonio census was enumerated. He had real estate valued at $400 and personal estate of $650. His wife, Ana Maria, was 27 and children at home included Luis, 23; Mauricio, 22; Jesus, 16; Basilia, 12; Juliana, 10; Longino, 7 and Severo, 5.

Salvador died on June 4, 1866, in Los Valles de San Agustin, San Miguel County, at age 76.[677]

Ana Maria Gomez married (2nd) Mariano Gonzales, son of Juan Gonzales, on July 3, 1870, in Anton Chico; Mariano was the widower of Teresa Roybal and Ana Maria Gomez the widow of Salvador Tapia from La Lyndre.[678]

v. Juan de Jesus Tapia was baptized on February 19, 1792, in Jemez and godparents were Francisco Antonio Borrego and Maria Borrego.[679]

Juan de Jesus died on May 21, 1796, in Cochiti at age 4.[680]

vi. Lorenso Tapia married Maria Francisca Sena, daughter of Ygnacio Sena and Maria Manuela Barranca, on January 20, 1816, in San Miguel del Bado. Lorenzo was originally from Pajarito (Albuquerque area) and Maria Francisca was from Santa Fe.[681]

Lorenzo was one of those who received parts of the Anton Chico land grant.

He died on November 19, 1836, in San Miguel del Bado; the record shows his wife as Francisca Martines.[682]

675Chavez, *DM's or Pre-Nuptial Investigations*, p. 1881; Padilla y Baca, *San Miguel Marriages, 1802-1865*, p. 217.

6761850 United States Federal Census, Territory of New Mexico. Roll 432-469; Salvador Tapia; San Miguel County, La Cuesta; family #485, p. 24B. Ancestry, www.ancestry.com, Provo, UT.

677Henrietta M. Christmas, *Anton Chico Burials, 1857-1956,* AASF/FHL Film 16628.

678Luis Gilberto Padilla y Baca, *New Mexico Marriages, Anton Chico, La Yglesia de San Jose, April 1857 - December 1940* (Albuquerque, NM: Hispanic Research Center of New Mexico, 2003), p. 33.

679Christmas, *Jemez Baptisms, 1704-1829*, AASF 5.

680Christmas, *Cochiti Burials, 1776 - 1873*: pp. 445-456, AASF Roll 35.

681Anderson, *Galisteo/Pecos Marriages, 1776-1828,* AASF Roll 27, frame 262.

682NMGS Volunteers, *Pecos, San Miguel del Bado, Ribera Burials, 1796-1850*, p. 60.

Salvador married (2nd) Maria Silvestre Montaño on April 17, 1806, in San Miguel del Bado, in the Pecos mission; Salvador Tapia, widower, with Maria Silvestra (no surname given).[683]

Maria Silvestre Montaño died on September 30, 1826, in San Miguel del Bado; she left a widower, Salvador Tapia of Cuesta.[684]

Salvador died on July 16, 1834, in San Miguel del Bado, married to Silvestre Montaño.[685]

Known children of Salvador Tapia and Maria Silvestre Montaño were as follows:

i. Jose Candelaria Tapia was baptized on February 22, 1810, in San Miguel del Bado, Spanish, of San Jose and godparents were Fernando Ulibarri and Ynes Gallegos.[686]

   Jose Candelaria married Guadalupe Sanchez, daughter of Ysidro Sanchez and Maria Francisca Atencio, on January 28, 1834, in San Miguel del Bado. The marriage investigation was dated January 1834 in San Miguel del Bado for a Jose Candelaria Tapia, age 24, with Maria Guadalupe Otero, age 15. No parents were given for either. Witnesses were Ramon Ulibarri, age 26, married; Rafael Salazar, 34 and Santiago Salazar, 26, all farmers.[687]

   Candelario was living in the Chaperito area when the 1870 census was enumerated. He was 60, a farm worker with real estate valued at $75. His wife, Guadalupe, was 55. Children in the home, relationship not stated, were: Jose Guadalupe, 16; Domingo, 5; Cayetano, 3; Maria Cruz, 26, washerwoman; Julian and Faustin, 3 months old. Also, Juan Tapia, age 25 and a farm worker. Maria de la Cruz and Juan were Candelario and Guadalupe's children.[688]

ii. Maria Soledad Tapia was baptized on August 27, 1812, in San Miguel del Bado; two days old and godparents were Tomas de Jesus Padilla and his wife, Maria Gertrudis Vigil.[689]

iii. Jose Guadalupe Tapia married Francisca Atencio on March 20, 1834, in San Miguel del Bado.

683Padilla y Baca, *New Mexico Marriages & Marriage Investigations; San Miguel del Vado, 1802-1865*, p. 216.

684NMGS Volunteers, *Pecos, San Miguel del Bado, Ribera Burials, 1796-1850*, p. 31.

685NMGS Volunteers, compiler, *Pecos, San Miguel del Bado & Ribera Burials, 1796 - 1850* (Albuquerque, NM: New Mexico Genealogical Society, 2014), p. 52.

686Padilla y Baca, *New Mexico Baptisms, San Miguel del Vado, Pecos Mission, 1799 - 1829*, p. 109.

687Chavez, *DM's or Pre-Nuptial Investigations*, p. 1881. Arellanes, Windham and Baca, *San Miguel del Bado Church, 12 November 1829 to 10 November 1878*, p. 8.

6881870 United States Federal Census, Territory of New Mexico. Roll M593-895; Candelario Tapia; San Miguel County, Chaperito; p. 21B. Ancestry, www.ancestry.com, Provo, UT.

689Padilla y Baca, *Pecos Mission Baptisms, 1799 - 1829*, p. 109.

iv. Juan de Jesus Tapia was baptized on October 25, 1817, in San Miguel del Bado, three days old and godparents were Diego Tapia and Polonia Gallegos.[690]

Juan de Jesus married Josefa Aragon, daughter of Juan Ygnacio Aragon and Maria Tomasa Flores, on February 2, 1841, in San Miguel del Bado; both were single.[691]

In the 1850 La Cuesta census, Juan was 30, a laborer with real estate worth $50. His wife, J., was 18 and they had one daughter, Guadalupe, age 3.[692]

In the 1860 La Cuesta census, Juan was age 50, a laborer with real estate valued at $160. His wife, Josefa, was 40. No children were shown.[693]

v. Maria Gregoria Tapia married Pedro Antonio Salas, son of Ramon Salas and Rosa Jaramillo, on September 22, 1834, in San Miguel del Bado; both were from this jurisdiction.[694]

Maria Gregoria died before November 1851 in San Miguel del Bado.

In the 1850 Las Vegas census, Pedro was identified as Pedro Salas Aragon. He was 40 years old, a farmer with real estate valued at $450. His wife, Gregoria, was 30. Children at home were: Santa Ana (f), 12; Jose Andres, 10; Manuel, 7; Eugenio, 5; Albino, 4 and Pomanino, 2. (Albino was actually Albina, and should be 10.).[695]

Pedro Antonio Aragon married (2nd) Maria Nicolasa Benavides on November 18, 1851, in San Miguel del Bado. Pedro was 40 years old and the widower of Maria Gregoria Tapia and Maria Nicolasa was 21 and the widow of Antonio Martin.[696]

In the 1860 Cañada de Aquilar, San Miguel County census, Pedro was 54, a farmer with real estate valued at $600 and personal estate valued at $550. His new wife, Maria Nicolasa, was 37. There were no children shown in the home.[697]

---

[690]Padilla y Baca, *Pecos Mission Baptisms, 1799 - 1829*, p. 110.

[691]Arellanes, Windham and Baca, *San Miguel del Bado Marriages, 1829-1878*, p. 28.

[692]1850 United States Federal Census, Territory of New Mexico. Roll M432-469; Juan Tapia; San Miguel County, La Cuesta; family #612, p. 31A. Ancestry, www.ancestry.com, Provo, UT.

[693]1860 United States Federal Census, Territory of New Mexico. Roll M653-713; Juan Tapia; San Miguel County, La Cuesta; family #1854, p. 245. Ancestry, www.ancestry.com, Provo, UT.

[694]Arellanes, Windham and Baca, *San Miguel del Bado Marriages, 1829-1878*, p. 9.

[695]1850 United States Federal Census, Territory of New Mexico. Roll M432-469; Pedro Salas Aragon; San Miguel County, Las Vegas; family #384, p. 19B. Ancestry, www.ancestry.com, Provo, UT.

[696]Arellanes, Windham and Baca, *San Miguel del Bado Marriages, 1829-1878*, p. 94.

[697]1860 United States Federal Census, Territory of New Mexico. Roll M653-713; Pedro Salas; San Miguel County, Canada de Aquilar; family #1663, p. 188. Ancestry, www.ancestry.com, Provo, UT.

vi. Juana Maria Tapia was baptized on March 10, 1822, in San Miguel del Bado, one day old, of San Jose and godparents were Manuel Duran and Soledad Vigil.[698]

Juana Maria married Pedro Gallegos, son of Juan Gallegos and Maria Ynes Valverde.

Enumerated in the 1860 La Cuesta census, Pedro was 39 and a laborer with no other information. Juana Maria was 37. Children in the home were: Clemete, 18; Apolonia, 12; Luz, 10; Romana, 5 and Leonor, age 1.[699]

San Jose Cemetery

[698]Padilla y Baca, *Pecos Mission Baptisms, 1799 - 1829*, p. 110.

[699]1860 United States Federal Census, Territory of New Mexico. Roll M653-713; Pedro Gallegos; San Miguel County, La Cuesta; family #1913, p. 251. Ancestry, www.ancestry.com, Provo, UT

Jose Manuel Tenorio

1. Jose Manuel Tenorio was born circa 1754 and married (1st) Maria Diega Blea, daughter of Domingo Antonio Blea and Rosalia Casillas, on January 14, 1782, in Santa Fe. Godparents for the marriage were Nerio (n.s.) and Felipa Ortega.[700]

In the 1790 Santa Fe census, living in household # 332 was Jose Tenorio, Spanish, age 36 and a farmer. Included in the household were his wife, Maria Blea, *color quebrado*, age 32, two sons, 4 and 2 and one daughter age 7. Also in the home were Modesto Rodriguez, *color quebrado*, 70, and his wife, Anna Maria Velasquez, *color quebrado*, 62. They had a grandson, age 12.[701]

Maria Diega Blea was born circa 1758 in Santa Fe and died on April 27, 1791, in Santa Fe, married to Manuel Tenorio.[702]

Manuel was a grantee of the San Jose del Bado settlement and was allotted 150 *varas* of land.[703]

Known children of Jose Manuel Tenorio and Maria Diega Blea were as follows:

i. Maria Luisa Tenorio was baptized on October 20, 1782, in Santa Fe, age two days and godparents were Antonio de Jesus Lucero and Antonia Rosalia Bernal.[704]

Maria Luisa married Juan Ygnacio Rodriguez on May 1, 1799, in Santa Fe and godparents were Francisco Urioste and Barbara Gallegos.[705]

She died on May 9, 1838, in San Miguel del Bado at age 55, adult, wife of Jose Rodriguez of La Cuesta.[706]

Juan Ygnacio Rodriguez died on May 30, 1835 in Cerrito. He was married to Lucia Tenorio.[707]

700Roybal, Pfeufer, Windham and Baca, *New Mexico Marriages, Santa Fe - St. Francis Parish and Military Chapel of Our Lady of Light (La Castrense), 1728-1857*, p. 56.

701Olmsted, *New Mexico Spanish & Mexican Colonial Censuses, 1790 * 1823 * 1845*, p. 66, household #332.

702Christmas, Gallegos and Rau, *New Mexico Burials, Santa Fe - St. Francis Parish and Military Chapel of Our Lady of Light (La Castrense), 1726-1834*, p. 124.

703Spanish Archives of New Mexico, Series I, *San Miguel del Bado Land Grant*, TW #887; Roll 5, frames 244-247.

704Windham and Baca, *Baptisms of Santa Fe, Parroquia de San Francisco de Asis, Vol. 1, 5 September 1747 to 17 July 1791*, p. 244.

705Roybal and Pfeufer, Windham and Baca, *Santa Fe Marriages, 1728-1857*, p. 76.

706NMGS Volunteers, compiler, *Pecos, San Miguel del Bado & Ribera Burials, 1796 - 1850* (Albuquerque, NM: New Mexico Genealogical Society, 2014), p. 65.

707NMGS Volunteers, *Pecos, San Miguel del Bado, Ribera Burials, 1796-1850*, p. 54.

ii. Maria Barbara Tenorio was baptized on March 3, 1786, in Santa Fe and godparents were Juan Ygnacio Moya and Juana Rodriguez.[708]

She died in April, 1786, in Santa Fe, buried on the 13th, child of Jose Manuel Tenorio and Maria Blea.[709]

iii. Juan Pedro Tenorio was baptized on June 29, 1789, in Santa Fe, born on the 25th and godparents were Antonio Sandoval and Petrona Baca.[710]

Juan Pedro married Maria Dolores Salas, daughter of Maria Petra Salas, on August 18, 1811, in San Miguel del Bado. Pedro was from Santa Fe and Maria Dolores was from "la Villa de La Cañada." In later baptismal records, her surname was given as Maese/Maes.[711]

When the 1841 San Miguel census was enumerated, Dolores Maes was a widow and age 50. She was living next door to her son-in-law, Luciano Mondragon, and family.[712]

iv. An unnamed Tenorio boy died on January 19, 1791, in Santa Fe, male, parvulo.[713]

Jose Manuel married (2nd) Maria Antonia Ramirez, daughter of Jose Antonio Ramirez and Getrudes Segura, on March 20, 1794, in Santa Fe. Jose Manuel was Spanish and the widower of Maria Blea. Maria Antonia was also Spanish.[714]

Known children of Jose Manuel Tenorio and Maria Antonia Ramirez were as follows:

i. Jose Eduardo Tenorio died on November 26, 1827, in San Miguel del Bado, adult, son of Manuel Tenorio and Maria Antonia Ramirez of Cerrito.[715]

ii. Francisco Tenorio married Dolores Mondragon, daughter of Antonio Mondragon and Maria Micaela Sanchez, on October 8, 1816, in San Miguel del Bado, both single and from Santa Fe.[716]

---

708 Windham and Baca, *Santa Fe Baptisms, Vol. 1, 1747-1791*, p. 274.

709 Christmas, Gallegos and Rau, *Santa Fe Burials, 1726-1834*, p. 109.

710 Windham and Baca, *Santa Fe Baptisms, Vol. 1, 1747-1791*, p. 307.

711 Padilla y Baca, *New Mexico Marriages & Marriage Investigations; San Miguel del Vado, 1802-1865*, p. 218.

712 Christmas, Tafoya and Olguin, *New Mexico Censuses, 1790, 1793, 1803, 1823, 1829, 1841*, p. 105.

713 Christmas, Gallegos and Rau, *Santa Fe Burials, 1726-1834*, p. 123.

714 Roybal and Pfeufer, Windham and Baca, *Santa Fe Marriages, 1728-1857*, p. 109.

715 NMGS Volunteers, *Pecos, San Miguel del Bado, Ribera Burials, 1796-1850*, p. 37.

716 Padilla y Baca, *San Miguel Marriages, 1802-1865*, p. 218.

iii. Juana Maria Tenorio was baptized on November 24, 1797, in Santa Fe, age three days and godparents were Xptobal Tenorio and Feliciana Leyba.[717]

iv. Maria Teresa Tenorio died on November 13, 1804, in San Miguel del Bado, daughter of Miguel Tenorio and Maria Antonia Ramirez.[718]

v. Maria Casilda Tenorio was baptized on April 11, 1800, in Santa Fe, born on the 6th and godparents were Pablo Sena and Josefa Blea, Spanish.[719]

Maria Casilda married Antonio Ysidro Lovato, son of Miguel Lovato and Teresa Fernandez.

She died on July 16, 1838, in San Miguel del Bado at age 38, wife of Ysidro Lobato of El Serrito.[720]

In the 1841 San Miguel census, Ysidro was a widower, a farmer and age 46. Others in the home were: Dario, single, farmer, 22; Siriaco, farmer, 18; Luisa, 12; Ramona, 6 and Culas, 4.[721]

vi. Juan Nepomuseno Tenorio was baptized on June 3, 1802, in Santa Fe, age three days, Spanish and godparents were Francisco Baca and Maria Antonia Lucero.[722]

He died on February 8, 1803, in Pecos.[723]

vii. Ygnes Maria Tenorio was baptized on July 5, 1804, in Pecos, Spanish and godparents were Juan Antonio Gallegos and Maria de la Cruz, also Spanish.[724]

viii. Jose Antonio Tenorio was baptized on October 4, 1805, in San Miguel del Bado, Spanish and godmother was Teodora Reyes, also Spanish.[725]

Jose Antonio married Maria Catarina Perea, daughter of Jacinto Perea and Maria Luciana Martin.

717May, Windham and Baca, *New Mexico Baptisms of Santa Fe, Parroquia de San Francisco de Asis, Vol. II, 15 August 1796 to 30 December 1822*, p. 002, p. 13.

718NMGS Volunteers, *Pecos, San Miguel del Bado, Ribera Burials, 1796-1850*, p. 6.

719May, Windham and Baca, *Santa Fe Baptisms, Vol. 2*, p. 43.

720NMGS Volunteers, *Pecos, San Miguel del Bado, Ribera Burials, 1796-1850*, p. 66.

721Christmas, Tafoya and Olguin, *New Mexico Censuses, 1790, 1793, 1803, 1823, 1829, 1841*, p. 105.

722May, Windham and Baca, *Santa Fe Baptisms, Vol. 2*, p. 67.

723Christmas, *New Mexico Burials, Pecos Mission, 1798 - 1829*, AASF Roll 35, frame 699.

724Padilla y Baca, *New Mexico Baptisms, San Miguel del Vado, Pecos Mission, 1799 - 1829*, p. 112.

725Christmas, *New Mexico Baptisms, San Miguel del Vado, Pecos Mission, 1799 - 1829*, AASF Roll 6, frame 360.

In the 1841 San Miguel census, Antonio Tenorio was a farmer and age 30. His wife, Catarina Perea, was 25 and there were two children: Santiago, 10 and Vicente, 8.[726]

In the 1850 La Cuesta census, Catarina was shown as 27 and son, Santiago, as 16. Vicente was given as age 40. The ages may be turned around and Catarina should be age 40, Santiago, 27 and Vicente, 16.[727]

In the 1841 San Miguel del Bado census, Manuel's 2nd wife, Antonia Ramirez, was shown as a widow and age 60. Others in the home were: Juana, 30; Manuel, 20, a farmer and Dolores, 7. They are living next door to Antonio Tenorio, another son.[728]

---

[726]Christmas, Tafoya and Olguin, *New Mexico Censuses, 1790, 1793, 1803, 1823, 1829, 1841*, p. 105.

[727]1850 United States Federal Census, Territory of New Mexico. M432-469; Catalina Perea; San Miguel County, La Cuesta; family #599, p. 30B. Ancestry, www.ancestry.com, Provo, UT.

[728]Christmas, Tafoya and Olguin, *New Mexico Censuses, 1790, 1793, 1803, 1823, 1829, 1841*, p. 105.

Jose de Jesus Trujillo

1. Jose de Jesus Trujillo married Maria Guadalupe Blea.

In 1803, Jose de Jesus was a grantee of the San Jose del Bado settlement and was allotted 50 *varas* of land.[729]

Maria Guadalupe Blea died on May 30, 1805, in Pecos; *genizara* is written in the margin.[730]

Known children of Jose de Jesus Trujillo and Maria Guadalupe Blea were as follows:

i. Jose Manuel Trujillo died on October 23, 1802 in Pecos.[731]

ii. Santiago Eusebio Trujillo was baptized on August 14, 1803, in Pecos and godparents were Santiago Ruivali and his wife (not named).[732]

iii. Maria Catalina Trujillo was baptized on May 1, 1805, in San Miguel del Bado, Spanish and godparents were Juan Jose Martin and Maria Antonia, residents of Jemez.[733]

She died on May 11, 1805, in San Miguel del Bado; child of Jose de Jesus Trujillo and Barbara (no surname), *genizara*. (Mother should be Guadalupe Blea.).[734]

729Spanish Archives of New Mexico, Series I, *San Miguel del Bado Land Grant*; TW #887; Roll 5, frames 244-247.

730Christmas, *New Mexico Burials, Pecos Mission, 1798 - 1829*, AASF Roll 35, frame 701.

731Christmas, *New Mexico Burials, Pecos Mission, 1798 - 1829.*

732Padilla y Baca, *New Mexico Baptisms, San Miguel del Vado, Pecos Mission, 1799 - 1829*, p. 113.

733Padilla y Baca, *Pecos Mission Baptisms, 1799 - 1829*, p. 113.

734NMGS Volunteers, compiler, *Pecos, San Miguel del Bado & Ribera Burials, 1796 - 1850* (Albuquerque, NM: New Mexico Genealogical Society, 2014), p. 6.

Manuel Trujillo

1. Manuel de Jesus Trujillo married Barbara Armijo.

Manuel was a grantee of the San Jose del Bado settlement and was allotted 300 *varas* of land.[735]

He died on May 14, 1828, in San Miguel del Bado; Manuel de Jesus, married to Maria Barbara Armijo of San Miguel.[736]

Barbara Armijo died on August 10, 1834, in San Miguel del Bado, married to Manuel Trujillo.[737]

Known children of Manuel Trujillo and Barbara Armijo, both born in San Miguel del Bado, were as follows:

i. Santiago de Jesus Trujillo was baptized on August 9, 1807, Spanish, of San Jose and godparents were Geronimo Lopez and Juana Gonzales.[738]

Santiago de Jesus married Micaela de Jesus Gonzales, daughter of Andres Gonzales and Maria Josefa Esquibel, on October 5, 1832, in San Miguel del Bado. This couple was on a list compiled by don Jose Felipe Ortiz.[739]

Micaela de Jesus Gonzales was baptized on March 10, 1814, in San Miguel del Bado, one day old and godparents were Jose Miguel Martin and his wife, Maria Salome Martinez.[740]

Enumerated in the 1850 San Miguel County, in the community of San Miguel, Santiago Trujillo was 42, a farmer with real estate worth $500. His wife, Micaela Gonzales, was 36. Children at home were: Miguel J., 15; Vicente, 7 and Santiago, 1.[741]

Santiago had moved his family to Anton Chico when the 1860 census was enumerated. He was 45, a laborer with real estate valued at $300 and personal

---

[735]Spanish Archives of New Mexico, Series I, *San Miguel del Bado Land Grant*; TW #887, Roll 5, frames 244-247. Albuquerque Genealogy Center, Albuquerque.

[736]NMGS Volunteers, compiler, *Pecos, San Miguel del Bado & Ribera Burials, 1796 - 1850* (Albuquerque, NM: New Mexico Genealogical Society, 2014), p. 39.

[737]NMGS Volunteers, *San Miguel del Bado, Ribera Burials, 1796-1850*, p. 52

[738]Padilla y Baca, *New Mexico Baptisms, San Miguel del Vado, Pecos Mission, 1799 - 1829*, p. 113.

[739]Arellanes, Windham and Baca, *San Miguel del Bado Church, 12 November 1829 to 10 November 1878*, p. 6.

[740]Padilla y Baca, *Pecos Mission Baptisms, 1799 - 1829*, p. 47.

[741]1850 United States Federal Census, Territory of New Mexico. Roll 432-469, Santiago Trujillo, San Miguel County, San Miguel, p. 52B, Ancestry, www.ancestry.com, Provo, UT.

estate valued at $300. His wife, Micaela, was 40. Children at home were Vicente, 18; Miguela, 14 and Santiago, 8.[742]

In the 1870 Lower Anton Chico census, Santiago was 62, a farm worker with real estate valued at $100. His wife, Micaela, was 56. Son, Santiago, was 22 and Antonia Gonzales, relationship unknown, was 12.[743]

ii. Juana Maria de Jesus Trujillo was baptized on June 4, 1810, in San Miguel del Bado, from San Jose and godparents were Jose Antonio Trujillo and Ana Victoria (no surname).[744]

San Jose Cemetery headstone

[742]1860 United States Federal Census, Territory of New Mexico. Roll M653-713; Santiago Trujillo; San Miguel County, Anton Chico, family #1077; p. 8. Ancestry, www.ancestry.com, Provo, UT.

[743]1870 United States Federal Census, Territory of New Mexico. Roll 593-895; Santiago Trujillo; San Miguel County, Lower Anton Chico; dwelling/family #30, p. 120B. Ancestry, www.ancestry.com, Provo, UT.

[744]Padilla y Baca, *Pecos Mission Baptisms, 1799 - 1829*, p. 114.

Manuel Antonio Trujillo

1. Manuel Antonio Trujillo married Maria Hilaria Montoya on July 2, 1787, in Santa Fe and godparents were Josef Quintana and Maria de la Luz Ortiz.[745]

Manuel Trujillo was a grantee of the San Jose del Bado settlement and was allotted 70 *varas* of land.[746]

Known children of Antonio Manuel Trujillo and Maria Hilaria Montoya were as follows:

i. Juana Margarita Trujillo was baptized on June 26, 1788, in Santa Fe, age 5 days and godparents were Jose Maria Montoya and Maria Francisca Lopez.[747]

ii. Maria Josefa Trujillo was baptized on March 24, 1791, in Santa Fe and godmother was Maria del Rosario de la Mora.[748]

iii. Juan Jose Trujillo married (1st) Maria Juliana Salazar, daughter of Bartolome Salazar and Maria Ursula Padilla, on September 17, 1817, in San Miguel del Bado. Juan Jose was originally from La Cienega and Juliana was originally from the Santa Clara Mission.[749]

Maria Juliana Salazar was baptized on April 25, 1797, in Santa Fe, age 2 days and godparents were Francisco Alonzo Real and Maria Juliana Baca.[750]

Juan Jose married (2nd) Maria Manuela Martin on April 7, 1836, in San Miguel del Bado. Juan Jose was the widower of Maria Juliana Salazar and Maria Manuela was single.[751]

iv. Manuel Baltazar de los Reyes Trujillo was baptized on January 13, 1798, in Santa Fe, age eight days and godparents were Juan Jose Silva and Maria Silva.[752]

Manuel Baltazar de los Reyes married Maria Dolores Urioste.

---

[745]Roybal, Pfeufer, Windham and Baca, *New Mexico Marriages, Santa Fe - St. Francis Parish and Military Chapel of Our Lady of Light (La Castrense), 1728-1857*, p. 98.

[746]Spanish Archives of New Mexico, Series I, *San Miguel del Bado Land Grant*; TW 887; Roll 5, frame 244-247.

[747]Windham and Baca, *Baptisms of Santa Fe, Parroquia de San Francisco de Asis, Vol. 1, 5 September 1747 to 17 July 1791*, p. 296.

[748]Windham and Baca, *Santa Fe Baptisms, Vol. 1, 1747-1791*, p. 325.

[749]Padilla y Baca, *New Mexico Marriages & Marriage Investigations; San Miguel del Vado, 1802-1865*, p. 221.

[750]May, Windham and Baca, *New Mexico Baptisms of Santa Fe, Parroquia de San Francisco de Asis, Vol. II, 15 August 1796 to 30 December 1822*, p. 002), p. 6.

[751]Arellanes, Windham and Baca, *San Miguel del Bado Church, 12 November 1829 to 10 November 1878*, p. 14.

[752]May, Windham and Baca, *Santa Fe Baptisms, Vol. 2*, p. 16.

When the October 23, 1850, census was enumerated in San Miguel, Reyes was 50 and his wife, Dolores F., was 30. Children at home were: Manuel Antonio, 28; Ruperto, 23; Casaria, 10; Juana Maria, 8; Nicolas, 7 and Ramon, 6.[753]

v. Maria Belen Trujillo was baptized on January 22, 1800, in Santa Fe, Spanish, born on the 14th and godparents were Mariano Bernal and Ana Maria Duran, also Spanish.[754]

Maria Belen married Juan Jose (Juan de Jesus) Sandoval, son of Juan Jose Sandoval and Maria Paula Martinez on December 19, 1813, in Pecos. Both were originally from Santa Fe and now residents of San Miguel del Bado.[755]

Juan de Jesus Sandoval married (2nd) Feliciana Baca, daughter of Jose Ramon Baca and Maria Alfonsa Martin on December 8, 1826, in San Miguel del Bado. He was the widower of 'Ana Maria' Trujillo and Feliciana was from El Puertecito.

vi. Francisca Trujillo was baptized on March 3, 1802, in Santa Fe, born on the 20th of February and godparents were Juan Cayetano Segura and Ana Petrona Armijo.[756]

She married Ygnacio Padilla, son of Antonio Anastacio Padilla and Teresa Romero.

In the 1845 Plaza del Burito (San Miguel) census, "Luciano" (Ygnacio) was 57 and his wife, Francisca, was 50. The children were: Jose Maria, 7; Diego, 4; Pomuseno, 2; Romano, 8 and Florentino, 7. Romano was actually Maria Ramona and Florentino was Florentina.[757]

vii. Miguel Antonio Trujillo was baptized on June 13, 1805, in San Miguel del Bado, Spanish and godparents were Jose Vigil and Maria Gertrudes (no surname), also Spanish.[758]

---

[753]Windham, *New Mexico 1850 Territorial Census, Vol. 3, Taos and San Miguel Counties* (Albuquerque, NM: New Mexico Genealogical Society, 1976), p. 154.

[754]May, Windham and Baca, *Santa Fe Baptisms, Vol. 2*, p. 39.

[755]Padilla y Baca, *San Miguel Marriages, 1802-1865*, p. 200.

[756]May, Windham and Baca, *Santa Fe Baptisms, Vol. 2*, p. 64.

[757]Olmsted, *New Mexico Spanish & Mexican Colonial Censuses, 1790 * 1823 * 1845*, p. 244.

[758]Padilla y Baca, *New Mexico Baptisms, San Miguel del Vado, Pecos Mission, 1799 - 1829*, p. 113.

Jose Francisco Ulibarri

1. Jose Francisco Ulibarri married Maria Antonia Vigil, daughter of Antonio de los Reyes Vigil and Barbara Josefa Madrid, on May 4, 1793, in Santa Fe and godparents were Antonio Jose Castillo and Equiteria Chavez.[759]

In 1803, Francisco was named as a grantee of the San Jose del Bado settlement and was allotted 66 *varas* of land.[760] In 1822, he was a resident of San Jose del Bado.[761]

He died on January 4, 1838, in San Miguel del Bado, adult, husband of Maria Antonia Vigil of San Jose.[762]

Maria Antonia Vigil was baptized on July 20, 1776, in Santa Cruz and godparents were Joseph Quintana and Maria de Jesus Lucero.[763]

Known children of Francisco Ulibarri and Maria Antonia Vigil were as follows:

i. Antonio Jose Ulibarri was baptized on January 4, 1794, in Santa Fe, born that day and godparents were Jose Maria Larrañga and Maria Paula, his sister.[764]

Antonio Jose married Maria Josefa Petra Martin, daughter of Alejandro Martin and Maria Teodora Marquez, circa 1823/1824. The marriage investigation in San Jose del Bado was started on the 29th of October and forwarded to Durango on the 27th of December 1822 for Antonio Jose Ulibarri, 28, a native of Santa Fe and resident of San Jose del Vado and Maria Josefa Petra Martin, 23, widow of 1st husband, Cristobal Aragon, and also a resident of San Jose del Vado.

One impediment was raised by Gregorio Vigil, 36, married and from Vado who said he had a relationship with Maria Josefa Martin. The Priest, Father Bragado, stated the impediment was difficult to believe as the couple were from honorable families. On the 11th of February 1823, Vicar General Millán Rodriguez granted a dispensation from an impediment of affinity in the 3rd degree.[765]

---

759 Roybal, Pfeufer, Windham and Baca, *New Mexico Marriages, Santa Fe - St. Francis Parish and Military Chapel of Our Lady of Light (La Castrense), 1728-1857*, p. 72.

760 Spanish Archives of New Mexico, Series I, *San Miguel del Bado Land Grant*; TW #887, frames 244-247. Albuquerque Genealogy Center, Albuquerque.

761 Hendricks and Colligan, *NM Prenuptial Investigations, Durango, 1800-1833*, p. 148.

762 NMGS Volunteers, compiler, *Pecos, San Miguel del Bado & Ribera Burials, 1796 - 1850* (Albuquerque, NM: New Mexico Genealogical Society, 2014), p. 64.

763 Olmsted, Windham and Baca, *New Mexico Baptisms, Santa Cruz de la Cañada Church, Vol. 1, 1710-1794*, p. 174.

764 Hendricks, Colligan, *NM Prenuptial Investigations, Durango, 1800-1833*, p. 148.

765 Hendricks, Colligan, *NM Prenuptial Investigations, Durango, 1800-1833*, p. 148.

In the 1845 Las Vegas census, Antonio was 45 and his wife, Juana Martin, was 40. Children at home were: Ramon, 20; Josefa, 19 and Susana, 5.[766]

Maria Josefa Petra Martin was baptized on April 20, 1799, in Santa Fe, three days old, daughter of soldier and Interpreter, Alejandro Martin and Teodora Marquez. Godparents were Tomas Sena and Josefa Quintana.[767]

ii. Maria Dolores Ulibarri was baptized March 3, 1797, in Santa Fe, age three days and godparents were Juan Felipe Archuleta and Maria Getrudes Madrid.[768]

Maria Dolores married Rafael Duran, son of Ysidro Duran and Maria Manuela Quintana.

Rafael Duran was baptized on December 3, 1790, in Santa Fe and godparents were Salvador Tenorio and Ana Maria Rael.[769]

In 1822, Rafael was one of the men who petitioned for the Anton Chico land grant.

In the 1845 Las Vegas census, Rafael Duran was 55 and his wife, Dolores Ulibarri, was 45. Children at home were: Gregoria, 15; Jesus Guadalupe, 12; Juan Jose, 10 and Manuel Antonio, 5.[770]

Rafael was back in La Cuesta when the 1850 census was taken. He was age 50 and no occupation was given. His wife, 'D', was also 50. Children at home were Jose G., 18; Juan, 14 and Jose Serapio, 12.[771]

iii. Jose de la Cruz Ulibarri died May 10, 1799, in Santa Fe, child of Francisco Ulibarri and Antonia Vigil, Spanish.[772]

iv. Jose Pedro Miguel Ulibarri was baptized on December 18, 1803, in Pecos and godparents were Señor Antonio Vigil and Barbara Madrid.[773]

---

[766]Olmsted, *New Mexico Spanish & Mexican Colonial Censuses, 1790 * 1823 * 1845*, p. 236.

[767]Hendricks, Colligan, *NM Prenuptial Investigations, Durango, 1800-1833*, p. 148.

[768]May, Windham and Baca, *New Mexico Baptisms of Santa Fe, Parroquia de San Francisco de Asis, Vol. II, 15 August 1796 to 30 December 1822*, p. 002), p. 4.

[769]Windham and Baca, *Baptisms of Santa Fe, Parroquia de San Francisco de Asis, Vol. 1, 5 September 1747 to 17 July 1791*, p. 319.

[770]Olmsted, *NM Spanish & Mexican Colonial Censuses, 1790 * 1823 * 1845*, p. 236.

[771]1850 United States Federal Census, Territory of New Mexico. Roll M432-469; Rafel Duran; San Miguel County, La Cuesta; family #616, p. 31B. Ancestry, www.ancestry.com, Provo, UT.

[772] Christmas, Gallegos and Rau, *New Mexico Burials, Santa Fe - St. Francis Parish and Military Chapel of Our Lady of Light (La Castrense), 1726-1834*, p. 144.

[773]Christmas, *Pecos, San Antonio Church Baptisms, 1726-1829*, AASF Roll 6, frame 356.

Pedro died on February 12, 1804, in Pecos.[774]

v. Maria Francisca Ulibarri was baptized on October 5, 1805, in San Miguel del Bado, Spanish and godparents were Juan Antonio Gallegos and Maria Gallegos, also Spanish.[775]

Maria Francisca married Julian Jimenez, son of Juan Jose Miguel Jimenez and Maria Guadalupe Garcia.

In the 1845 Las Vegas census, Julian was 50 and his wife, Francisca Ulibarri, was 40. Children were Teresa, 20 and Donaciana, 18. There was a servant, Matiana, 10.[776]

In the October 1850 Las Vegas census, the census taker wrote the name of Julian 'Kimenes.' He was 28 and a farmer with real estate valued at $700. His wife, 'F. Ribile Kimenes,' was 25. No children listed. (Both of these people were actually in their 40's.)[777]

Enumerated in the 1860 San Antonio, San Miguel County, census, Julian was 50, a laborer with real estate valued at $200. His daughter, Matiana, was 23.[778]

vi. Lauriana Ulibarri married Nicolas Tapia, son of Diego Antonio Tapia and Maria Apolonia Gallegos, on March 6, 1824, in San Miguel del Bado, both Spanish and single.[779]

In the 1850 San Miguel census, Nicolas was 46 and a farmer with real estate valued at $200. His wife, Laureana, was 36 and children at home were: Damiana, 17; Victoria, 15; Isabel, 12; Tomas, 10; Pedro, 3 and Juan B., 2. Also in the home was Pedro J. Ruibal, 16 and a servant.[780]

Living in San Jose when the 1860 census was enumerated, Nicolas was age 50 and his wife, 'Deluvina' was 53. Sons Tomas, 19, a farm worker; Pedro, 16 and Juan B., 12 were also listed in the census.[781]

---

[774]Christmas, *New Mexico Burials, Pecos Mission, 1798 - 1829*, AASF Roll 35, frame 700, p. 15.

[775] Christmas, *Pecos, San Antonio Church Baptisms, 1726-1829,* AASF Roll 6, frame 360.

[776]Olmsted, *NM Spanish & Mexican Colonial Censuses, 1790 * 1823 * 1845*, p. 237.

[777]1850 United States Federal Census, Territory of New Mexico. Roll M432-469; Julian Kimenes; San Miguel County, Las Vegas; family #72, p. 4B. Ancestry, www.ancestry.com, Provo, UT.

[778]1860 United States Federal Census, Territory of New Mexico. Roll M653-713; Julian Jimenez; San Miguel County, San Antonio; family #1516, p. 190. Ancestry, www.ancestry.com, Provo, UT.

[779]Padilla y Baca, *New Mexico Marriages & Marriage Investigations; San Miguel del Vado, 1802-1865*, p. 216

[780]1850 United States Federal Census, Territory of New Mexico. Roll M432-469; Nicolas Tapia; San Miguel County, San Miguel; family #1229, p. 63A. Ancestry, www.ancestry.com, Provo, UT.

[781]1860 United States Federal Census, Territory of New Mexico. Roll 653-713; Nicolas Tapia; San Miguel County, San Jose; family #3094, p. 104. Ancestry, www.ancestry.com, Provo, UT.

vii. Jose Miguel Ulibarri was baptized on August 7, 1812, in San Miguel del Bado and godparents were Toribio Gallegos and his wife, Bernarda Baca.[782]

Jose Miguel married Maria Teresa de Jesus Gonzales, daughter of Juan Cristoval Gonzales and Maria Trinidad Lucero, on November 14, 1836, in San Miguel del Bado, both single.[783]

In the 1845 Tecolote census, Miguel was 27 and his wife, Teresa Gonzales, was 20. Children at home were Limona, 4; Marsalino (m), 2 and Josefa, 1. (Limona was Simona and Marsalino was Marselina).[784]

Living in Tuckeleta in San Miguel County in 1850, Jose Ulibaria, was 36 and a farmer with real estate valued at $400. His wife, Teresa, was 26. Children at home were: Maria Marcelina, 10; Josefa, 8; Jose Dario, 6; Maria Josefa, 4; Sacramenta, 1. Also listed was Matias Carades?, 60.[785]

In the 1860 San Geronimo census, Jose 'Ulibari' was 40 and a farmer with real estate valued at $1600. His wife, Teresa, was 33. Children at home were: Simona, 23; Maredina, 19 (Marselina); Josefa, 16; Dario, 14; Maria Josefa, 13; Valentina, 9; Jose Dimas, 6 and Luisa, 3.[786]

Maria Teresa de Jesus Gonzales was baptized on October 20, 1810, in Jemez, resident of San Ysidro and godparents were Jose Ygnacio Chaves and Maria de la Luz Valdez.[787]

viii. Anna Maria Ulibarri married Antonio Serafin Aragon, son of Manuel Cristobal Aragon and Josefa Martin, on January 27, 1834, in San Miguel del Bado and witnesses were Miguel Urioste, Anastacio Hernandez and Tomas Becerra.[788]

Antonio Serafin Aragon was baptized on October 30, 1814, in San Miguel del Bado, Spanish and godparents were Juan Montaño and Maria Rosa de Herrera.[789]

---

[782]Padilla y Baca, *New Mexico Baptisms, San Miguel del Vado, Pecos Mission, 1799 - 1829*, p. 117.

[783]Arellanes, Windham and Baca, *San Miguel del Bado Church, 12 November 1829 to 10 November 1878*, p.. 14.

[784]Olmsted, *NM Spanish & Mexican Colonial Censuses, 1790 * 1823 * 1845*, p. 242.

[785]1850 United States Federal Census, Territory of New Mexico. Roll M432-469; Jose Ulibaria; San Miguel County, Tuckeleta, family #1484, p. 76B. Ancestry, www.ancestry.com, Provo, UT.

[786]1860 United States Federal Census, Territory of New Mexico. Roll M653-713; Jose Ulibari; San Miguel County, San Geronimo; family #2296, p. 88. Ancestry, www.ancestry.com, Provo, UT.

[787]Padilla y Baca, *New Mexico Baptisms, Pueblo Missions, San Felipe, Santa Ana, Santo Domingo, Cochiti, Jemez*, p. 155.

[788]Arellanes, Windham and Baca, *San Miguel del Bado Marriages, 1829-1878*, p. 7.

[789]Padilla y Baca, *Pecos Mission Baptisms, 1799 - 1829*, p. 6.

In the 1845 Tecolote census, Antonio was 28 and his wife, Ana Maria Ulibarri, was 20. Children were: Jose Bitor, 10; Encarnacion, 8; Tomasa, 6 and Maria Rita, 1.[790]

In the 1850 Tuckeleta, San Miguel County, census, Antonio was 34 and a farmer with real estate valued at $150. His wife, Anna Maria, was 28. Children were: Rita, 11; Encarnacion, 9; Tomasita, 6; Micaela, 4 and Jose Gregorio, 1.[791]

When the 1860 San Geronimo census was enumerated, Anna Maria was the head of house, age 36, and a farmer with real estate valued at $200 and personal estate valued at $300. Her children at home were: Encarnacion, 18; Maria Tomasa, 15; Micaela, 13; Gregorio, 11 and Manuelito, 8. There was also Sabina Montoya, a servant, age 17.[792]

Antonio died before 1860.

---

[790]Olmsted, *NM Spanish & Mexican Colonial Censuses, 1790 * 1823 * 1845*, p. 242.

[791]1850 United States Federal Census, Territory of New Mexico. Roll M432-469; Anton Arragon; San Miguel County, Tuckelata; family #1485, p. 76B. Ancestry, www.ancestry.com, Provo, UT.

[792]1860 United States Federal Census, Territory of New Mexico. Roll M653-713; Ana Ma Ulibari; San Miguel County, San Geronimo; family #2295, p. 87. Ancestry, www.ancestry.com, Provo, UT.

Jose Antonio Ulibarri

1. Jose Antonio Ulibarri, son of Fernando Ulibarri and Maria Olaya Armenta, was baptized on March 29, 1767, in Santa Fe and godparents were Nerio Antonio Montoya and Maria Barbara de la Peña.[793]

Jose Antonio married (1st) Maria Rosa Garcia, daughter of Francisco Garcia de Noriega and Rita Padilla, on September 26, 1787, in Santa Fe and witnesses were Antonio Anaya and Getrudis Ortiz.[794]

In the 1790 Santa Fe census, Jose Antonio Ulibarri was Spanish, age 19 and a farmer. He was married to Rosa Garcia, also Spanish and age 18. They had one son, age 1.[795]

Maria Rosa Garcia was baptized on September 7, 1770, in Santa Fe and godparents were Joseph Rodriguez and Juliana Rivera.[796]

Jose Antonio was named as one of the grantees of the San Jose del Bado settlement and was allotted 60 *varas* of land.[797]

Known children of Jose Antonio Ulibarri and Maria Rosa Garcia were as follows:

i. Jose Fernando Ulibarri was baptized on February 17, 1790, in Santa Fe, age two days and godparents were Antonio Gonzales and Maria Francisca Lopez.[798]

ii. Bernardo Ulibarri married Maria Victoria "Bitaria" Gallegos, daughter of Jose Toribio Gallegos and Maria Bernarda Baca, on November 10, 1810, in San Miguel del Bado and no other information.[799]

Bernardo received part of the Anton Chico land grant on the 24th of January 1822. He died before January 1848.

iii. Jose Francisco Ulibarri married Maria Beatriz Lucero, daughter of Cristobal Lucero and Catarina Gertrudia Sedillo.

---

793 Windham and Baca, *Baptisms of Santa Fe, Parroquia de San Francisco de Asis, Vol. 1, 5 September 1747 to 17 July 1791*, p. 117.

794 Roybal, Pfeufer, Windham and Baca, *New Mexico Marriages, Santa Fe - St. Francis Parish and Military Chapel of Our Lady of Light (La Castrense), 1728-1857*, p. 98.

795 Olmsted, *New Mexico Spanish & Mexican Colonial Censuses, 1790 * 1823 * 1845*, p. 61.

796 Windham and Baca, *Santa Fe Baptisms, Vol. 1, 1747-1791*, p. 148.

797 Spanish Archives of New Mexico, Series I, *San Miguel del Bado Land Grant*; TW #887, Roll 5, frames 244-247.

798 Windham and Baca, *Santa Fe Baptisms, Vol. 1, 1747-1791*, p. 314.

799 Padilla y Baca, *New Mexico Marriages & Marriage Investigations; San Miguel del Vado, 1802-1865*, p. 225.

He died on July 27, 1834, in San Miguel del Bado, married to Maria Beatrix Lucero of San Jose.[800]

Maria Beatriz married (2nd) Jose Rafael Blea, son of Alexandro Santiago Blea and Maria Concepcion (Garcia) Griego, on December 24, 1834, in San Miguel del Bado. Jose Rafael was 25 and Maria Beatriz was the widow of Jose Francisco Ulibarri.[801]

iv. Jose Miguel Ulibarri was baptized on September 27, 1801, in Santa Fe, age three days and godparents were Miguel Lovato and Rosalia Armijo.[802]

Jose Miguel married Maria Lorenza Lucero, daughter of Juan Francisco Lucero and Maria Josefa Gallegos.

Miguel Ulibarri was enumerated in the 1850 San Miguel census as 50 years old, a laborer, with real estate valued at $50. His wife was Lorenza, age 47. [803]

He died on March 18, 1864, in San Miguel del Bado, 70 years old, the husband of Lorenza Lucero.[804]

v. Maria Barbara Josefa Ulibarri was baptized on August 23, 1811, in Pecos, Spanish and godparents were Juan Estevan Lopez and his wife, Maria Teresa Ulibarri.[805]

Maria Barbara Josefa married Jose Felipe Blea, son of Alexandro Santiago Blea and Maria Concepcion (Garcia) Griego, on November 26, 1828, in San Miguel del Bado.[806]

Jose Felipe Blea was baptized on May 2, 1806, in Santa Fe, age two days and godparents were Jose Francisco Griego and Francisca Lucero.[807]

In the 1845 Plaza de Ariva (San Miguel) census, Felipe was 28 and his wife, Barbara Ulibarri, was 22. Children at home were: Maria Dolores, 12;

---

[800]NMGS Volunteers, compiler, *Pecos, San Miguel del Bado & Ribera Burials, 1796 - 1850* (Albuquerque, NM: New Mexico Genealogical Society, 2014), p. 52.

[801]Padilla y Baca, *San Miguel Marriages, 1802-1865*, p. 35.

[802]May, Windham and Baca, *New Mexico Baptisms of Santa Fe, Parroquia de San Francisco de Asis, Vol. II, 15 August 1796 to 30 December 1822*, p. 59.

[803]1850 United States Federal Census, Territory of New Mexico. Roll 432-469; Miguel Ulibari; San Miguel County, San Miguel, p. 59B; dwelling/household #1161. Ancestry, www.ancestry.com, Provo, UT.

[804]Anderson, *Ribera/San Miguel del Bado Burials, 1848-1955*, AASF/FHL Film 0016879.

[805]Padilla y Baca, compiler, *New Mexico Baptisms, San Miguel del Vado, Pecos Mission, 1799 - 1829*, p. 117.

[806]Padilla y Baca, *San Miguel Marriages, 1802-1865*, p. 35.

[807]May, Windham and Baca, *Santa Fe Baptisms, Vol. 2*, p. 104.

Guadalupe, 10; Tomasa, 8 and Juan Jose, 6. It is possible this census was taken at the end of 1845 and that Juan Jose was six months old.[808]

When the 1850 census was enumerated, Felipe and family were living in the Las Vegas vicinity. He was age 30, a laborer with real estate valued at $50. His wife, Barbara, was 28. Children at home were: Miguel Antonio, 12; Juan B., three months; Janacia (Tomasa), 13; Esquipula, 8; Maria Antonia, 6 and Maria Ramona, 5.[809]

vi. Maria Josefa de Jesus Ulibarri died on February 9, 1838, in San Miguel del Bado, adult, the daughter of Jose Antonio Ulibarri and Maria Rosa Garcia.[810]

Jose Antonio married (2nd) Maria Concepcion Blea, daughter of Alexandro Santiago Blea and Maria Concepcion (Garcia) Griego, on March 18, 1833, in San Miguel del Bado.

In the 1845 Agua Zarca (San Miguel) census, Jose Antonio was 76 and his wife, Concepcion Blea, was 30. A daughter at home, Maria de Jesus, was 8.[811] He died before 1850.[812]

Known children of Jose Antonio Ulibarri and Maria Concepcion Blea were as follows:

i. Maria Josefa Ulibarri was baptized on September 30, 1833, in San Miguel del Bado and godparents were Jose Miguel Ulibarri and Maria Polonia Perea.[813]

Maria Josefa married Juan Antonio Argûello, son of Estevan Argûello and Maria Manuela Ortiz.

ii. Maria del Rosario de Jesus Ulibarri was baptized on December 27, 1837, and godparents were Jose Rafael Blea and Maria Beatris Lucero.[814]

Maria del Rosario de Jesus married Jesus Maria Vigil, son of Juan Vigil and Madalena Lucero, on November 18, 1850, in San Miguel del Bado. Jesus Maria was 23 and Maria del Rosario was 16. Both were single.[815]

---

[808]Olmsted, *NM Spanish & Mexican Colonial Censuses, 1790 * 1823 * 1845*, p. 239.

[809]1850 United States Federal Census, Territory of New Mexico. Roll M432-469; Felipe Brea; San Miguel County, Las Vegas, family #130, p. 7A. Ancestry, www.ancestry.com, Provo, UT.

[810]NMGS Volunteers, *Pecos, San Miguel del Bado, Ribera Burials, 1796-1850*, p. 64.

[811]Olmsted, *NM Spanish & Mexican Colonial Censuses, 1790 * 1823 * 1845*, p. 241.

[812]1850 United States Federal Census, Territory of New Mexico. Roll M432-469; Consision Blea; San Miguel County, Tuckeleta, family #1534, p. 79A. Ancestry, www.ancestry.com, Provo, UT.

[813]Arellanes, Pfeufer, Olmsted, Windham and Baca, *New Mexico Baptisms, San Miguel del Bado Church, Vol. I, 1 January 1829 ~ 12 May 1844*, p. 45.

[814]Arellanes, Windham and Baca, *San Miguel del Bado Marriages, 1829-1878*, p. 106

[815]Arellanes, Windham and Baca, *San Miguel del Bado Marriages, 1829-1878*, p. 87.

In the 1860 El Salitre, San Miguel County, census, Jesus was 26, a laborer with real estate valued at $140. His wife, Rosaria, was 28. Children were Crisantos, 1 and Leandra, 5.[816]

Enumerated in the 1870 Ojitos Frios, San Miguel County, census, Jesus was 30, a farm worker with real estate valued at $100. His wife, Rosario, was also 30. Children at home were: Leandra, 14; Crisantos, 11 and Clementa (son), 7. (Notice that Jesus only aged 4 years and Rosario aged 2 years between 1860 and 1870.).[817]

iii. Jose Hernando Ulibarri was baptized on May 9, 1846, in San Miguel del Bado, twin, born on the 7th and godparents were Jesus Gonzales and Maria de Jesus Ulibarri.[818] He was not listed on the 1850 census.

iv. Juana Maria Ulibarri was baptized on May 9, 1846, in San Miguel del Bado, twin, born on the 7th and godparents were Jesus Gonzales and Maria de Jesus Ulibarri.[819] She was not listed on the 1850 census.

v. Jose Pablo Ulibarri died on November 14, 1847, in San Miguel del Bado, child of Jose Antonio Ulibarri and Concencion Blea.[820]

In the 1850 Tuckeleta, San Miguel County, census, Concepcion Blea, Jose Antonio's 2nd wife, was living with a family by the name of "Longlad." Joseph Longlad was 45, from Canada, and no occupation was shown. His wife, Rufina Longlad, was 38 and born in New Mexico. Concepcion's age was given as 30 and she was a farmer with real estate valued at $200. Her children were Rosario, 12 and Jose Carlos, age 6.[821]

Maria Concepcion Blea married (2nd) Jose de la Asencion Montaño, son of Gregorio Montaño and Encarnacion Garcia, on September 21, 1851, in San Miguel del Bado. Jose de la Asencion was 23 and single, married to Maria Concepcion, widow of Jose Antonio Ulibarri.[822]

---

816 1860 United States Federal Census, Territory of New Mexico. Roll M653-713; Jesus MA Vigil; San Miguel County, El Salitre; family #2264, p. 57. Ancestry, www.ancestry.com, Provo, UT.

817 1870 United States Federal Census, Territory of New Mexico. Roll M593-895; Jesus MA Vigil; San Miguel County, Ojitos Frios, p. 161A. Ancestry, www.ancestry.com, Provo, UT.

818 Arellanes, Pfeufer, Bradford, Windham and Baca, *New Mexico Baptisms, San Miguel del Bado Church, Vol. II, 12 May 1844 to 6 July 1853*, p. 55.

819 Arellanes, Pfeufer and Bradford, Windham and Baca, *San Miguel del Bado Baptisms, Vol. II, 1844-1853*, p. 55.

820 NMGS Volunteers, *Pecos, San Miguel del Bado, Ribera Burials, 1796-1850*, p. 144.

821 1850 United States Federal Census, Territory of New Mexico. Roll M432-469; Consision Blea; San Miguel County, Tuckeleta, family #1534, p. 79A. Ancestry, www.ancestry.com, Provo, UT.

822 Arellanes, Windham and Baca, *Marriages, San Miguel del Bado Church, 12 November 1829 to 10 November 1878*, p. 92.

Jose Antonio Ulibarri

1. Jose Antonio Ulibarri, son of Asencio Ulibarri and Maria Francisca Armijo, was baptized on November 26, 1776, in Santa Fe, Spanish, born on the 21st and godparents were Domingo Romero and Lugarda Montoya.[823]

Jose Antonio married (1st) Maria Manuela de la Ascencion Montoya, daughter of Jose Maria Montoya and Maria Antonia Gomez, on April 30, 1797, in Santa Fe.[824]

Maria Manuela de la Ascencion Montoya was baptized on May 31, 1764, in Santa Fe, Spanish and godparents were Juan Antonio Montoya and Margarita Gallegos.[825]

Manuela died on July 23, 1807, in Pecos, at age 43.[826]

Jose Antonio was named as a grantee of the San Jose del Bado settlement and was allotted 200 *varas* of land.[827]

Known children of Jose Antonio Ulibarri and Maria Manuela de la Ascencion Montoya were as follows:

i. Ascencio Albino Ulibarri was baptized on March 4, 1798, in Santa Fe, age four days and godparents were Manuel Jose Baca and Maria Baca.[828]

Ascencio Albino married Maria Soledad Baca, daughter of Francisco Baca and Maria Ana Josefa Ortega, on January 6, 1822, in San Miguel del Bado, both Spanish and single. (Bride's surname was missing, but later found in their children's baptismal record.)[829]

---

[823]Windham and Baca, *Baptisms of Santa Fe, Parroquia de San Francisco de Asis, Vol. 1, 5 September 1747 to 17 July 1791*, p. 204.

[824]Roybal, Pfeufer, Windham and Baca, *New Mexico Marriages, Santa Fe - St. Francis Parish and Military Chapel of Our Lady of Light (La Castrense), 1728-1857*, p. 114.

[825]Windham and Baca, *Santa Fe Baptisms, Vol. 1, 1747-1791*, p. 98.

[826]Christmas, *New Mexico Burials, Pecos Mission, 1798 - 1829*, AASF Roll 35, frame 703.

[827]Spanish Archives of New Mexico, Series I, *San Jose Land Grant*; TW #887; Roll 5, frames 244-247. Albuquerque Genealogy Center, Albuquerque.

[828]May, Windham and Baca, *New Mexico Baptisms of Santa Fe, Parroquia de San Francisco de Asis, Vol. II, 15 August 1796 to 30 December 1822*, p. 18.

[829]Padilla y Baca, *San Miguel Marriages, 1802-1865*, p. 225.

In the 1850 La Cuesta, San Miguel County, census, Ascencio was 54 and a farmer with real estate valued at $600. Two of his children are living with him: Teodosio, 13 and Felicita, 9.[830]

The 1860 Lower Gallinas, San Miguel County, census is confusing as it shows Albino's daughter, Viviana, living with Albino while her husband, Esperidon Braseda, and children are living next door. Albino was 61 and Viviana was 25. Esperidion was a blacksmith, age 30, and children are Francisca, 8; Ysabel, 5 and Jose, 2.[831]

Albino was still alive when the 1870 Lower La Cueva, San Miguel County census was enumerated. He was age 73 and a farm worker with real estate valued at $200 and personal estate valued at $300. His daughters, Biviana, 40 and Felicita, 29 were living with him as well as some of their children and some of the children of his deceased son, Teodosio.[832]

ii. Maria Ygnacia Ulibarri was baptized on October 6, 1805, in San Miguel del Bado, Spanish and godparents were Alexandro Martin and Teodora Marquez.[833]

Maria Ygnacia married (1st) Jose Antonio Gallegos, son of Jose Toribio Gallegos and Maria Bernarda Baca.

Jose Antonio Gallegos was baptized on July 12, 1804, in San Miguel del Bado, Spanish and godparents were Estevan Lopez and Maria Manuela Montoya.[834]

Jose Antonio died on March 17, 1840, in San Miguel del Bado at age 35, married to Ygnacia Ulibarri.[835]

Maria Ygnacia married (2nd) Jose Rafael de Jesus Martin, son of Manuel Martin and Maria Rosa Sena, on February 8, 1841, in San Miguel del Bado. Rafael was single and Ygnacia Ulibarri was the widow of Antonio Gallegos.[836]

Ygnacia died before March 1852.

---

[830]1850 United States Federal Census, Territory of New Mexico. Roll M432-469; Ascencio A Ulibari; San Miguel County, La Cuesta, family #890, p. 45B. Ancestry, www.ancestry.com, Provo, UT.

[831]1860 United States Federal Census, Territory of New Mexico. M653-713; Albino Ulibari; San Miguel County, Lower Gallinas, family #1719, p. 353. Ancestry, www.ancestry.com, Provo, UT.

[832]1870 United States Federal Census, Territory of New Mexico. M593-895; Alline Ulibarri; San Miguel County, Lower La Cuesta; p. 127A. Ancestry, www.ancestry.com, Provo, UT.

[833]Padilla y Baca, compiler, *New Mexico Baptisms, San Miguel del Vado, Pecos Mission, 1799 - 1829*, p. 117.

[834]Padilla y Baca, *Pecos Mission Baptisms, 1799 - 1829*, p. 40.

[835]NMGS Volunteers, compiler, *Pecos, San Miguel del Bado & Ribera Burials, 1796 - 1850* (Albuquerque, NM: New Mexico Genealogical Society, 2014), p. 77.

[836]Arellanes, Windham and Baca, *San Miguel del Bado Church, 12 November 1829 to 10 November 1878*, p. 29.

Jose Rafael de Jesus Martin was baptized on September 27, 1810, in Jemez, born the 24th in San Ysidro and godparents were Lorenzo Montoya and Juana Maria Montoya.[837]

Rafael Martinez was enumerated in the 1850 San Miguel census. He was age 30 (should be 40) and a grocery keeper. His wife, Ygnacia, was 40 and children shown are: Maria Justa, 8; Maria Leonicia, 7 and Cristina B., 9. Also in the home was Cristina Moya, age 20.[838]

Jose Rafael de Jesus married (2nd) Maria Agapita de los Dolores Mares, daughter of Jose Maria Mares and Maria Josefa Casados, on March 8, 1852, in San Miguel del Bado. Rafael was a widower and his deceased wife was not named.[839]

Jose Antonio married (2nd) Maria Simona Gallegos, daughter of Jose Toribio Gallegos and Maria Bernarda Baca, on December 28, 1814, in San Miguel del Bado. Jose Antonio was the widower of Maria Manuela Montoya. Both were from Santa Fe.[840]

Jose Antonio Ulibarri died before August 1834.

Known children of Jose Antonio Ulibarri and Maria Simona Gallegos were as follows:

i. Maria de la Cruz Ulibarri died on January 11, 1838, in San Miguel del Bado, adult daughter of Jose Antonio Ulibarri and Simona Gallegos of San Jose.[841]

ii. Maria Dolores Esquipulas Ulibarri was baptized on February 13, 1821, in San Miguel del Bado and godparents were Santiago Ulibarri and Maria Petra Duran.[842]

Maria Dolores Esquipulas married Jose Miguel Padilla, son of Diego Padilla and Maria Nicolasa Lopez, in November 1837 in San Miguel del Bado. The marriage investigation began the 30th of October 1837 for Jose Miguel Padilla, age 21, son of Diego Padilla, deceased, and Nicolasa Lopez, with Maria Dolores Esquipulas Ulibarri, age 17, daughter of Antonio Ulibarri, deceased, and Maria Simona Gallegos.[843]

---

[837]Padilla y Baca, compiler, *New Mexico Baptisms, Pueblo Missions, San Felipe, Santa Ana, Santo Domingo, Cochiti, Jemez,* p. 133.

[838]1850 United States Federal Census, Territory of New Mexico. Roll M432-469; Rafel Martinez; San Miguel County, San Miguel; family #1109, p. 56B. Ancestry, www.ancestry.com, Provo, UT.

[839]Arellanes, Windham and Baca, *San Miguel del Bado Marriages, 1829-1878*, p. 95.

[840]Padilla y Baca, *New Mexico Marriages & Marriage Investigations; San Miguel del Vado, 1802-1865*, p. 225.

[841]NMGS Volunteers, *Pecos, San Miguel del Bado, Ribera Burials, 1796-1850*, p. 64.

[842]Padilla y Baca, *Pecos Mission Baptisms, 1799 - 1829*, p. 118.

[843]Chavez, *New Mexico Roots Ltd., DM's or Pre-Nuptial Investigations (1678-1869)*, p. 1455.

Dolores died on November 13, 1839, in San Miguel del Bado at age 18, married to Miguel Padilla.[844]

Jose Miguel Padilla was baptized on April 8, 1818, in San Miguel del Bado, five days old and godparents were Pedro Sandoval and Barbara Arias.[845]

Jose Miguel married (2nd) Maria Dolores Montaño.

iii. Jose Feliz Ulibarri married (1st) Maria Ygnacia Peña, daughter of Juan Pena and Maria de los Angeles Montoya, on November 2, 1845, in San Miguel del Bado, both were single.[846]

Maria Ygnacia Peña died on May 15, 1847, in San Miguel del Bado; married to "Pedro" Ulibarri.[847]

Jose Feliz married (2nd) Maria Felipa Alarcon, daughter of Jacinto Alarcon and Maria Serafina Apodaca, circa 1850.

Maria Felipa Alarcon was baptized on June 2, 1836, in San Miguel del Bado; born in La Cuesta and godparents were Jose Andres Garcia and Ynes Gallegos.[848]

In the 1860 El Chaperito census, Felix was age 34, a merchant with real estate worth $2000 and personal estate valued at $2000. His wife, Felipa, was 20. Others in the home were Francisca, 8; Leonarda, 6; Marcelita, 3 and Santiago, 1. There was a Santos Chacon, age 9 and Francisco Padilla, age 19 and a clerk.[849]

When enumerated in the 1870 Chaperito census, Felix was a freighter, age 47, with real estate valued at $500 and personal estate worth $2000. His wife, Felipa, was 26. Children at home were: Marcela, 12; Santiago, 10; Jose, 8; Josefa, 6 and Lucaria, 1. Also in the home was Francisca Valdez, age 1 and Pedro Ulibarri, age 10.[850]

---

[844]NMGS Volunteers, *Pecos, San Miguel del Bado, Ribera Burials, 1796-1850*, p. 75.

[845]Padilla y Baca, *Pecos Mission Baptisms, 1799 - 1829*, p. 91.

[846]Arellanes, Windham and Baca, *San Miguel del Bado Marriages, 1829-1878*, p. 49.

[847]NMGS Volunteers, *Pecos, San Miguel del Bado, Ribera Burials, 1796-1850*, p. 109.

[848]Arellanes, Pfeufer, Olmsted, Windham and Baca, *New Mexico Baptisms, San Miguel del Bado Church, Vol. I, 1 January 1829 ~ 12 May 1844*, p. 85.

[849]1860 United States Federal Census, Territory of New Mexico. Roll M653-713; Felix Ulibari; San Miguel County, El Chaperito; family #1385, p. 33. Ancestry, www.ancestry.com, Provo, UT.

[850]1870 United States Federal Census, Territory of New Mexico. Roll M593-895; Jose F Ulibarri; San Miguel County, Chaperito; family #77, p. 25A. Ancestry, www.ancestry.com, Provo, UT.

iv. Juan Francisco Ulibarri was baptized on December 27, 1829, in San Miguel del Bado, born on the 12th and godparents were Juan Esquibel and Maria Rosalia Gallegos.[851]

Juan Francisco married Maria Josefa Alarcon, daughter of Jacinto Alarcon and Maria Serafina Apodaca, on February 11, 1858, in San Miguel del Bado. Francisco was from Chaperito and both were single.[852]

Maria Josefa Alarcon was baptized on March 21, 1841, in San Miguel del Bado, born yesterday and godparents were Ysidro Flores and Nepomucena Garcia.[853]

v. Juan de Jesus Ulibarri was born circa 1833 in San Miguel County.[854]

Maria Simona married (2nd) Manuel Duran, son of Ygnacio Duran and Maria Feliciana Sandoval, on August 28, 1834, in San Miguel del Bado. Manuel was a widower of his first marriage to Francisca Ulibarri and 2nd marriage to Maria Soledad Vigil. Simona was the widow of Jose Antonio Ulibarri.[855]

(See the chapter on Manuel de Jesus Duran, also a grantee of the San Jose del Bado settlement.)

In the 1845 Las Vegas census, Simona was 40 and a widow. Children at home were: Jesus Felix Ulibarri, 18; Juan de Jesus, 12 and Francisco, 5. Juan de Jesus was probably the son of Manuel and Soledad Vigil, born 1830. Francisco, at age 5, would have been a Duran, son of Manuel.[856]

---

[851]Arellanes, Pfeufer and Olmsted, Windham and Baca, *San Miguel del Bado Baptisms, Vol. I, 1829-1844*, p. 3.

[852]Arellanes, Windham and Baca, *San Miguel del Bado Marriages, 1829-1878*, p. 119.

[853]Arellanes, Pfeufer and Olmsted, Windham and Baca, *San Miguel del Bado Baptisms, Vol. I, 1829-1844*, p. 163.

[854] Olmsted, *New Mexico Spanish & Mexican Colonial Censuses, 1790 * 1823 * 1845*, p. 236.

[855]Arellanes, Windham and Baca, *San Miguel del Bado Marriages, 1829-1878*, p. 5.

[856]Olmsted, *New Mexico Spanish & Mexican Colonial Censuses, 1790 * 1823 * 1845*, p. 236.

Jose de Jesus Ulibarri

1. Jose de Jesus Ulibarri, son of Asencio Ulibarri and Maria Francisca Armijo, was baptized on February 10, 1778, in Santa Fe, age one day and godparents were Antonio Jose Sandoval and Getrudis Tafoya.[857]

Jose de Jesus married Juana Baca on June 18, 1801, in Santa Fe, both Spanish of Santa Fe.[858]

Jose de Jesus was a grantee of the San Jose del Bado settlement and was allotted 50 *varas* of land.[859]

On the 12th of November 1820 in San Jose del Bado, Jose de Jesus purchased 30 *varas* of land from his wife, Juana Baca, who inherited the land from her late husband (unnamed). Jesus paid her one burro and one *peso* in *reales*. At the time, his brother, Santiago, was the *Alcalde* of San Jose del Bado and witnessed the sale.[860]

He died before February 1827.

Known children of Jose de Jesus Ulibarri and Juana Baca, all born in Santa Fe, were as follows:

i. Jose Pantaleon Ulibarri was baptized on July 29, 1802, age two days and godparents were Juan Antonio Anaya and Getrudis Ortiz.[861]

He died on October 6, 1802, in Pecos. The record shows him as Jose Bartolome.[862]

ii. Jose Pablo Ulibarri was baptized on January 16, 1803, age two days, Spanish and godparents were Antonio Tafoya and Maria Encarnacion Baca.[863]

Jose Pablo married Francisca Ramona Vigil, daughter of Gregorio Vigil and Francisca Antonia Sanchez, on February 25, 1827, in San Miguel del Bado; both were single.[864]

---

[857]Windham and Baca, *Baptisms of Santa Fe, Parroquia de San Francisco de Asis, Vol. 1, 5 September 1747 to 17 July 1791*, p. 216.

[858]Roybal, Pfeufer, Windham and Baca, *New Mexico Marriages, Santa Fe - St. Francis Parish and Military Chapel of Our Lady of Light (La Castrense), 1728-1857*, p. 120.

[859]Spanish Archives of New Mexico, Series I, *San Miguel del Bado Land Grant*; TW #887, Roll 5, frames 244-247. Albuquerque Genealogy Center, Albuquerque.

[860]Christmas, *Joe & Diane Stein Collection*, Accession 1983-062; Box 1, folder 4.

[861]May, Windham and Baca, *New Mexico Baptisms of Santa Fe, Parroquia de San Francisco de Asis, Vol. II, 15 August 1796 to 30 December 1822*, p. 69.

[862]Christmas, *New Mexico Burials, Pecos Mission, 1798 - 1829*, AASF Roll 35, frame 698, p. 14.

[863]May, Windham and Baca, *Santa Fe Baptisms, Vol. 2*, p. 81.

[864]Padilla y Baca, *New Mexico Marriages & Marriage Investigations; San Miguel del Vado, 1802-1865*, p. 225.

In the 1850 San Miguel census, Pablo was 44, a farmer and had real estate valued at $300. His wife, Romana, was 33. Children were: Atanacio, 15; Josefa, 14; Lucia, 9; Gertrudes, 7; Esquipula, 5 and Larseta, 1. Also in the home was Pedro Jose Ulibarri, 14, possibly the son of Pablo's brother, Julian.[865]

When the 1860 San Jose, San Miguel County, census was enumerated, Pablo was 55, a farmer with real estate valued at $800 and personal estate valued at $350. His wife, Romana, was 43. Children at home were: Luis, 9; Laureano, 7 and Eutimia, 2.[866]

In both the 1870 and 1880 censuses, Pablo was still living in San Jose.

iii. Julian Ulibarri was baptized on February 21, 1807, age two days and godparents were Jose Baca and Maria Getrudis Ulibarri.[867]

Julian married Francisca Martin, daughter of Bernardo Martin and Maria Rita Rael. Francisca had married (1st) Diego Olguin, son of Enriques (Antonio) Olguin and Gertrudis Garcia, on January 10, 1827, in San Miguel del Bado, both single.[868]

Julian died, possibly in Las Vegas, September 28, 1839.[869]

Francisca died before August 1860.

---

[865] 1850 United States Federal Census, Territory of New Mexico. Roll M432-469; Bablo Ulibin; San Miguel County, San Miguel; family #1189, p. 61A. Ancestry, www.ancestry.com, Provo, UT.

[866] 1860 United States Federal Census, Territory of New Mexico. Roll M653-713; Pablo Ruibali; San Miguel County, San Jose, family #3034, p. 98. Ancestry, www.ancestry.com, Provo, UT.

[867] May, Windham and Baca, *Santa Fe Baptisms, Vol. 2*, p. 113.

[868] Padilla y Baca, *San Miguel Marriages, 1802-1865*, p. 159.

[869] NMGS Volunteers, compiler, *Pecos, San Miguel del Bado & Ribera Burials, 1796 - 1850* (Albuquerque, NM: New Mexico Genealogical Society, 2014), p. 75.

Andres Valencia

1. Andres Valencia, natural son of Barbara Valencia, married Ana Maria Apodaca, daughter of Miguel Apodaca and Maria de la Luz Sandoval, on June 24, 1791, in Cochiti, both Spanish. The groom was shown as Valenzuela.[870]

Andres was a grantee of the San Jose del Bado settlement and was allotted 200 *varas* of land.[871]

Known children of Andres Valencia and Ana Maria Apodaca were as follows:

i. Felipe Valencia was baptized on February 10, 1790, in Cochiti, age five days and godparents were Jose Miguel Apodaca and Maria Francisca Leyba.[872]

Felipe married Juana Maria Montaño, daughter of Antonio Jose Montaño and Maria Francisca Jirón, on December 5, 1810, in San Miguel del Bado, both residents of San Jose.[873]

Felipe died on February 1, 1865, in San Miguel del Bado, 70 years old, husband of Juana Montaño.[874]

Juana Maria Montaño was baptized on September 16, 1794, in Cochiti, age 8 days and godparents were Juan Antonio Gallegos and Maria de la Cruz Gallegos.[875]

ii. Maria Trinidad de la Valencia was baptized on February 11, 1792, in Cochiti, age six days and godparents were Antonio Valentin Romero and Juana Theresa Lovato. (Maria Trinidad's father was shown as Valenzuela.).[876]

Maria Trinidad married Jose de Jesus Gonzales, son of Juan Miguel Gonzales and Maria Manuela Gomez, on January 25, 1812, in San Miguel del Bado. Jose de Jesus was from Rancho de San Ildefonso and Maria Trinidad was from Santa Fe.[877]

---

[870]Padilla y Baca, *New Mexico Marriages - Pueblo Missions: San Felipe, Santa Ana, Santo Domingo y vecindario, Cochiti, Jemez*, p. 27.

[871]Spanish Archives of New Mexico, Series I, *San Miguel del Bado Land Grant*; TW 877; Roll 5, fames 244-247.

[872]Dressen and Baca, *New Mexico Baptisms, San Buenaventura de Cochiti Church, 1736-1873*, p. 72.

[873]Padilla y Baca, *New Mexico Marriages & Marriage Investigations; San Miguel del Vado, 1802-1865*, p. 231.

[874]Anderson, *Ribera/San Miguel del Bado Burials, 1848-1955*, AASF/FHL Film 0016879.

[875]Dressen and Baca, *New Mexico Baptisms, San Buenaventura de Cochiti Church, 1736-1873*, p. 87.

[876]Dressen and Baca, *New Mexico Baptisms, San Buenaventura de Cochiti Church, 1736-1873*, p. 79.

[877]Padilla y Baca, *San Miguel Marriages, 1802-1865*, p. 85.

In the 1845 Tecolote census, Jesus was 40 and his wife, Trinidad Valencia, was 38. No children were shown.[878]

iii. Maria Teodora Valencia died on February 1, 1796, in Cochiti, daughter of Andres Valencia and Ana Maria Apodaca, residents of la Cañada.[879]

iv. Maria Josefa Valencia died on June 18, 1795, in Cochiti, daughter of Andres Valencia and Ana Maria Apodaca, residents of la Cañada.[880]

v. Maria Teodora Pasquala Valencia was baptized on May 23, 1796, in Cochiti, age five days and godparents were Juan Francisco Lucero and Maria Lorenza Lucero.[881]

vi. Jose Francisco Valencia was born on May 15, 1801, in Cochiti, age eight days and godparents were Jose Agaton Mireles and Maria Francisca Guerrero.[882]

Francisco died on October 20, 1803, in Pecos at age 2.[883]

---

[878]Olmsted, *New Mexico Spanish & Mexican Colonial Censuses, 1790 * 1823 * 1845*, p. 242.

[879]Christmas, *Cochiti Burials, 1776 - 1873*. AASF Roll 35: frames 451/452.

[880]Christmas. *Cochiti Burials, 1776 - 1873*. AASF Roll 35: frames 447.

[881]Dressen and Baca, *New Mexico Baptisms, San Buenaventura de Cochiti Church, 1736-1873*, p. 96.

[882]Dressen and Baca, *New Mexico Baptisms, San Buenaventura de Cochiti Church, 1736-1873*, p. 118.

[883]Christmas, *New Mexico Burials, Pecos Mission, 1798 - 1829*, AASF Roll 35, frame 700, p. 15.

Antonio de los Reyes Vigil

1. Antonio de los Reyes Vigil, son of Juan Bautista Montes Vigil and Maria Candelaria Medina, was baptized on January 8, 1749, in Santa Cruz; and godparents were Manuel Montoya and his wife, not named.[884]

Antonio de los Reyes married Barbara Josefa Madrid, daughter of Juan Cristoval Madrid and Margarita Sanchez.

Barbara Josefa Madrid was baptized on December 11, 1758, in Santa Cruz; and godparents were Juan Bustos and Teresa Sanchez.[885]

On the 11th of January 1779 Antonio Reyes "Bejil," son of Lieut. don Juan Bautista "Bejil" and doña Candelaria Medina, Villa of Santa Cruz, enlisted in the Santa Fe Presidio. He was a laborer, 5'2" and 29 years old. He had black hair and eyebrows, dark eyes, swarthy skin, somewhat imperfect nose, heavy black beard, scars below chin and point of left eyebrow. He was married and signed by his mark. He was on the invalid roster on the 12th of July 1800.[886]

Because of his enlistment in the Santa Fe Presidio in 1779, direct descendants are eligible for membership in both the DAR (Daughters of the American Republic) and SAR (Sons of the American Republic). Soldiers at the Presidio donated monies to be spent for clothing, guns and ammunition for the American Revolution soldiers fighting against England.

In the Santa Fe 1790 census, residing in household #39, Antonio was Spanish, born in New Mexico and age 41. His wife, Maria Josefa Madrid, was 31 and they had two sons, ages 6 and 1, and two daughters, ages 12 and 8.[887]

In the March 31st 1800 service muster of the Santa Fe Presidio, Antonio was age 50, served for 25 years, two months, twenty days, served in 33 campaigns and was currently injured or ill.[888]

In 1803, Jose Vigil was named as a grantee for the San Jose del Bado settlement and was allotted 170 *varas*.[889]

"In the summer of 1805, Manuel Baca, interim deputy justice of the district, ordered Ignacio Duran, in charge at San Jose, to beat the drum for the people to come work on the church."

Another San Jose grantee, Reyes Vigil, and his sons, refused. Words were exchanged with Reyes telling Ignacio that he could "eat shit, eat a bucket of shit!" Ignacio paid a call on Reyes

---

884Olmsted, Windham and Baca, *New Mexico Baptisms, Santa Cruz de la Cañada Church, Vol. 1, 1710-1794*, p. 62.

885Olmsted, Windham and Baca, *Santa Cruz Baptisms, Vol. 1, 1710-1794*, p. 10.

886Olmsted, "Spanish Enlistment Papers of New Mexico, 1732-1820," *National Genealogical Society Quarterly* Vol 67:3 (September 1979), p. 233.

887Olmsted, *New Mexico Spanish & Mexican Colonial Censuses, 1790 * 1823 * 1845*, p. 104.

888Christmas, compiler. *Military Records ~ Colonial New Mexico ~ Notas y Revistas*, p. 19.

889Spanish Archives of New Mexico, Series I, *San Miguel del Bado Land Grant*; TW #887, frames 244-247.

and in his corral, they got into a "name-calling, rock-throwing, hair-pulling brawl." This record is incomplete and does not tell what happened afterwards.[890]

Known children of Antonio de los Reyes Vigil and Barbara Josefa Madrid were as follows:

i. Maria Antonia Vigil was baptized on July 20, 1776, in Santa Cruz and godparents were Joseph Quintana and Maria de Jesus Lucero.[891]

Maria Antonia married Francisco Ulibarri on May 4, 1793, in Santa Fe and godparents were Antonio Jose Castillo and Equiteria Chavez.[892]

In 1803, Francisco was named as a grantee of the San Jose del Bado settlement and was allotted 66 *varas* of land.[893]

In 1822, he was counted as a resident of San Jose del Bado.[894]

Francisco died on January 4, 1838, in San Miguel del Bado; adult, husband of Maria Antonio Vigil of San Jose.[895]

(See chapter on Francisco Ulibarri, also a grantee of the San Jose del Bado settlement.)

ii. Jose Ramon Vigil died on February 19, 1781, in Santa Fe, child of soldier Reyes Vigil and Barbara Josefa Madrid.[896]

iii. Maria de la Luz Vigil died on March 20, 1797, in Santa Fe, adult, daughter of soldier Reyes Vigil and Barbara Madrid.[897]

iv. Jose Vigil died on February 5, 1808, in San Miguel del Bado; single, son of Antonio Reyes Vigil and Barbara "Fernandez," residents of the plaza of San Miguel del Bado.[898]

890Kessell, *Kiva, Cross and Crown*, p. 424.

891Olmsted, Windham and Baca, *Santa Cruz Baptisms, Vol. 1, 1710-1794*, p. 174.

892Roybal, Pfeufer, Windham and Baca, *New Mexico Marriages, Santa Fe - St. Francis Parish and Military Chapel of Our Lady of Light (La Castrense), 1728-1857*, p. 72.

893Spanish Archives of New Mexico, Series I, *San Miguel del Bado Land Grant*; TW #887, frames 244-247.

894Hendricks and Colligan, *New Mexico Prenuptial Investigations from the Archivos Historicos del Arzobispado de Durango, 1800-1893*, p. 148.

895NMGS Volunteers, compiler, *Pecos, San Miguel del Bado & Ribera Burials, 1796 - 1850* (Albuquerque, NM: New Mexico Genealogical Society, 2014), p. 64.

896Christmas, Gallegos and Rau, *New Mexico Burials, Santa Fe - St. Francis Parish and Military Chapel of Our Lady of Light (La Castrense), 1726-1834*, p. 221.

897Christmas, Gallegos and Rau, *Santa Fe Burials, 1726-1834*, p. 239.

898NMGS Volunteers, *Pecos, San Miguel del Bado, Ribera Burials, 1796-1850*, p. 8.

v. Antonio Jose Vigil died on May 21, 1790, in Santa Fe, child of Antonio Reyes Vigil and Barbara Madrid.[899]

vi. Gregorio Vigil married Maria Clara Perea, daughter of Rafael Perea and Maria Ysabel Gutierrez.

In the 1850 San Miguel census, Gregorio was 62, a farmer with real estate valued at $1,000. No wife was shown in this census. Children at home were: Jose A., 14; Jose T., 10 and Francisco, 6.[900] In the 1860 San Miguel census, Gregorio was 72, still farming with real estate worth $550 and personal estate worth $600. His wife, Clara Perea, was given as age 33. Children at home were: Jose, age 20 and a farm worker; Francisco, 15 and Sofera, age 10.[901]

Gregorio died on July 30, 1863, in San Miguel del Bado, 75 years old, husband of Maria Clara Perea.[902]

Maria Clara married (2nd) Juan Miguel Lovato, son of Rafael Lovato and Lorenza Archuleta, on August 22, 1870, in San Miguel del Bado.

Miguel was the widower of Estefana Gutierrez and Maria Clara was the widow of Gregorio Vigil.[903]

vii. Maria Soledad Vigil married Manuel Duran, son of Ygnacio Duran and Maria Feliciana Sandoval, on December 22, 1814, in San Miguel del Bado; all residents of this jurisdiction.[904]

She died before August 1834 in San Miguel del Bado.

Manuel died on January 16, 1842, in San Miguel del Bado; adult.[905]

(See chapter on Manuel Duran, also a grantee of the San Jose del Bado settlement.)

viii. Maria Concepcion Vigil died on February 3, 1800, in Santa Fe, child of Reyes Vigil and Josefa Barbara Madrid.[906]

---

[899]Christmas, Gallegos and Rau, *Santa Fe Burials, 1726-1834*, p. 233.

[900]1850 United States Federal Census, Territory of New Mexico. Roll M432-469; Gregorio Vigil; San Miguel County, San Miguel, family #1156, p. 59A. Ancestry, www.ancestry.com, Provo, UT.

[901]1860 United States Federal Census, Territory of New Mexico. Roll M653-713; Gregorio Vigil; San Miguel County, San Miguel, family #129, p. 118. Ancestry, www.ancestry.com, Provo, UT.

[902]Anderson, *Ribera/San Miguel del Bado Burials, 1848-1955*, AASF/FHL Film 0016879.

[903]Arellanes, Windham and Baca, *San Miguel del Bado Church, 12 November 1829 to 10 November 1878*, p. 149.

[904]Padilla y Baca, *New Mexico Marriages & Marriage Investigations; San Miguel del Vado, 1802-1865*, p. 52.

[905]NMGS Volunteers, *Pecos, San Miguel del Bado, Ribera Burials, 1796-1850*, p. 90.

[906]Christmas, Gallegos and Rau, *Santa Fe Burials, 1726-1834*, p. 243.

ix. Maria Josefa Vigil was baptized on April 29, 1800,in Santa Fe, born on the 25th and godparents were Anselmo Gallegos and Maria de la Cruz Silva.[907]

Maria Josefa married Rafael Garcia, son of Antonio Garcia and Maria Francisca Gutierrez, on November 7, 1817, in San Miguel del Bado. The marriage investigation began the 20th of September 1817 in Jemez for Jose Rafael Garcia, age 22, son of Antonio Garcia, deceased, and Maria Francisca Gutierrez, with Maria Josefa Vigil of El Vado, Pecos district, daughter of Jose Antonio Reyes Vigil and Barbara Madrid. They married in San Miguel del Bado and the marriage record states that Rafael was originally from Jemez.[908]

Antonio de los Reyes married (2nd) Maria Antonia Benavides, daughter of Miguel 'Domingo' Benavides and Maria Guadalupe Garcia.

Antonio died on May 12, 1832, in San Miguel del Bado at age 83.[909]

Maria Antonia married (2nd) Francisco Matias Garcia, son of Antonio Jose Garcia de Noriega and Marta Lopez, on February 3, 1834, in San Miguel del Bado. Francisco was from Taos and Maria Antonia was the widow of Reyes Vigil.[910]

Known children of Antonio de los Reyes Vigil and Maria Antonia Benavides were as follows:

i. Juan de la Cruz Vigil was baptized on November 26, 1826, in San Miguel del Bado, three days old and godparents were doña Guadalupe Garcia and her son, Juan Cristoval Benavides.[911]

Juan de la Cruz married Maria Juana Martin, daughter of Pedro Martin and Trinidad Garcia, on May 16, 1846, in San Miguel del Bado, both were single.[912]

In the 1860 Las Manuelitas, San Miguel County census, Juan was age 30, a laborer with no real estate value given. His wife, Juana, was 27. They had one daughter, Ramona, who was 10.[913]

---

[907]May, Olmsted, Windham and Baca, *New Mexico Baptisms of Santa Fe, Parish of Saint Francis of Assisi, Vol. III, 1 January 1823 to 26 June 1833; Castrense Register, June 1798 to 26 June 1833*, p. 6.

[908]Chavez, *New Mexico Roots Ltd., DM's or Pre-Nuptial Investigations (1678-1869)*, p. 616.

[909]Christmas, *San Miguel del Bado Burials, 1829-1833*, AASF/FHL Film 0017002, frame 194.

[910]Arellanes, Windham and Baca, *San Miguel del Bado Marriages, 1829-1878*, p. 8.

[911]Padilla y Baca, *New Mexico Baptisms, San Miguel del Vado, Pecos Mission, 1799 - 1829*, p. 122.

[912]Arellanes, Windham and Baca, *San Miguel del Bado Marriages, 1829-1878*, p. 52.

[913]1860 United States Federal Census, Territory of New Mexico. Roll M653-713; Juan Vigil; San Miguel County, Las Manuelitas, family #2643, p. 288. Ancestry, www.ancestry.com, Provo, UT.

Maria Juana Martin was baptized on September 26, 1831, in San Miguel del Bado, born on the 24th and godparents were Rafael Garcia and Micaela Lovato.[914]

ii. Maria Dimas Vigil was baptized on April 25, 1831, in San Miguel del Bado and godparents were Jose Antonio Casaus and Maria de Jesus Ortiz.[915]

Maria Dimas married (1st) Juan Nepomuseno Vivian Armijo, son of Juan Antonio Armijo and Maria Josefa Martin, on August 22, 1848, in San Miguel del Bado, both were single.[916]

In the 1850 census, Vivian was age 20, a laborer with real estate valued at $50. His wife, Dimas, was 22. They had one daughter, Felipa, age 1.[917]

When the 1860 San Geronimo census was enumerated, Vivian was a farmer with real estate valued at $1,000 and personal estate valued at $300. His wife, Dimas, was 29. Children living with them were: Felipa, 11; Teofila, 9 and Jose Cenobio, eight months.[918]

Maria Dimas married (2nd) Tomas Luis Rael, son of Alonzo Rael and Maria Manuela de Jesus Armijo, on April 23, 1866, in Las Vegas. Luis was the widower of Francisca Ruiz and Dimas was the widow of Vivian Armijo. They were both from Los Valles de San Geronimo.[919]

Tomas Luis Rael was baptized on March 9, 1814, in Santa Fe, Spanish and godparents were Jose Tomas (no surname) and Maria Antonia Chavez.[920]

When the 1870 San Geronimo census was enumerated, Dimas was remarried to Luis Rael. He was age 50, a farm worker with real estate worth $300. She was age 40. The children were: Felipa, 20; Teofila, 18; Zenovio, 10 and Carmen, 2. They were all given the surname of Rael, yet Felipa, Teofila and Zenovio were Armijo children and Carmen was Rael.[921]

---

[914]Arellanes, Pfeufer, Olmsted, Windham and Baca, *New Mexico Baptisms, San Miguel del Bado Church, Vol. I, 1 January 1829 ~ 12 May 1844,* p. 20.

[915]Arellanes, Pfeufer and Olmsted, Windham and Baca, *San Miguel del Bado Baptisms, Vol. I, 1829-1844*, p. 17.

[916]Arellanes, Windham and Baca, *San Miguel del Bado Marriages, 1829-1878*, p. 68.

[917]1850 United States Federal Census, Territory of New Mexico. Roll M432-469; Vivian Armijo; San Miguel County, Tuckelata, family #1480, p. 76A. Ancestry, www.ancestry.com, Provo, UT.

[918]1860 United States Federal Census, Territory of New Mexico. Roll M653-713; Vivian Armijo; San Miguel County, San Geronimo, family # 2294, p. 87. Ancestry, www.ancestry.com, Provo, UT.

[919] Padilla y Baca, *New Mexico Marriages, Las Vegas, Nuestra Señora de los Dolores, January 1853 - December 1882,* p. 59.

[920]May, Windham and Baca, *New Mexico Baptisms of Santa Fe, Parroquia de San Francisco de Asis, Vol. II, 15 August 1796 to 30 December 1822,* p. 177.

[921]1870 United States Federal Census, Territory of New Mexico. Roll 593-895; Dimas Rael; San Miguel County, San Geronimo, p. 200A. Ancestry, www.ancestry.com, Provo, UT.

Introduction to the Mystery Grantees of San Jose del Bado

Due to missing baptismal and marriage records between 1798 and 1829 in Pecos, Galisteo, and San Miguel del Bado, there could be several men of the same name that are possible grantees. It is possible that several of these were *genizaros* or Indians.

The San Jose grantees seem to appear in San Miguel between 1800 and 1803 and these mystery people were among those appearing by March of 1803 and then disappearing before they had children or married. The grantees were to hold the land for a period of time before they could sell. If they did not stay, then their *varas* of land were given to new arrivals.

While the records we found are sourced, we **cannot prove** these were the land grantees!

1. Jose Francisco Chaves – two possibilities

2. Miguel Duran - two possibilities for land grantee.

    a. Miguel Duran, married to Barbara Rivera, was a *genizaro*. He married in Santa Fe in 1806, but may have been in San Miguel in 1803 to receive the land and traveled back and forth.

    b. Miguel Duran, married to Maria Antonia Dolores Benavides, does not appear until their children marry. However, a search of records in Albuquerque, Sandia, the Jemez, Cochiti, San Felipe, Galisteo area, San Juan, Santa Clara, Abiquiu, Santa Cruz and Santa Fe does not show any baptismal records for the children of this couple. Two of the sons had *matrimoniales diligencias* (marriage investigations) performed which shed little light on their place of birth.

3. Miguel Gonzales – only one is found in the San Miguel records. His wife was first thought to be Maria de la Luz, but a further examination of church records revealed she was Alcaria de la Luz Garcia.

4. Julian Roybal/Ruibal was a big problem as we were not sure if he was Ruibal or Ruibali (Ulibarri). The Rafael Julian Roybal, Comanche Interpreter, may fit as the San Miguel land grant was originally set up as outposts to guard against Comanche raids in Santa Fe. He may have been stationed in San Jose at some point.

Jose Francisco Chaves

There are no baptismal, marriage, or burial records for any Francisco Chaves or any children in Pecos or San Miguel del Bado until 1817. There is one mentioned as a godparent. Presented below are two different Francisco Chaves men for consideration.

1. Francisco Chaves and Geronima Sandoval were godparents for Maria Polonia Martin, baptized on April 26, 1803, daughter of Bernardo Martin and Maria Antonia Trujillo.[922] Geronima Sandoval was the wife of Jose Lucero, married on November 18, 1802, in Pecos.[923]

~~~~~~~~~~~~~~~~~~~

2. Jose Francisco Chavez, son of Jose Vicente Chaves and Maria Casilda Jaramillo, married Maria Manuela Valencia, daughter of Jose Valencia and Maria Manuela Gonzales, on November 7, 1817, in San Miguel del Bado. Jose Francisco was from Jemez Mission and Maria Manuela was the widow of Juan Gonzales.[924]

   Maria Manuela Valencia was (1st) married to Juan Manuel Gonzales, son of Diego Gonzales and Ana Maria Hurtado, on November 3, 1797, in Cochiti, both Spanish.[925]

   (See the chapter for Manuel Gonzales, also a grantee of the San Jose del Bado settlement.)

922Padilla y Baca, *New Mexico Baptisms, San Miguel del Vado, Pecos Mission, 1799 - 1829*, p. 69.

923Christmas, *Galisteo/Pecos Marriages, 1772-1862*; AASF Roll 27; frame 241.

924Padilla y Baca, *New Mexico Marriages & Marriage Investigations; San Miguel del Vado, 1802-1865*, p. 43.

925Padilla y Baca, *New Mexico Marriages - Pueblo Missions: San Felipe, Santa Ana, Santo Domingo y vecindario, Cochiti, Jemez,* p. 30.
~~~~~~~~~~~~~~~~~~~

Miguel Duran

1. Miguel married Barbara Rivera on January 8, 1806, in Santa Fe, both widowed and genizaros. Godparents were Rafael Gonzales and Juana Esquibel.[926]

Barbara Rivera married (1st) Pedro Armijo on April 14, 1798, in Santa Fe, both genizaros and godparents were Rafael Blanco and Maria de la Asencion (no surname).[927]

This Miguel Duran **may** be the one who received 150 *varas* in the San Jose del Bado settlement.[928]

Known children of Miguel Duran and Barbara Rivera were as follows:

i. Miguel de Jesus Duran died on May 19, 1807, in Santa Fe, child of Miguel Duran and Maria Barbara Rivera.[929]

ii. Juan Duran was baptized on July 14, 1811, in Santa Fe, Yndios and godparents were Juan Manriquez and Francisca Trujillo. (Surname was given as Duran, but only the father's first name, Pedro, was given. Should it be Miguel?).[930]

iii. Jose de Jesus Duran was baptized on March 12, 1814, in Santa Fe, Indian, age three days and godmother was Juana Maria Lucero.[931]

iv. Jose Francisco Duran died on February 15, 1815, in Santa Fe, son of Miguel Duran and Barbara Rivera.[932]

v. Jose de Esquipulas Duran was born on May 12, 1818, in San Miguel del Bado, four days old and godparents were Cristoval Sena and Josefa Fernandez.[933]

---

[926]Roybal, Pfeufer, Windham and Baca, *New Mexico Marriages, Santa Fe - St. Francis Parish and Military Chapel of Our Lady of Light (La Castrense), 1728-1857*, p. 126.

[927]Roybal and Pfeufer, Windham and Baca, *Santa Fe Marriages, 1728-1857*, p. 116.

[928]Spanish Archives of New Mexico, Series I, *San Jose Land Grant*; TW #887; Roll 5, frames 244-249. Albuquerque Genealogy Center, Albuquerque, NM.

[929]Christmas, Gallegos and Rau, *New Mexico Burials, Santa Fe - St. Francis Parish and Military Chapel of Our Lady of Light (La Castrense), 1726-1834*, p. 180.

[930]May, Windham and Baca, *New Mexico Baptisms of Santa Fe, Parroquia de San Francisco de Asis, Vol. II, 15 August 1796 to 30 December 1822*, p. 152.

[931]May, Windham and Baca, *Santa Fe Baptisms, Vol. 2*, p. 177.

[932]Christmas, Gallegos and Rau, *Santa Fe Burials, 1726-1834*, p. 204.

[933]Padilla y Baca, *New Mexico Baptisms, San Miguel del Vado, Pecos Mission, 1799 - 1829*, p. 31.

Jose de Esquipulas married Maria Barbara Archuleta, daughter of Juan de Jesus Archuleta and Soledad Lovato, on November 28, 1839, in San Miguel del Bado; both were single and Maria Barbara was from Anton Chico.[934]

Enumerated in the 1850 La Cuesta (San Miguel County) census, Jose was 30 and a servant. Wife, Barbara, was 26. Children were: 'Alearia,' 5; Josefa, 4 and Manuela, age 1.[935]

---

[934]Arellanes, Windham and Baca, *San Miguel del Bado Church, 12 November 1829 to 10 November 1878*, p. 22.

[935]1850 United States Federal Census, Territory of New Mexico. Roll M432-469; San Miguel County, San Miguel, p. 46B. Ancestry, www.ancestry.com, Provo, UT.

Miguel Gonzales

This was the only Miguel Gonzales mentioned in baptismal, marriage or burial records for San Miguel del Bado. If this was the correct Miguel Gonzales, his family stayed in Albuquerque until 1803 and were back in Albuquerque by 1826. The church records put Miguel and his family in San Miguel in 1803 and 1807.

1. Miguel Gonzales was born circa 1778 and married Alcaria de la Luz Garcia on July 29, 1798, in Albuquerque and godparents were Juàn Duran and Ursula Duran.[936]

Miguel was **possibly** the grantee of the San Jose del Bado settlement and was allotted 178 *varas* of land.[937]

Known children of Miguel Gonzales and Alcaria de la Luz Garcia were as follows:

i. Juana Maria Gonzales was baptized on January 30, 1800, in Albuquerque, age four days and godparents were Geronimo Jaramillo and Maria Gertrudes Lucero.[938]

ii. Juan de Jesus Gonzales was baptized on April 8, 1802, in Albuquerque, Spanish, age three days and godparents were Pedro Duran and Josefa Antonia Jaramillo.[939]

Juan de Jesus died on October 27, 1803, in San Miguel del Bado at age 1, child of Miguel Gonzales and Maria de la Luz Garcia.[940]

iii. Maria Bacilia Gonzales was baptized on June 12, 1807, in San Miguel del Bado, Spanish, of San Jose and godparents were Jose and Maria de la Luz (no surnames).[941]

Maria Bacilia married Miguel Armijo on March 6, 1826, in Albuquerque. The marriage investigation began the 22nd of February 1826 in Albuquerque for Jose

---

936 Dressen, Gooch, Windham and Baca, *New Mexico Marriages, San Felipe de Neri Church in Albuquerque, 16 June 1726 ~ 16 January 1855*, p. 60.

937 Spanish Archives of New Mexico, Series I, *San Jose Land Grant*, TW #887; Roll 5, frames 244-249. Albuquerque Genealogy Center, Albuquerque.

938 NMGS Volunteers, *Albuquerque Baptisms, 1706 - 1850*, p. 261.

939 NMGS Volunteers, *Albuquerque Baptisms, 1706-1850*, p. 260.

940 NMGS Volunteers, *Pecos, San Miguel del Bado & Ribera Burials, 1796 - 1850*, p. 5.

941 Padilla y Baca, *New Mexico Baptisms, San Miguel del Vado, Pecos Mission, 1799 - 1829*, p. 47.

Miguel Armijo, age 23, indio, son of Santiago Armijo, with Maria Basilia Gonzales, age 20, daughter of Miguel Gonzales and Maria Luz Garcia.[942]

iv. Maria Dolores Gonzales was born circa 1820 and married Juan Andres Nuane on March 8, 1841, in Albuquerque. The marriage investigation began on the 8th of March 1841, in Albuquerque for Juan Andres Nuane, age 63, widower of his lst marriage to Maria Concepcion Martinez, with Maria Dolores Gonzales, age 18-23, daughter of Miguel Gonzales, deceased, and Maria Luz Garcia. Witnesses were Pedro Armijo, 35 and Antonio Felix Garcia, 40.

The marriage record reveals that Maria Dolores and her parents were residents of Albuquerque.[943]

---

[942]Dressen and Gooch, Windham and Baca, *Albuquerque Marriages, 1726-1855*, pp. 97/98. Chavez, *New Mexico Roots Ltd, DM's or Pre-Nuptial Investigations*, p. 131.

[943]Chavez, *Roots Ltd., DM's or Pre-Nuptial Investigations*, p. 1376. Dressen and Gooch, Windham and Baca, *Albuquerque Marriages, 1726-1855*, p. 135.

Rafael Julian Roybal

This Julian Roybal is a **possible** San Jose del Bado grantee, receiving 150 *varas* of land. If you will notice, he marries in 1791, but the first baptismal record is not found for a child until 1802. There was a Julian Roybal who buried a daughter on the 27th of September 1802 in San Miguel del Bado. The wife was given as Josefa Garcia, but may have been a mistake of the part of the priest or scribe. The daughter was Maria de los Reyes and no baptismal record has been found for her, but she could have been as old as three years.

This Julian was a Comanche Interpreter for the Presidio of Santa Fe in later years and could have been assigned to San Miguel/San Jose to help with the Indian problems as those communities were established as an outpost to warn Santa Fe of possible Indian attacks. The communities of Pecos, San Miguel and San Jose were also trading posts between the Spanish and Comanche Indians.

~~~~~~~~~~~~~~~~~~~

1. Rafael Julian Roybal, son of Tomas Roybal and Ana Josefa Ginzo Ron y Tobar, was baptized on March 9, 1768, in Santa Fe and godparents were Carlos Fernandes and Juana Padilla.[944]

Rafael Julian married Maria Francisca Garcia on February 5, 1791, in Santa Fe and godparents were Juan Xptoval Sanchez and Maria Antonia Marquez.[945]

In Santa Fe, on the 2nd of September 1807, Julian Roybal and Maria Francisca Garcia were godparents for Juan Estevan Armijo, son of Soldier Salvador Armijo and Maria Manuela Garcia.[946]

In Santa Fe, on the 29th of January 1809, Julian Ruibal and Francisca Garcia were godparents for Maria Marcelina Garcia, daughter of Soldier Manuel Garcia and Antonia Baca.[947]

In Santa Fe, on the 20th of August 1812, Julian Roybal and Francisca Garcia were godparents for Juan Bauptista Tafoya, son of Soldier Jesus Tafoya and Ana Maria Lopez.[948]

---

[944]Windham and Baca, *Baptisms of Santa Fe, Parroquia de San Francisco de Asis, Vol. 1, 5 September 1747 to 17 July 1791*, pp. 121/22.

[945]Roybal, Pfeufer, Windham and Baca, *New Mexico Marriages, Santa Fe - St. Francis Parish and Military Chapel of Our Lady of Light (La Castrense)*, 1728-1857, p. 71.

[946]May, Olmsted, Windham and Baca, *New Mexico Baptisms of Santa Fe, Parish of Saint Francis of Assisi, Vol. III, 1 January 1823 to 26 June 1833; Castrense Register, June 1798 to 26 June 1833*, p. 22.

[947]May and Olmsted, Windham and Baca, *Santa Fe Baptisms, Vol. III*, p. 26.

[948]May and Olmsted, Windham and Baca, *Santa Fe Baptisms, Vol. III*, p. 34.
~~~~~~~~~~~~~~~~~~~

Rafael Ruibal was listed as present in the muster list of the Santa Fe Presidio on the 1st of January 1819 as a Comanche Soldier Interpreter.[949]

Rafael Ruibal was listed as the Comanche Interpreter in the muster of 1823 at the Santa Fe Presidio.[950]

Known children of Rafael Julian Roybal and Maria Francisca Garcia were as follows:

i. Maria Ysabel Roybal was baptized on July 12, 1802, in Santa Fe, age two days and godparents were Jose Manuel Garcia and Maria Antonia Baca.[951]

   Maria Ysabel married Jose Maria Gallegos, son of Anselmo Gallegos and Maria de la Cruz Silva, on April 20, 1816, in Santa Fe. Jose Maria was a soldier. Godparents were Jose Manuel Gallegos and Francisca Quiros.[952]

   Jose Maria Gallegos enlisted at the Santa Fe Presidio on the 3rd of September 1804. He was the son of Anselmo Gallegos and Cruz Silva of Santa Fe, a farmer, age 20. He had chestnut hair and eyebrows, blue-green eyes, large nose, fair skin, new beard, and a scar on his left shoulder. He signed by his mark.

   He was discharged on the 1st of October 1821.[953]

   Enumerated in the 1823 Santa Fe census, don Jose Maria Gallegos was age 40, married and a farmer. His wife, doña Isabel Ruibal, was 18 and they had two children: Paubla, 5 and Jose, 2.[954]

   In the 1841 Santa Fe, San Miguel, census, Ysabel Roibal was 37 and a widow. Children in the home were: Maria Paula Gallegos, single; Filomeno (Miguel) Gallego, 18, single, hat maker; and Dolores Gallego, 5. Also in the home were Juan Andres Roibal, 8; Junio Roibal, 6; Rosario Roibal, age 5, and their mother, Marselina Roibal, 26 and married.[955]

---

[949]Christmas, *Military Records ~ Colonial New Mexico ~ Notas y Revistas,* p. 234.

[950]Olmsted, *New Mexico Spanish & Mexican Colonial Censuses, 1790 * 1823 * 1845*, p. 177.

[951]May, Windham and Baca, *New Mexico Baptisms of Santa Fe, Parroquia de San Francisco de Asis, Vol. II, 15 August 1796 to 30 December 1822*, p. 68.

[952]Roybal and Pfeufer, Windham and Baca, *Santa Fe Marriages, 1728-1857*, p. 82.

[953]Olmsted, "Spanish Enlistment Papers of New Mexico, 1732-1820," *National Genealogical Society Quarterly* Vol 67:3 (September 1979), p. 236.

[954]Olmsted, *NM Spanish & Mexican Colonial Censuses, 1790 * 1823 * 1845*, p. 163.

[955]Christmas, Tafoya and Olguin, *New Mexico Censuses, 1790, 1793, 1803, 1823, 1829, 1841*, p. 52.

ii. Marcelina Roybal married Pedro Andres Coy, son of Willian 'Guillermo' Coy and Mary 'Maria' Tracy, on December 16, 1832 in Santa Fe. Pedro was 'extrangero y vago (stranger and idle).'[956]

Pedro Andres Coy was born circa 1801, but was baptized on November 30, 1832, in Santa Fe, age 31 years, from 'Quintoque' (Kentucky) and godparents were Jose Rafael Numen and Maria Altagracia Esquibel.[957] The surname eventually became McCoy.

In 1841, Marcelina was living with her sister, Ysabel Roibal in Santa Fe, district of San Miguel. Marcelina was 26 and married. Her children were: Juan Andres, 8; Junio, 6 and Rosario, 5.[958]

In the 1850 Santa Fe census, Marcelina was the head of the house and age 29. Children at home were: Yginino, 15; Maria Rosario, 14; Alvino, 8; Nabor, 5 and Camilia, just born.[959]

In the 1860 Santa Fe County census, living on the farm of Senora de la Luz, Marcelina McCoy was given as a male and a laborer, age 46. McCoy children at home were: Iginio, 22, silversmith; Rosaria, 20, laborer; Nabor, 15, laborer and Camilia, age 9. There was another child in the home, Casimiro Leyba, 3, relationship unknown.[960]

When the 1870 San Geronimo, San Miguel County, census was enumerated, Marcelina Ruibal had moved. She was age 50, and McCoy children at home were: Rosario, 25, and Nabor, 23. There was a Casimiro Leyba, age 12.[961]

iii. Maria Dolores (patron) Roybal was baptized on March 7, 1820, in Santa Fe, parents unknown, servant in the house of Interpreter Julian Roybal and godmother was Francisca Garcia, his wife.[962]

iv. Maria del Carmen (patron) Roybal was baptized on November 3, 1823, in Santa Fe, parents unknown, servant in the home of Interpreter Rafael Ruibal and Francisca Garcia. Godparents were Nestor Armijo and Maria Soledad Ruibal.[963]

---

[956]Roybal and Pfeufer, Windham and Baca, *Santa Fe Marriages, 1728-1857*, p. 180.

[957]May and Olmsted, Windham and Baca, *Santa Fe Baptisms, Vol. III*, p. 203.

[958]Christmas, Tafoya and Olguin, *New Mexico Censuses, 1790, 1793, 1803, 1823, 1829, 1841*, p. 52.

[959]1850 United States Federal Census, Territory of New Mexico. Roll M432-468; Santa Fe County, Santa Fe, p. 338A. Ancestry, www.ancestry.com, Provo, UT.

[960]1860 United States Federal Census, Territory of New Mexico. Roll M653-714; Santa Fe County, Farm of MI Senora de la Luz, p. 365. Ancestry, www.ancestry.com, Provo, UT.

[961]1870 United States Federal Census, Territory of New Mexico. Roll M593-895; San Miguel County, San Geronimo, p. 200B. Ancestry, www.ancestry.com, Provo, UT.

[962]May and Olmsted, Windham and Baca, *Santa Fe Baptisms, Vol. III*, p. 49.

[963]May and Olmsted, Windham and Baca, *Santa Fe Baptisms, Vol. III*, p. 58.

v. Jose Andres (adopted) Roybal was baptized on November 29, 1831, in Santa Fe, age eleven days, adopted by Julian Roybal and Francisca Garcia, and godparents were Miguel Filomeno Gallegos and Ysabel Roibal.[964]

[964]May and Olmsted, Windham and Baca, *Santa Fe Baptisms, Vol. III*, p. 188.

ADDENDUMS

Pecos River above San Jose, on the San Juan road

The San Miguel del Bado land grant and the two settlements were doors which opened up more land grants further east. The largest being Las Vegas in 1835, but also Anton Chico, Chaperito, Tecolote and many more. The children of the first grantees are seen in the lists below. A few of the ‘aged’ grantees did make it to these other grants, but quickly passed on. The eastward expansion or migration in New Mexico from Pecos to what we now call the Texas border grew rapidly and kept on growing as many more settlers after 1860 homesteaded out in these vast plains.

Las Vegas Land Grantees

SPANISH ARCHIVES OF NEW MEXICO (SANM), SERIES I, REEL 15

(Frame 15-18) April 6, 1835. List showing the number of individuals who occupy the new settlement entitled “Nuestra Señora de los Dolores de Las Vegas,” and showing the number of yards of land each one has received, which is as follows, to-wit:

Citizen Asension Baca	175		Citizen Juan de Dios Maes	250
“” Simon Blea	100	“ “	Juan Jose Baca	200
“ “ Jose de Jesus Ulibarri	150	“ “	Francisco Lopez	100
“ “ Santiago Ortega selected				
In Balendre, 150 yards of land	150			

For gardens 125 *varas* towards the north, and 25 for a road to the watering place, one each side, and towards the south 750 *varas* for gardens, from whence the distribution continues, to the individuals contained in the list, noting that the number of yards herein stipulated for gardens and roads is opposite to the square plaza, which I marked out on either side. I left this number of yards for the inhabitants of the place, to be divided equally between them:

[all noted as Citizen] (frame 65)

Jose Guadalupe Baca	150	Felipe Tafolla	250
Miguel Rendon	150	Jose de Jesus Duran	100
Rafael Rendon	100	Manuel Duran	175
Cruz Rendon	150	Antonio Romo	200

Jose Lucero	200	Simon Romo	100
Toribio Crespin	100	Jose Maria Martin	200
Pablo Ulibarri	150	Miguel Martin	200
Antonio Ulibarri	185	Antonio Martin	200
Juan Pedro Archuleta	150	Juan Nepomucento Martin	100
Eulogia Segma	100	Miguel Martin, Jr.	100
Ramon Ulibarri	100	Juan Jose Martin	100
Teodocio Quintana	200		

List of the Names of Persons who may apply for and receive lands after April 6, 1835.

(frame 18-20) [all citizens]

Victorino Baca	150	A portion in another valley	
Antonio Gallegos	455	Mariano Gonzales, sr.	150
Jose Antonio Ulibarri, Sr.,		Desiderio Maese	100
Jose Miguel Garcia took		Rafael Duran	200
The place of Ulibarri, sr.,		Vicente Romero	200
And entered upon his land	125	Santiago Ulibarri	600
Rufino Gonzales	100	Jose Leon Romero	200
Ambrocio Gonzales	100	Jose Antonio Flores	200
Santos Gonzales	100	Rafael Duran	200
Francisco Sanchez	356	Rafael Romero	200
Rafael Rodriguez	165	Miguel Romero	200
Julian Ulibarri	225	Juan Christobal Armijo	230
Manuel Tafolla received a		Jose Miguel Sanchez	200
Portion in the valley…		Francisco Maese	111
Mariano Gonzales received		Francisco Lucero	112

Miguel Caerio	150
Rafael Castillo	100
Jose Fernando Gallegos	100
Jose Dolores Sena	185
Jose Ramon Sena	125
Francisco Sena	200
Vicente Villanueva	100
Jose Pablo Baca	100
Ramon Baca	100
Fernando Chavez (Ramon	
Pena took his land, the other	
Having left	100
Toribio Archuleta	100
Tobirio Martin	100
Miguel Montaño	100
Jesus Pando	100
Juan Felipe Sanches	100
Maria Encarnacion Armijo	100
Jose Flores	75
Cruz Martin, on the opposite	
Side of the river and two	
Little valleys	100
Polonio Herrera	100
Ferrer Herrera	50
Fabian Archuleta	100
Simon Romo	100
Ramon Vigil	100
The remainder was given	
To Juan Jose Vigil	170
Francisco Sanchez, also a	
Little valley	150
Pedro Barela	100
Julian Jiminez	100
Ramon Benavides	100
Antonia Garcia	100
Rafael Rodriguez	100
Pedro Gonzales	200
Andres Trugueque	100
Gabriel Crispin	100
Ascensio Baca	100
Miguel Archuleta	1,087
Jose Maria Tafoya	700
Jose Miguel Cairello	100
Christobal Baca	500
Miguel Martin	125
Martin Romero, 50 more	100
Domingo Gama, 50 more	100
Santiago Sandoval	50

Names of those in the cañada of Pecos from road dividing Lo de Mora to the arroyo of Pecos:

(frames 21, 68) [all citizens]

Jesus Maria Montoya	200	Valley above the ravine on the	
Santiago Montoya	100	River	150
Antonio Jose Saiz	100	Christobal Baca	250
Asensio Sanez	100	Pablo Pando	100
Tomas Ulibarri	100	Jesus Pando	100
Rafael Rodriguez (Antonio		Pedro Garcia	100
Saenz takes the place of		Acensio Garcia	100
Rodriguez by purchase)	100	Esquipula Baca	100
Domingo Peña	200	Julian Archuleta	100
Nerio Montoya (Anastacia		Sebastian Duran	200
Gonzales takes his place)	150	Rafael Nieto	200
Luis Maria Gonzales	170	Andres Trugueque	100
Patricio Benavides (Guillerma		Francisco Lucero	340
and Valeriano take his place,		Jose Flores	100
With 75 *varas* each in the		Francisco Sanchez	400

Leaving 50 *varas* for a public road on the bank below where the plaza is situated, where 50 *varas* are to be left. Pedro Barela, two little valleys at the springs…

Names of citizens placed in possession of lands at the Puertocito, which is attached to the general list of distribution: that is, the lower Puertocito [west of Las Vegas]: (frame 69)

Ramon Cisneros, no *varas*		(Upper Puertocito)	150
Jose Pablo Maes, no *varas*		Juan Martin, for himself and his	
Juan Sais	250	Father and from the boundary	
Antonio Saiz	250	of Mariano Gonzales to the road	
Felipe Tafoya	125	Mariano Gonzales, jr.	100
Jose Dolores Duran	125	Don Lorenzo Baca	100
Rafael Castiyo	100	Ana Maria Chama	100
Rafael Garcia	125	Augustin Quintana	100
Francisco Antonio Sanchez		(And a small valley in the river	

Not measures)	on one side of the arroyo,
Jose Martin, from the boundary	from a rock in the middle of the
of Augustine to the road	valley to the lower rock…
Juan Gallegos, at the mouth of	Sebastian Duran 100
the canyon of the Agua Sarca,	Jesus Duran 100

(frame 23) One hundred varas of land were given to Gregorio Vigil of the remaining lands of the Agua Sarca, designating as boundaries: on the west the little canon of the Agua Sarca, on the east the arroyo of Abayo, on the north a hill near the creston, and the south the common boundary, respecting the tracts already donated.

June 11, 1841 (frame 70)

I have given to each one 25 varas in length, with the precise condition that they should fence them in; and in case of not doing so, they cannot claim damages. The individuals are as follows:

Francisco Sanchez	25
Antonio Saenz	25
Simona Gallegos	25

(frame 25) Vegas, June 11, 1841

Felipe Tafoya	150	Prudencio Griego	150
Francisco Antonio Sanchez	100	Jose Zamora	100
Miguel Tafoya	100		

(frames 26, 71) Lands distributed on the new ditch:

Jose Manuel Martin	150	Manuel Archuleta	100
Jose Manuel Angel	100	Crisantos Salas	100
Pedro Bustos	200	Felipe Martin	100
Jesus Castillo	100	Antonio Jose Sais	50
Jose Flores	100		

At the springs the foreigners William and Anthony Donaldson; Jose Manuel Angel, a little corner in the Cerrito, not measured; Don Ramon Vigil, a valley on the other side of the arroyo of the Pecos, from the wagon road to the blue hills, not measured.

Las Vegas, 25 November 1846, distribution as follows:

Miguel Antonio Padiya	200	Jesus Maria Maese	200
Gertrudis Salazar	200	Rafael Duran	200
Juan Jaramillo	200	Miguel Martin, Jr.	200
Martin Romero	200	Anisteo Quintana, from	
Jose Maria Garcia	200	boundary of Miguel Martin	
Vicente Segura	200	to the road without	
Juan Jose Montoya	200	measurement	

(frame 73) on the 17th (torn) requesting a tract of public land

Juan Pedro Archuleta	50	Rafael Rodriguez	50
Jesus Gallego	50	Jose Martin	50
Jose Candelario Garcia	50	Elogio Gonzales	50

Anton Chico Land Grantees

SPANISH ARCHIVES OF NEW MEXICO (SANM), SERIES I, REEL 25

(frame 708) at Anton Chico January 24, 1822

Salvador Tapia
Francisco Baca
Rafael Duran
Juan Sebastian Duran
Diego Antonio Tapia
Bernardo Ulibarri
Felipe Valencia
Luis Gonzales
Juan Cristobal Garcia.

Tomas Martin
Juan Jose Martin
Miguel Martin
Jose Medina
Simon Estrada
Lorenzo Tapia
Mariano Aragon
Jose Duran

San Miguel del Bado Settlement Grantees[965]

Anaya, Matias
Archibeque, Jose Manuel
Archuleta, Ramon
Arias, Jose de la Cruz
Armijo, Jose Pablo
Armijo, Juan Asencio
Armijo, Juan Domingo
Baca, Diego Manuel
Baca, Diego Pedro Manuel
Baca, Ramon
Benavides, Juan Domingo
Brito, Jose Miguel
Bustamante, Ventura
Cazache, Jose Miguel
Cheferi, Juan Antonio (Father)
Duran, Antonio Encarnacion
Esquibel, Jose
Fragoso de Adorno, Francisco
Fuentes, Manuel
Garduño, Francisco
Garduño, Jose Maria
Guerrero, Cristoval
Guerrero, Juan Cayetano
Jaramillo, Felipe
Lopez, Antonio Geronimo
Lopez, Geronimo
Lovato, Jose Maria
Lucero, Antonio Jose (1)
Lucero, Antonio Jose (2)
Lujan, Juan de Dios
Maes, Manuel
Maese, Pablo
Maestas, Jose Manuel
Marquez, Juan Antonio
Marquez, Pedro Jose
Martin, Antonio
Martin, Francisco
Martin, Jose Cornelio
Martin, Jose Francisco
Martin, Juan Domingo
Martinez, Juan Eusebio
Moran, Maria Balvaneda
Ortega, Antonia Damiana
Ortega, Antonio
Ortega, Antonio Lorenzo
Padilla, Diego
Rael de Aguilar, Jose Antonio
Ribera, Antonio Maria
Rodriguez, Apolonia
Sandoval, Felipe
Sandoval, Juan Jose
Sandoval, Matias
Sandoval, Pedro
Troncoso, Jose Maria (Manuel)
Urioste, Jose Miguel

[965] Christmas and Anderson, *The San Miguel del Bado del Rio de Pecos - The 1803 Land Grantees.*

ANTA FE WEE GAZETTE
"INDEPENDENT IN ALL THI IN NOTHING."
me VIII. SANTA FE, NEW MEXICO. JULY 28, 1866.
WILSON, BRAEC y Co.
NEGOCIANTES POR MAYOR DE
Quinquilleria Estranjera y Domestica, Herramientos, etc. etc

Report of Capt. Rufus C. Vose

Fort Sumner N.M.

June 22, 1866

To: Lt. W. R. Savage, 1st Cavalry, California Volunteers, Post Adjutant, Fort Sumner, N.M.

Sir, I have the honor to report that in obedience to Special Order No. (67) dated Headquarters, Fort Sumner, N.M., June 8th 1866, I left the post on Friday June 8th 1866 with fifteen enlisted men of Company "B", 1st Cavalry, California Volunteers, taking with me three pack mules and fifteen days of rations for the command. Started from the post at 1 p.m. and arrived at Gerhardt's Ranch on the Pecos River at sunset, where I camped for the night. (Note: John Gerhartdt lived at Los Ojitos, a small village on the Pecos River about 25 miles from Fort Sumner). Distance traveled 25 miles.

June 9th. I left Gerhardt's Ranch at 6 a.m. and halted at Capt. Henderson's camp on the Pecos, where we got dinner; started again at 2 p.m. for Giddings Ranch where we camped for the night. (Note: James Giddings was a very prominent man in New Mexico History. His wife's name was Petra Gutierrez. Petra was either the daughter of "Dona Tulles" Barcelo or was raised by her). Distance traveled 20 miles.

June 10th. Left Giddings Ranch at 6 a.m. and traveled up the Pecos River to Las Colonias. Just as we arrived there we met two men hurrying out with guns on their shoulders. They reported to me that Indians had just taken a lot of cattle from Don Antonio Gallegos. I took them back with me to show me where Gallegos lived and found the neighbors gathering in and preparing to follow the Indians. I told them to go out into the hills and hunt for the cattle until they found them or their trail, and that I would camp here on the river until I heard from them; that if they found the tracks of any Indians to send in someone to me, and that I would then immediately take up the trail and overtake the Indians. A little before sundown, they returned and reported to me that they had found the cattle at a Salt Spring up the river bottom and that no sign of the Indians had been discovered. At this place I saw the brother of Salazar, who was killed at the Pintada a few weeks ago, also a number of other men who were out with the party who found the bodies of the two men who were killed by the Indians.

They all think that the same party killed these two men who killed the Fort Bascom Express man, as they found a great many letters there. (Note: the Fort Bascom Express man, named Chambers, disappeared and was believed killed by Indians. He delivered mail and military dispatches between Fort Bascom on the Canadian River and the Santa Fe Military Headquarters).

June 13th. Spent the night at the Middle Spring on the Las Vegas Road: Distance traveled 24 miles.

June 14th. Started at sunrise for Las Vegas where I was obliged to have some of my animals shod, they having lost their shoes in the mountains. Left Las Vegas at 5 p.m. and arrived at Los Valles de San Agustin on the Gallinas River at 9 p.m., the trail from the mesa down being rocky and precipitous. Distance traveled that day 23 miles.

This is the place where Miguel Gonzales was killed on the 26th of last month. I went to see the alcalde and learned from him the full particulars of the case. Gonzales had gone out on the mesa three or four miles from the town to look after some stock. He was on foot and had a Colt's Pistol on at the time. He was evidently waylaid from behind a bush near which he passed and after having been knocked down with clubs, was shot through the head with his own pistol. He was then stripped and dragged into the bushes so that although searched for the next morning, he was not found for several days. They found near the place a Navajo blanket and the cross poles of a loom, also a flat stick, which the Navajo call a guitar, and which is used in weaving by them. These were stained with blood, and had been used in the murder. The Indians took away from him quite a number of horses and went in the direction of Canon Largo. The articles above mentioned I have brought with me.

June 15th. Started towards the Canon Largo and after a march of four hours halted at Monia Springs for dinner. Left here at 1 p.m. and arrived at the head of the Conchas at sundown where we camped for the night. Distance traveled 23 miles.

June 16th. Started early and traveled in a N.E. direction over very rough country and reached the Cañon Largo after a march of five hours. Camped for dinner, after which we traveled down the canon quite smoothly for a few miles when we came to very rough and rocky places where it was very tedious and difficult to march. Arrived at the point where Capt. Benjamin J. Fox entered the canon a month ago and found the trail of the animals. Camped here for the night. Distance traveled 20 miles.

June 17th. Started early and followed the canon down about six miles where I was obliged to travel the sides of the canon on account of the rough bottom. After traveling along awhile the guide discovered tracks of Indians and horses. Halted at a favorable place and examined the ground carefully. Counted the tracks of eighteen (18) horses also found tracks of several bucks, one squaw and a child three or four years old. They answered the descriptions of the party who killed Gonzales so well that I am quite sure of their being the same. Followed their trail five or six miles to where they had camped in a small ravine. From all appearances they must have been joined at this point by more Indians, as there had been no less then six different fires. The tracks and signs about camp seem to be about 10 weeks old. I found here some wool and pieces of rawhide; also fragments of a Navajo Belplata or a woman's dress and an awl such as they use in the making moccasins.

After leaving this place I found it impossible to follow their trail further, on account of it's age and the rocky character of the country. I then struck out for the Mesa Rica and camped at 2 p.m. near water, the horses being very tired, and many of them without shoes, having torn them off amongst the rocks. Started again at 5 p.m. and soon after entered the Trementina Valley down which we traveled till 9 p.m., where we camped for the night. Distance traveled 28 miles

June 18th. Started early and traveled till half past ten a.m. where we halted for dinner. Found several stray sheep which were as wild as deer along the top of the mesa among the bushes. Shot one or two of them, started again at 3 p.m. and in about an hour came upon a flock of sheep numbering some 280 head. They had come down from the mesa late this evening for water and when they discovered us tried to escape again into the bushes. But we surrounded them and prevented the rest of them from doing so. Only some half a dozen getting away from us.

I looked about here for any ranch or herder of sheep to which these might belong but found none in the vicinity. The place where they were found is about 20 miles from any habitation, and they have evidently been run off from different flocks by Indians or wolves, and again been lost by them. They have at least four or five different earmarks and are covered with a very heavy fleece. Drove them down with some difficulty to where the Bascom road crosses the Conchas and camped there for the night. Distance traveled 18 miles.

June 19th. Started early and traveled along the West Side of the Mesa Rica, which I examined carefully as I went, and could find no trails of Indians or horses. I went up myself with the guide but would discover nothing with the glass. As I now had only three-day rations, I concluded that it would be impractical for me to continue and returned to Fort Sumner.

Your obedient servant,

Rufus C. Vose, Captain,
1st Calvary, California Volunteers, Commanding Scout. [966]

[966]Report of Capt. Rufus C. Vose, *Santa Fe Weekly Gazette,* Santa Fe, NM, July 28, 1866

Joe & Diane Stein Collection

New Mexico State Archives, Santa Fe, New Mexico
Accession 1983-062

Folder 1, partitioning of land at SJB, 1803.

Folder 2, 20 May 1805, at SMB, before the *alcalde* Juan Antonio Anaya Almazan, Juan Jesus Rael de Aguilar sells to Manuel Rivera, both from this place. The price of 60 *pesos*.

Folder 3, SJB Manuel Duran also sells land to Santiago Ulibarri. (same paper).

Folder 4, SJB, 4 Nov 1820, Before the *alcalde* don Santiago Ulibarri, Luis Cordoba and Jose Jesus Ulibarri residents, sold 25 *varas* of land he rec'd as lands via don Jose Antonio Ulibarri for one fat cow and one ewe.

Folder 4, SJB, 12 Nov 1820, Don Santiago Ulibarri, Juana Baca to Jose de Jesus Ulibarri, 30 *varas* of land her deceased husband (land grant) sold for one burro and one *peso* in *reales*.

Folder 5, 1 Dec 1820, *Alcalde* Luis Maria Cabeza de Baca, present Santiago de Jesus Aragon, land granted at a place called the A*ncon de Sarrasino*, 52 *varas* certified. Signed Luis Maria Cabeza de Baca, Jose Ronquillo and Antonio Nieto.

Folder 6, 7 Apr 1823, Santiago Ulibarri, commission as Captain of the 5th Cavalry Company 1st Regiment of the National Militia.

Folder 7, 19 Oct 1825, Antonio Estrada, sells lands to Santiago Ulibarri at *Ancon de Sarracino*, lands from the land grant, hoop earrings of solid silver, five varas each of *sabania* (woven yardage), a *quartilla* of wheat, signed Tomas Sena, Alcalde.

Folder 8, 29 March 1826, SJB. At the *plaza* de la Cuesta. Antonio Flores sells land to Miguel Flores, at *Ancon de Sarracino*, 60 pesos in *reales* and 15 rams, from a land grant. Signed Jose Ramon Alarid, *alcalde*; Jose Antonio Tapia, Manuel Lobato.

Folder 10, 3 Dec 1831, Rosa Gutierrez sells to Jose de Jesus Gonzales, SJB. 120 *varas*, one of the boundaries is the river.

Folder 11, 1831, Rosa Ramires? To Jose Gonzales, exchange at SJB on the river.

Folder 12, 31 May 1832, Francisco Ulibarri sold to Santiago Ulibarri at *Ancon de Sarracino*, 12 *varas*, for one heifer, a ram and three gold pieces. Signed Jose de Jesus Ulibarri, *alcalde*.

Folder 13, 3 Nov 1833, Toribio Baca, sold to Santiago Ulibarri, at *Ancon de Sarracino*, SJB, 50 *varas*, and on the *acequia madre*. Signed Nicolas Tapia, Antonio Nieto.

Folder 14, 7 July 1834, Jose Archibeque sold to Santiago Ulibarri, at *Ancon de NS Guadalupe*, SMB, 120 *varas* and on the river. Juan Jose Cabeza de Baca, Jose Archibeque, Jose Antonio Cabeza. Santiago Narvais states some trespass issues on a separate paper.

Folder 15, 9 Feb 1835, Blas Baca sold to Salvador Xaramillo, for 60 *pesos* and one horse, a place called *Los Trigos*. Mariano Gonzales, Antonio Nieto and Jose Ulibarri, Blas Baca signs.

Folder 16, 11 Nov 1835, Manuel Duran granted land at Las Vegas, signed *alcalde* Jose de Jesus Ulibarri, Antonio Nieto.

Folder 17, 6 Feb 1837, Andres Gonzales sells to Salbador Xaramillo, SMB, Vicente Rivera *alcalde*, 30 pesos. *Ancon de Pedro Jose Marquez*. Bicente Rivera, Bartole Martin, Jose Antonio Casaus.

Folder 18, 28 May 1838, Tomas Baca appoints executors for his wife's estate of six children, Maria Miquela Ulibarri, SJB. Santiago and Jose de Jesus Ulibarri appointed.

SMB = San Miguel del Bado

SJB = San Jose del Bado

Reference: New Mexico State Records Center and Archives, Joe & Diane Stein Collection, Accession 1983-062, Box 1, Folders as indicated.

Bibliography

Arellanes, Eloise, extractor. Compiled by Margaret Leonard Windham and Evelyn Lujan Baca. *New Mexico Marriages, San Miguel del Bado Church, 12 November 1829 to 10 November 1878*. Albuquerque: New Mexico Genealogical Society, 1997.

Baca, Evelyn Lujan, compiler. "Spanish Enlistment Papers, 1770 -1816 ~ Filiaciones Español." *The Genealogist*, March-June 1998. Online archives. *NMGS.org*. http://www.nmgs.org/filiciones. htm/ : 2016.

Chávez, Fr. Angélico, compiler. *New Mexico Roots Ltd., A demographic perspective from genealogical, historical and geographic data found in the Diligencias Matrimoniales or Pre-Nuptial Investigations (1678-1869) of the Archives of the Archdiocese of Santa Fe*. Santa Fe: Museum of New Mexico Press, 1982.

Christmas, Henrietta M., extractor and compiler. *Military Records ~ Colonial New Mexico ~ Notas y Revistas*. Albuquerque: Hispanic Genealogical Research Center of New Mexico, 2004.

_____, Jeanette Gallegos, and Patricia S. Rau, extractors, compilers, and editors. *New Mexico Burials, Santa Fe - St. Francis Parish and Military Chapel of Our Lady of Light (La Castrense), 1726-1834*. Albuquerque: New Mexico Genealogical Society, 2007.

_____, Ernestino Tafoya, and Ruby Olguin, extractors, transcribers, and editors. *New Mexico Census: 1790, 1793, 1803, 1823, 1829, 1841*. Albuquerque: Hispanic Genealogical Research Center of New Mexico, 2008.

Christmas, Henrietta Martinez and Nancy Anderson, compilers. *The San Miguel del Bado del Rio de Pecos - The 1803 Land Grantees*. Albuquerque: New Mexico Genealogical Society, 2013.

Colligan, John B., compiler. Edited by Rick Hendricks. *New Mexico Prenuptial Investigations from the Archivos Historicos del Arzobispado de Durango, 1800-1893*. Las Cruces, New Mexico: Rio Grande Historical Collection, New Mexico State University Library, 2000.

Dressen, Donald S., and Evelyn Lujan Baca, extractors. Compiled by Margaret Leonard Windham and Evelyn Lujan Baca. *New Mexico Baptisms, San Buenaventura de Cochiti Church, 1736-1873*. Albuquerque: New Mexico Genealogical Society, 2000.

______, and Consuelo Gooch, extractors. Compiled by Margaret Leonard Windham and Evelyn Lujan Baca. *New Mexico Marriages, San Felipe de Neri Church in Albuquerque, 16 June 1726 ~ 16 January 1855*. Albuquerque: New Mexico Genealogical Society, 2005.

Ebright, Malcolm. *Land Grants & Lawsuits in Northern New Mexico*. Albuquerque, New Mexico: University of New Mexico Press, 1994.

______, and Rick Hendricks, *The Witches of Abiquiu: The Governor, the Priest, the Genizaro Indians, and the Devil*, Albuquerque, New Mexico: University of New Mexico Press, 2006.

Gutiérrez, Ramón A. *When Jesus Came, the Corn Mothers Went Away: Marriage, Sexuality, and Power in New Mexico, 1500-1846*. Stanford, California: Stanford University Press, 1991.

Hall, G. Emlen. "San Miguel del Bado and the Loss of the Common Lands of New Mexico Community Land Grants," *New Mexico Historical Review* 66, (October 1991).

Kavanagh, Thomas W. *Comanche Political History: an Ethnohistorical Perspective, 1706-1875.* Lincoln, Nebraska: University of Nebraska Press, 1996.
Kessell, John L. *Kiva, Cross and Crown: the Pecos Indians and New Mexico, 1540-1840.* Washington, D. C.: National Park Service, U. S. Department of the Interior, 1979.
Levine, Francis. *Our Prayers Are in This Place: Pecos Pueblo Identity Over the Centuries*, Albuquerque, New Mexico: University of New Mexico Press, 1999.
May, Ella Louise, extractor. Windham, Margaret L. and Evelyn L. Baca, compilers. *New Mexico Baptisms of Santa Fe, Parroquia de San Francisco de Asis, Vol. 1, 5 September 1747 to 17 July 1791.* Albuquerque: New Mexico Genealogical Society, 2002.
_____, extractor. Compiled by Margaret Leonard Windham and Evelyn Lujan Baca. *New Mexico Baptisms of Santa Fe: Parroquia de San Francisco de Asis, Volume II, 15 August 1796 to 30 December 1822.* Albuquerque: New Mexico Genealogical Society, 2002.
_____, and Virginia L. Olmsted, extractors. Compiled by Margaret Leonard Windham and Evelyn Lujan Baca. *New Mexico Baptisms of Santa Fe, Parish of Saint Francis of Assisi, Volume III, 1 January 1823 to 26 June 1833; Castrense Register, 9 June 1798 to 26 June 1833.* Albuquerque: New Mexico Genealogical Society, 2002.
Mocho, Jill. *Murder and Justice in Frontier New Mexico, 1821-1846.* Albuquerque: University of New Mexico Press, 1997.
New Mexico Genealogical Society Volunteers, compilers. *Albuquerque Baptisms, Archdiocese of Santa Fe, 1706-1850.* Albuquerque: New Mexico Genealogical Society, 1983.
_____. *New Mexico Baptisms, Church in San Juan de los Caballeros, 1726-1798.* Albuquerque: New Mexico Genealogical Society and Archdiocese of Santa Fe, 2016.
_____. *San Miguel del Bado, NM Burials: 1829-1848, also includes Pecos from 1796-1829 and Ribera from 1847-1850.* Albuquerque: New Mexico Genealogical Society, 2015.
Nostrand, Richard L. *El Cerrito, New Mexico: Eight Generations In A Spanish Village.* Norman: University of Oklahoma, 2003.
Olmsted, Virginia Langham, transcriber. Compiled by Margaret Leonard Windham and Evelyn Lujan Baca. *New Mexico Baptisms, Santa Cruz de la Cañada Church, Vol. II, 1795-1827.* Albuquerque: New Mexico Genealogical Society, 1995.
_____, transcriber. Compiled by Margaret Leonard Windham and Evelyn Lujan Baca. New Mexico Baptisms, *Santa Cruz de la Cañada Church, Vol. 3, 1827-1856.* Albuquerque: New Mexico Genealogical Society, 1997.
_____, transcriber and compiler. *New Mexico Spanish & Mexican Colonial Censuses, 1790 * 1823 * 1845.* Albuquerque: New Mexico Genealogical Society, 1975.
_____, compiler. *Spanish and Mexican Censuses of New Mexico, 1750 to 1830.* Albuquerque: New Mexico Genealogical Society, 1981.
_____. "Spanish Enlistment Papers of New Mexico, 1732-1820." *National Genealogical Society Quarterly* 67 (September 1979) through 68 (June 1980).
Padilla y Baca, Luis Gilberto, compiler. *Baptisms for San Miguel del Bado, from 1799 to 1829: extracted from the Pecos Mission.* Albuquerque: L. & F. Enterprises, 1999.
_____. *New Mexico Marriages & Marriage Investigations: San Miguel del Vado, 1802-1865.* Albuquerque: Hispanic Genealogical Research Center of New Mexico, ca. 2000.
_____. *New Mexico Marriages Anton Chico: La Yglesia de San Jose, April 1857 - December 1940.* Albuquerque: Hispanic Genealogical Research Center of New Mexico, 2003.

_____. *New Mexico Marriages, Pueblo Missions: San Felipe, Santa Ana, Santo Domingo y vecindario, Cochiti, Jemez*. Albuquerque: Hispanic Genealogical Research Center of New Mexico, ca. 2000.

Roybal, Marie J., and Lila Armijo Pfeufer, extractors. Compiled by Margaret Leonard Windham and Evelyn Lujan Baca. *New Mexico Marriages, Santa Fe - St. Francis Parish and Military Chapel of Our Lady of Light (La Castrense), 1728-1857*. Albuquerque: New Mexico Genealogical Society, 1997.

San Miguel County, New Mexico Wills, Book A. San Miguel County, N. M. Records, 1847-1942. New Mexico State Records Center and Archives, Santa Fe.

Simpson, James H. *Journal of a Military Reconnaissance from Santa Fé, New Mexico, to the Navajo Country*. Philadelphia: Lippincott, Grambo, and Company, 1852.

Spanish Archives of New Mexico (SANM), Series I. Surveyor General and Court of Private Land Claims Records microfilm collection 1972-007, 63 rolls. New Mexico State Records Center and Archives, Santa Fe, New Mexico.

Tafoya, Ernestino. "More Information on the Genealogy of the Alcalde of Santa Fe, Captian don Antonio de Ulibarri," *Herencia, Quarterly Journal of HGRC* Vol. 10:2 (April 2002)

_____, Marlin Aker, Jr., and Joyce Aker, compilers. *New Mexico Marriages: San Miguel del Vado, November 19, 1878 - December 12, 1900*. Albuquerque: Hispanic Genealogical Research Center of New Mexico, 2000.

Windes, Thomas C. "A Dendrochronological Study of Nineteenth-Century San Miguel del Vado and San José del Vado in Northeastern New Mexico," *New Mexico Historical Review*, 86 (Fall 2011)

Archives of the Archdiocese of Santa Fe (AASF) & Family History Library (FHL) Microfilms

Anton Chico Burials, 1857-1956. San Buenaventura de Cochiti Burials, 1776-1873. Archives of Archdiocese of Santa Fe, Santa Fe, NM, AASF/FHL Film 0016628. Genealogy Center, Albuquerque/Bernalillo County Library, Albuquerque, NM.

Cochiti Burials, 1776-1873. Archives of Archdiocese of Santa Fe, Santa Fe, NM, Roll 35. Genealogy Center, Albuquerque/Bernalillo County Library, Albuquerque, NM.

Cochiti Marriages, 1776-1827. Archives of Archdiocese of Santa Fe, Santa Fe, NM, Roll 27. Genealogy Center, Albuquerque/Bernalillo County Library, Albuquerque, NM.

Galisteo/Pecos Marriages, 1776-1828. Archives of Archdiocese of Santa Fe, Santa Fe, NM, Roll 27. Genealogy Center, Albuquerque/Bernalillo County Library, Albuquerque, NM.

Jemez Baptisms, 1704-1829. Archives of Archdiocese of Santa Fe, Santa Fe, NM, Roll 5. Genealogy Center, Albuquerque/Bernalillo County Library, Albuquerque, NM.

Pecos/San Miguel del Bado Baptisms, 1726-1829. Archives of Archdiocese of Santa Fe, Santa Fe, NM, Roll 6. Genealogy Center, Albuquerque/Bernalillo County Library, Albuquerque, NM.

Pecos/San Miguel del Bado Marriages, 1772-1828. Archives of Archdiocese of Santa Fe, Santa Fe, NM, Roll 27. Genealogy Center, Albuquerque/Bernalillo County Library, Albuquerque, NM.

Ribera/San Miguel del Bado Burials, 1848-1955. San Buenaventura de Cochiti Burials, 1776-1873. Archives of Archdiocese of Santa Fe, Santa Fe, NM, AASF/FHL Film 0016879. Genealogy Center, Albuquerque/Bernalillo County Library, Albuquerque, NM.

San Juan de los Caballeros Baptisms, 1726-1820. Archives of Archdiocese of Santa Fe, Santa Fe, NM, Roll 9. Genealogy Center, Albuquerque/Bernalillo County Library, Albuquerque, NM.

Nicolas Apodaca

8. Joseph de Apodaca
b. ca 1657
at
m.[11] Aug 12, 1686
at Guadalupe Del Paso
d.
at

4. Juan Antonio Apodaca
b. ca 1687
at Guadalupe Del Paso, NM
m.[8] Jan 2, 1710
at Santa Cruz
d.[9] Oct 27, 1758
at Santa Fe

9. Isabel Gutierrez
b. ca 1676
at
d.[12] May, 1693
at El Paso del Norte

2. Marcos Apodaca
bap.[4] May 6, 1713
at Santa Cruz
m.[5] Aug 19, 1733
at Santa Fe
d.[6] Jan 16, 1766
at Santa Fe

10. Salvador Duran
b. ca 1646
at
m. ca 1666
at
d.[13] before Mar 24, 1697
at

5. Maria Duran
b. ca 1680
at
d.[10] before Oct 6, 1716
at

11. Ana Marquez
b.
at
d.[14] before Mar 24, 1697
at

1. Nicolas Apodaca
bap.[1] Sep 10, 1753
at Santa Fe
m.[2] Oct 14, 1782
at Cochiti
d.[3] May 24, 1818
at San Miguel del Bado

sp. Maria Rosa Gutierrez
b. ca 1747
at
d.
at

3. Monica de Jesus Valverde
b.
at
d.[7] Nov 30, 1790
at Cochiti

Endnotes

1. Margaret L. Windham and Evelyn L. Baca, compiler, *Baptisms of Santa Fe, Parroquia de San Francisco de Asis, Vol. 1, 5 September 1747 to 17 July 1791* (Albuquerque, NM: New Mexico Genealogical Society, 2002), p. 33.

2. Luis Gilberto Padilla y Baca, *New Mexico Marriages - Pueblo Missions: San Felipe, Santa Ana, Santo Domingo y vecindario, Cochiti, Jemez* (Albuquerque, NM: Hispanic Genealogical Research Center of New Mexico, 2000), p. 23.

3. NMGS Volunteers, compiler, *Pecos, San Miguel del Bado & Ribera Burials, 1796 - 1850* (Albuquerque, NM: New Mexico Genealogical Society, 2014), p. 16.

4. Margaret Langham Olmsted, transcriber, Margaret Leonard Windham and Evelyn Lujan Baca, compilers, *New Mexico Baptisms, Santa Cruz de la Cañada Church, Vol. 1, 1710-1794* (Albuquerque, NM: New Mexico Genealogical Society, 1994), p. 3.

5. Marie J. Roybal and Lila Armijo Pfeufer, extractors, Margaret Leonard Windham and Evelyn Lujan Baca, compilers, *New Mexico Marriages, Santa Fe - St. Francis Parish and Military Chapel of Our Lady of Light (La Castrense), 1728-1857* (Albuquerque: New Mexico Genealogical Society, 1997), p. 5.

6. Henrietta M. Christmas, Jeanette Gallegos and Patricia S. Rau, compiler, *New Mexico Burials, Santa Fe - St. Francis Parish and Military Chapel of Our Lady of Light (La Castrense), 1726-1834* (Albuquerque, NM: New Mexico Genealogical Society, 2007), p. 63.

7. Henrietta M. Christmas, extractor. Cochiti Burials, 1776 - 1873. AASF #35: frame 428. Albuquerque Genealogy Center, Albuquerque, NM.

8. Fr. Angelico Chavez, compiler, *New Mexico Roots Ltd., A demographic perspective from genealogical, historical and geographic data found in the Diligencias Matrimoniales or Pre-Nuptial Investigations (1678-1869) of the Archives of the Archdiocese of Santa Fe* (Santa Fe: Museum of New Mexico Press, 1982), p. 44.

9. Christmas, Gallegos and Rau, *Santa Fe Burials, 1726-1834*, p. 52.

10. Chavez, *DM's or Pre-Nuptial Investigations*, p. 44.

11. Chavez, *DM's or Pre-Nuptial Investigations*, p. 41.

12. Chavez, *DM's or Pre-Nuptial Investigations*, p. 42.

13. Chavez, *DM's or Pre-Nuptial Investigations*, p. 1377.

14. Chavez, *DM's or Pre-Nuptial Investigations*, p. 1377.

Chart of Maria Francisca Armijo

1. Maria Francisca Armijo
b. ca 1757
at
m.[1] Jun 24, 1771
at Santa Fe
d.
at

sp. Ascencio Antonio Ulibarri
b. ca 1740
at
d.[2] Feb 6, 1796
at Santa Fe

2. Manuel S. de la C. Duran y Armijo
b. ca 1713
at
m.[3] Oct 19, 1734
at Santa Fe
d.[4] Dcc 4, 1764
at Albuquerque

3. Francisca Alfonsa Lucero de Godoy
b.
at
d.[5] Jan, 1786
at Albuquerque

4. Vicente Ferrer Duran y Armijo
b. ca 1679
at Zacatecas
m.[6] after Aug 29, 1703
at Santa Fe
d.[7] after Nov 15, 1743
at Santa Fe

5. Maria Magdalena Apodaca
b.
at
d.
at

6. Juan Lucero de Godoy
b. ca 1678
at
m.[8] May 7, 1703
at Santa Fe
d.[9] Nov 23, 1741
at Santa Fe

7. Maria Isabel Lopez Lujan
b. ca 1688
New Mexico
d.[10] Aug 9, 1771
at Santa Fe

8. Jose de Armijo
b. ca 1650
at
m.[11] ca 1674
at
d. ca 1706
at Santa Fe

9. Catalina Duran
b. ca 1660
at
d.
at

10.
.

11. Juana de la Cruz Apodaca
b.
at
d.
at

12. Antonio Lucero de Godoy
b.[12] ca 1655
at Santa Fe
m. ca 1681
at El Paso del Norte
d.
at

13. Antonia Varela de Losada Perea
b. ca 1667
'native of New Mexico'
d.[13] after Jan 13, 1712
at Santa Fe

14. Pedro Lujan
b.[14] ca 1669
at
m.[15] Jan 10, 1689
at Guadalupe Del Paso, NM
d.
at

15. Francisca Salazar Martin
b. ca 1675
at Santa Cruz
d.
at

1. Marie J. Roybal and Lila Armijo Pfeufer, extractors, Margaret Leonard Windham and Evelyn Lujan Baca, compilers, *New Mexico Marriages, Santa Fe - St. Francis Parish and Military Chapel of Our Lady of Light (La Castrense), 1728-1857* (Albuquerque: New Mexico Genealogical Society, 1997), p. 40..

2. Henrietta M. Christmas, Jeanette Gallegos and Patricia S. Rau, compiler, *New Mexico Burials, Santa Fe - St. Francis Parish and Military Chapel of Our Lady of Light (La Castrense), 1726-1834* (Albuquerque, NM: New Mexico Genealogical Society, 2007), p. 137.

3. Roybal and Pfeufer, Windham and Baca, *Santa Fe Marriages, 1728-1857*, p. 6.

4. Jackie Luna, (website: http://home.earthlink.net/index.html), "electronic": *San Felipe de Neri Church, Burials/Deaths 1726-1776, Book #1, LDS Reel #0016645.*

5. Luna, (website: http://home.earthlink.net/index.html), *San Felipe de Neri Church, Burials/Deaths 1726-1776, Book #1, LDS Reel #0016645.*

6. Fr. Angelico Chavez, compiler, *New Mexico Roots Ltd., A demographic perspective from genealogical, historical and geographic data found in the Diligencias Matrimoniales or Pre-Nuptial Investigations (1678-1869) of the Archives of the Archdiocese of Santa Fe* (Santa Fe: Museum of New Mexico Press, 1982), p. 125.

7. John L, Kessel, Rick Hendricks and Meredith D. Dodge, compiler, *Blood on the Boulders, The Journals of don Diego de Vargas, New Mexico, 1694-97, Book I* (Albuquerque: University of New Mexico Press, 1998), p. 562, n25.

8. Chavez, *DM's or Pre-Nuptial Investigations*, p. 966.

9. Christmas, Gallegos and Rau, *Santa Fe Burials, 1726-1834*, p. 28.

10. Christmas, Gallegos and Rau, *Santa Fe Burials, 1726-1834*, p. 67.

11. *Origins of New Mexico Families, A Genealogy of the Spanish Colonial Period.*, Fray Angelico Chavez, (Santa Fe, NM, Museum of New Mexico Press:1910, Revised 1992).

12. Chavez, *Origins of New Mexico Families*. p. 209.

13. 1598 New Mexico, online http://1598nm.blogspot.com/, Henrietta Martinez Christmas, Antonia Varela de Losada.

14. Chavez, *DM's or Pre-Nuptial Investigations*, p. 1011.

15. Chavez, *DM's or Pre-Nuptial Investigations*, p. 1011.

Jose Antonio Ulibarri

1. Jose Antonio Ulibarri
bap.[1] Nov 26, 1776
at Santa Fe
m.[2] Apr 30, 1797
at Santa Fe
d. before Aug, 1834
at

sp. Maria Manuela de la A. Montoya
bap.[3] May 31, 1764
at Santa Fe
d.[4] Jul 23, 1807
at Pecos

2. Ascencio Antonio Ulibarri
b. ca 1740
at
m.[5] Jun 24, 1771
at Santa Fe
d.[6] Feb 6, 1796
at Santa Fe

3. Maria Francisca Armijo
b. ca 1757
at
d.
at

4. Captain Antonio de Ulibarri
b.[7] ca 1680
at San Luis de la Paz, Guanajuato, Mexico
m.[8] after Jan 25, 1725
at Santa Fe
d. Nov 2, 1762
at Santa Fe, NM

5. Antonia Teresa Rael de Aguilar
b. ca 1706
at
d.
at

6. Manuel S. de la C. Duran y Armijo
b. ca 1713
at
m.[9] Oct 19, 1734
at Santa Fe
d.[10] Dec 4, 1764
at Albuquerque

7. Francisca Alfonsa Lucero de Godoy
b.
at
d.[11] Jan, 1786
at Albuquerque

8. Joseph Henriques delos Reyes
b.
at
m.[12] after Jan 10, 1672
at San Luis de La Paz
d.
at

9. Maria de Hinojosa
bap.[13] Jun 17, 1652
at San Luis de la Paz, Mexico
d.
at

10. Captain Alonso J. Rael de Aguilar
bap.[14] Feb 14, 1661
at la Iglesia de San Mateo, Lorca, Spain
m. ca 1670
at
d.[15] Apr 10, 1735
at Santa Fe

11. Josefa Garcia de Noriega
b. ca 1655
at
d.[16] Aug 12, 1734
at

12. Vicente Ferrer Duran y Armijo
b. c 1679
at Zacatecas
m.[17] after Aug 29, 1703
at Santa Fe
d.[18] after Nov 15, 1743
at Santa Fe

13. Maria Magdalena Apodaca
b.
at
d.
at

14. Juan Lucero de Godoy
b. ca 1678
at
m.[19] May 7, 1703
at Santa Fe
d.[20] Nov 23, 1742
at Santa Fe

15. Maria Isabel Lopez Lujan
b. ca 1692
at NM
d.[21] Aug 9, 1771
at Santa Fe

Endnotes

1. Margaret L. Windham and Evelyn L. Baca, compiler, *Baptisms of Santa Fe, Parroquia de San Francisco de Asis, Vol. 1, 5 September 1747 to 17 July 1791* (Albuquerque, NM: New Mexico Genealogical Society, 2002).

2. Marie J. Roybal and Lila Armijo Pfeufer, extractors, Margaret Leonard Windham and Evelyn Lujan Baca, compilers, *New Mexico Marriages, Santa Fe - St. Francis Parish and Military Chapel of Our Lady of Light (La Castrense), 1728-1857* (Albuquerque: New Mexico Genealogical Society, 1997).

3. Windham and Baca, *Santa Fe Baptisms, Vol. 1, 1747-1791.*

4. Henrietta M. Christmas, *New Mexico Burials, Pecos Mission, 1798 - 1829*, AASF Roll #35.

5. Roybal and Pfeufer, Windham and Baca, *Santa Fe Marriages, 1728-1857.*

6. Henrietta M. Christmas, Jeanette Gallegos and Patricia S. Rau, compiler, *New Mexico Burials, Santa Fe - St. Francis Parish and Military Chapel of Our Lady of Light (La Castrense), 1726-1834* (Albuquerque, NM: New Mexico Genealogical Society, 2007).

7. Fr. Angelico Chavez, compiler, *New Mexico Roots Ltd., A demographic perspective from genealogical, historical and geographic data found in the Diligencias Matrimoniales or Pre-Nuptial Investigations (1678-1869) of the Archives of the Archdiocese of Santa Fe* (Santa Fe: Museum of New Mexico Press, 1982).

8. Fray Angelico Chavez, compiler, *New Mexico Diligencias* (Albuquerque: New Mexico Genealogical Society, 2010).

9. Roybal and Pfeufer, Windham and Baca, *Santa Fe Marriages, 1728-1857.*

10. Jackie Luna, (website: http://home.earthlink.net/index.html), "electronic": *San Felipe de Neri Church, Burials/Deaths 1726-1776, Book #1, LDS Reel #0016645.*

11. Luna, *San Felipe de Neri Church, Burials/Deaths 1726-1776, Book #1, LDS Reel #0016645.*

12. Ernestino Tafoya, "More Information on the Genealogy of the Alcalde of Santa Fe, Captain don Antonio de Ulibarri." HERENCIA, 10 (April 2002), p. 2.

13. Tafoya, "More Information on the Genealogy of Captain don Antonio de Ulibarri," p. 2.

14. Jose Antonio Esquibel, et al. Beyond Origins of New Mexico Families, online https://sites.google.com/site/beyondoriginsofnmfamilies/. Hereinafter cited as Beyond ONMF.

15. Christmas, Gallegos and Rau, *Santa Fe Burials, 1726-1834.*

16. Christmas, Gallegos and Rau, *Santa Fe Burials, 1726-1834.*

17. Chavez, *DM's or Pre-Nuptial Investigations.*

18. John L, Kessel, Rick Hendricks and Meredith D. Dodge, compiler, *Blood on the Boulders, The Journals of don Diego de Vargas, New Mexico, 1694-97, Book I* (Albuquerque: University of New Mexico Press, 1998).

19. Chavez, *DM's or Pre-Nuptial Investigations.*

20. Christmas, Gallegos and Rau, *Santa Fe Burials, 1726-1834.*

21. Christmas, Gallegos and Rau, *Santa Fe Burials, 1726-1834.*

Jose de Jesus Ulibarri

1. Jose de Jesus Ulibarri
bap.[1] Feb 10, 1778
at Santa Fe
m.
at
d. before Feb, 1827
at

sp. Juana de la Cruz Baca
bap.[2] Oct 26, 1783
at Santa Fe
d.
at

2. Ascencio Antonio Ulibarri
b. ca 1740
at
m.[3] Jun 24, 1771
at Santa Fe
d.[4] Feb 6, 1796
at Santa Fe

3. Maria Francisca Armijo
b. ca 1757
at
d.
at

4. Captain Antonio de Ulibarri
bap.[5] Dec 28, 1680
at San Luis de la Paz, Guanajuato, Mexico
m.[6] after Jan 25, 1725
at Santa Fe
d.[7] Nov 2, 1762
at Santa Fe, NM

5. Antonia Teresa Rael de Aguilar
b. ca 1706
at
d.
at

6. Manuel S. de la C. Duran y Armijo
b. ca 1713
at
m.[8] Oct 19, 1734
at Santa Fe
d.[9] Dec 4, 1764
at Albuquerque

7. Francisca Alfonsa Lucero de Godoy
b.
at
d.[10] Jan, 1786
at Albuquerque

8. Joseph de los Reyes
b.
at
m.[11] after Jan 10, 1672
at San Luis de La Paz
d.
at

9. Maria de Hinojosa y Robledo
bap.[12] Jun 17, 1652
at San Luis de la Paz, Mexico
d.
at

10. Captain Alonso J. Rael de Aguilar
bap.[13] Feb 14, 1661
at la Iglesia de San Mateo, Lorca, Spain
m. ca 1670
at
d.[14] Apr 10, 1735
at Santa Fe

11. Josefa Garcia de Noriega
b. ca 1655
at
d.[15] Aug 12, 1734
at

12. Vicente Ferrer Duran y Armijo
b. ca 1679
at Zacatecas
m.[16] after Aug 29, 1703
at Santa Fe
d.[17] after Nov 15, 1743
at Santa Fe

13. Maria Magdalena Apodaca
b.
at
d.
at

14. Juan Lucero de Godoy
b. ca 1678
at
m.[18] May 7, 1703
at Santa Fe
d.[19] Nov 23, 1742
at Santa Fe

15. Maria Isabel Lopez Lujan
b. ca 1692
at NM
d.[20] Aug 9, 1771 at Santa Fe

Endnotes

1. Margaret L. Windham and Evelyn L. Baca, compiler, *Baptisms of Santa Fe, Parroquia de San Francisco de Asis, Vol. 1, 5 September 1747 to 17 July 1791* (Albuquerque, NM: New Mexico Genealogical Society, 2002).

2. Windham and Baca, *Santa Fe Baptisms, Vol. 1, 1747-1791.*

3. Marie J. Roybal and Lila Armijo Pfeufer, extractors, Margaret Leonard Windham and Evelyn Lujan Baca, compilers, *New Mexico Marriages, Santa Fe - St. Francis Parish and Military Chapel of Our Lady of Light (La Castrense), 1728-1857* (Albuquerque: New Mexico Genealogical Society, 1997).

4. Henrietta M. Christmas, Jeanette Gallegos and Patricia S. Rau, compiler, *New Mexico Burials, Santa Fe - St. Francis Parish and Military Chapel of Our Lady of Light (La Castrense), 1726-1834* (Albuquerque, NM: New Mexico Genealogical Society, 2007).

5. Ernestino Tafoya, "More Information on the Genealogy of the Alcalde of Santa Fe, Captain don Antonio de Ulibarri," *HERENCIA, Quarterly Journal of HGRC* Vol. 10:2 (April 2002).

6. Fray Angelico Chavez, compiler, *New Mexico Diligencias* (Albuquerque: New Mexico Genealogical Society, 2010).

7. Tafoya, "More Information on the Genealogy of Captain don Antonio de Ulibarri," April 2002.

8. Roybal and Pfeufer, Windham and Baca, *Santa Fe Marriages, 1728-1857.*

9. Jackie Luna, (website: http://home.earthlink.net/index.html), "electronic": *San Felipe de Neri Church, Burials/Deaths 1726-1776, Book #1, LDS Reel #0016645.*

10. Luna, (website: http://home.earthlink.net/index.html), *San Felipe de Neri Church, Burials/Deaths 1726-1776, Book #1, LDS Reel #0016645.*

11. Tafoya, "More Information on the Genealogy of Captain don Antonio de Ulibarri," April 2002.

12. Tafoya, "More Information on the Genealogy of Captain don Antonio de Ulibarri," April 2002.

13. Jose Antonio Esquibel, et al. Beyond Origins of New Mexico Families, online https://sites.google.com/site/beyondoriginsofnmfamilies/..

14. Christmas, Gallegos and Rau, *Santa Fe Burials, 1726-1834.*

15. Christmas, Gallegos and Rau, *Santa Fe Burials, 1726-1834.*

16. Fr. Angelico Chavez, compiler, *New Mexico Roots Ltd., A demographic perspective from genealogical, historical and geographic data found in the Diligencias Matrimoniales or Pre-Nuptial Investigations (1678-1869) of the Archives of the Archdiocese of Santa Fe* (Santa Fe: Museum of New Mexico Press, 1982).

17. John L, Kessel, Rick Hendricks and Meredith D. Dodge, compiler, *Blood on the Boulders, The Journals of don Diego de Vargas, New Mexico, 1694-97, Book I* (Albuquerque: University of New Mexico Press, 1998).

18. Chavez, *DM's or Pre-Nuptial Investigations.*

19. Christmas, Gallegos and Rau, *Santa Fe Burials, 1726-1834.*

20. Christmas, Gallegos and Rau, *Santa Fe Burials, 1726-1834.*

Jose Santiago Ulibarri

1. Jose Santiago Ulibarri
bap.[1] Nov 20, 1782
at Santo Domingo
m.[2] May 10, 1805
at Galisteo
d.
at

sp. Josefa Duran
b.
at
d.[3] May 22, 1841
at San Miguel del Bado

2. Ascencio Antonio Ulibarri
b. ca 1740
at
m.[4] Jun 24, 1771
at Santa Fe
d.[5] Feb 6, 1796
at Santa Fe

3. Maria Francisca Armijo
b. ca 1757
at
d.
at

4. Captain Antonio de Ulibarri
bap.[6] Dec 28, 1680
at San Luis de la Paz, Guanajuato, Mexico
m.[7] after Jan 25, 1725
at Santa Fe
d.[8] Nov 2, 1762
at Santa Fe, NM

5. Antonia Teresa Rael de Aguilar
b. ca 1706
at
d.
at

6. Manuel S. de la C. Duran y Armijo
b. ca 1713
at
m.[9] Oct 19, 1734
at Santa Fe
d.[10] Dec 4, 1764
at Albuquerque

7. Francisca Alfonsa Lucero de Godoy
b.
at
d.[11] Jan, 1786
at Albuquerque

8. Joseph de los Reyes
b.
at
m.[12] after Jan 10, 1672
at San Luis de La Paz
d.
at

9. Maria de Hinojosa y Robledo
bap.[13] Jun 17, 1652
at San Luis de la Paz, Mexico
d.
at

10. Captain Alonso J. Rael de Aguilar
bap.[14] Feb 14, 1661
at la Iglesia de San Mateo, Lorca, Spain
m. ca 1670
at
d.[15] Apr 10, 1735
at Santa Fe

11. Josefa Garcia de Noriega
b. ca 1655
at
d.[16] Aug 12, 1734
at

12. Vicente Ferrer Duran y Armijo
b. ca 1679
at Zacatecas
m.[17] after Aug 29, 1703
at Santa Fe
d.[18] after Nov 15, 1743
at Santa Fe

13. Maria Magdalena Apodaca
b.
at
d.
at

14. Juan Lucero de Godoy
b. ca 1678
at
m.[19] May 7, 1703
at Santa Fe
d.[20] Nov 23, 1742
at Santa Fe

15. Maria Isabel Lopez Lujan
b. ca 1692
at NM
d.[21] Aug 9, 1771 at Santa Fe

Endnotes

1. Luis Gilberto Padilla Y Baca, compiler, *New Mexico Baptisms, Pueblo Missions, San Felipe, Santa Ana, Santo Domingo, Cochiti, Jemez.* (Albuquerque, NM: Hispanic Genealogical Research Center, 2000).

2. Henrietta Christmas, extractor, *New Mexico Baptisms, Galisteo Marriages, 1776 - 1828*, AASF Roll #27.

3. NMGS Volunteers, compiler, *Pecos, San Miguel del Bado & Ribera Burials, 1796 - 1850* (Albuquerque, NM: New Mexico Genealogical Society, 2014).

4. Marie J. Roybal and Lila Armijo Pfeufer, extractors, Margaret Leonard Windham and Evelyn Lujan Baca, compilers, *New Mexico Marriages, Santa Fe - St. Francis Parish and Military Chapel of Our Lady of Light (La Castrense), 1728-1857* (Albuquerque: New Mexico Genealogical Society, 1997).

5. Henrietta M. Christmas, Jeanette Gallegos and Patricia S. Rau, compiler, *New Mexico Burials, Santa Fe - St. Francis Parish and Military Chapel of Our Lady of Light (La Castrense), 1726-1834* (Albuquerque, NM: New Mexico Genealogical Society, 2007).

6. Ernestino Tafoya, "More Information on the Genealogy of the Alcalde of Santa Fe, Captain don Antonio de Ulibarri," *HERENCIA, Quarterly Journal of HGRC* Vol. 10:2 (April 2002).

7. Fray Angelico Chavez, compiler, *New Mexico Diligencias* (Albuquerque: New Mexico Genealogical Society, 2010). Hereinafter cited as *Cinn. DM's.*

8. Tafoya, "More Information on the Genealogy of the Alcalde of Santa Fe, Captain don Antonio de Ulibarri," April 2002.

9. Roybal and Pfeufer, Windham and Baca, *Santa Fe Marriages, 1728-1857.*

10. Jackie Luna, (website: http://home.earthlink.net/index.html), "electronic": *San Felipe de Neri Church, Burials/Deaths 1726-1776, Book #1, LDS Reel #0016645.*

11. Luna, (website: http://home.earthlink.net/index.html), *San Felipe de Neri Church, Burials/Deaths 1726-1776, Book #1, LDS Reel #0016645.*

12. Tafoya, "More Information on the Genealogy of the Alcalde of Santa Fe, Captain don Antonio de Ulibarri," April 2002.

13. Tafoya, "More Information on the Genealogy of the Alcalde of Santa Fe, Captain don Antonio de Ulibarri," April 2002.

14. Jose Antonio Esquibel, et al. Beyond Origins of New Mexico Families, online https://sites.google.com/site/beyondoriginsofnmfamilies/.

15. Christmas, Gallegos and Rau, *Santa Fe Burials, 1726-1834.*

16. Christmas, Gallegos and Rau, *Santa Fe Burials, 1726-1834.*

17. Fr. Angelico Chavez, compiler, *New Mexico Roots Ltd., A demographic perspective from genealogical, historical and geographic data found in the Diligencias Matrimoniales or Pre-Nuptial Investigations (1678-1869) of the Archives of the Archdiocese of Santa Fe* (Santa Fe: Museum of New Mexico Press, 1982).

18. John L, Kessel, Rick Hendricks and Meredith D. Dodge, compiler, *Blood on the Boulders, The Journals of don Diego de Vargas, New Mexico, 1694-97, Book I* (Albuquerque: University of New Mexico Press, 1998).

19. Chavez, *DM's or Pre-Nuptial Investigations.*

20. Christmas, Gallegos and Rau, *Santa Fe Burials, 1726-1834.*

21. Christmas, Gallegos and Rau, *Santa Fe Burials, 1726-1834.*

Chart of Juan Jose Duran

1. Juan Jose Duran
b. ca 1771
at
m.[1] Dec 8, 1791
at Santa Fe
d.[2] Dec 23, 1841
at

sp. Getrudis Alire
b.
at
d.[3] Mar 9, 1837
at San Miguel del Bado

2. Ygnacio Duran
b. between 1738-1740
at
m.[4] Oct 21, 1767
at Santa Fe
d.
at

3. Maria Feliciana Sandoval
bap.[5] Sep 21, 1748
at Santa Fe
d.[6] May 26, 1811
at Pecos

4. Juan Jose Duran
b.
at
m. ca 1738
at
d.[7] Nov 23, 1789
at Santa Fe

5. Felipa Trujillo
b. ca 1720
at
d.[8] May 20, 1806
at Santa Fe

6. Andres Sandoval Martinez
b. ca 1704
at Santa Fe
m.[9] Jun 29, 1729
at San Juan de los Caballeros
d.[10] May 30, 1785
at Santa Fe

7. Maria Marquez
b. ca 1712
at
d.
at

8. Sebastian Duran
b.
at
m.
at
d.[11] Nov 20, 1761
at Santa Fe

9. Ana Martin
b.
at
d.
at

10. Bartolome Trujillo
b. ca 1699
at Santa Cruz
m.[12] May 1, 1719
at Santa Cruz
d.[13] after May 6, 1764
at Chama

11. Maria Margarita Torres
b. ca 1702
at
d.[14] Mar 27, 1742
at Santa Cruz

12. Miguel de Dios Sandoval Martinez
b.[15] ca 1678
at Mexico City
m.[16] Oct 28, 1697
at Santa Fe
d.[17] Nov 27, 1755
at Santa Fe

13. Lucia Gomez Robledo
b. ca 1670
at
d.[18] Aug 20, 1758
at Santa Fe

14. Juan Marquez
b. ca 1684
at
m.[19] Aug 18, 1709
at Santa Cruz
d.
at

15. Josefa Apodaca
b. ca 1693
at Guadalupe Del Paso, NM
d. Mar 2, 1758
at Santa Fe, NM

Endnotes

1. Marie J. Roybal and Lila Armijo Pfeufer, extractors, Margaret Leonard Windham and Evelyn Lujan Baca, compilers, *New Mexico Marriages, Santa Fe - St. Francis Parish and Military Chapel of Our Lady of Light (La Castrense), 1728-1857* (Albuquerque: New Mexico Genealogical Society, 1997).

2. NMGS Volunteers, compiler, *Pecos, San Miguel del Bado & Ribera Burials, 1796 - 1850* (Albuquerque, NM: New Mexico Genealogical Society, 2014).

3. NMGS Volunteers, *Pecos, San Miguel del Bado, Ribera Burials, 1796-1850.*

4. Roybal and Pfeufer, Windham and Baca, *Santa Fe Marriages, 1728-1857.*

5. Margaret L. Windham and Evelyn L. Baca, compiler, *Baptisms of Santa Fe, Parroquia de San Francisco de Asis, Vol. 1, 5 September 1747 to 17 July 1791* (Albuquerque, NM: New Mexico Genealogical Society, 2002).

6. Henrietta M. Christmas, *New Mexico Burials, Pecos Mission, 1798 - 1829*, AASF Roll #35.

7. Henrietta M. Christmas, Jeanette Gallegos and Patricia S. Rau, compiler, *New Mexico Burials, Santa Fe - St. Francis Parish and Military Chapel of Our Lady of Light (La Castrense), 1726-1834* (Albuquerque, NM: New Mexico Genealogical Society, 2007).

8. Christmas, Gallegos and Rau, *Santa Fe Burials, 1726-1834.*

9. M. Eloise Arellanes, extractor and translator, Margaret L. Windham and Evelyn L. Baca compiler. *New Mexico Marriages, Church in San Juan Pueblo, 1726-1776, 1831-1855 & Church in Santa Clara Pueblo, 1726-1832.*. (New Mexico Genealogy Society: Albuquerque, NM, 1998.)

10. Christmas, Gallegos and Rau, *Santa Fe Burials, 1726-1834.*

11. Christmas, Gallegos and Rau, *Santa Fe Burials, 1726-1834.*

12. Fr. Angelico Chavez, compiler, *New Mexico Roots Ltd., A demographic perspective from genealogical, historical and geographic data found in the Diligencias Matrimoniales or Pre-Nuptial Investigations (1678-1869) of the Archives of the Archdiocese of Santa Fe* (Santa Fe: Museum of New Mexico Press, 1982).

13. 1598 New Mexico, online http://1598nm.blogspot.com/, Henrietta Martinez Christmas.

14. Henrietta Martinez Christmas, "Selected Santa Cruz de la Cañada Deaths, 1726-1859," *New Mexico Genealogist* Vol. 39, #4 (December 2000).

15. Jose Antonio Esquibel and John B. Colligan, compiler, *The Spanish Recolonization of New Mexico, An Account of the Families Recruited at Mexico City in 1693.* (Albuquerque, NM: Hispanic Genealogical Research Center of New Mexico, 1999).

16. Chavez, *DM's or Pre-Nuptial Investigations.*

17. Christmas, Gallegos and Rau, *Santa Fe Burials, 1726-1834.*

18. Christmas, Gallegos and Rau, *Santa Fe Burials, 1726-1834.*

19. Chavez, *DM's or Pre-Nuptial Investigations.*

Chart of Manuel de Jesus Duran

1. Manuel de Jesus Duran
b. ca 1783
at
m.[1] May 10, 1805
at San Miguel del Bado
d.[2] Jan 16, 1842
at San Miguel del Bado

sp. Maria Francisca Ulibarri
b. ca 1788
at
d. before Dec, 1814
at

2. Ygnacio Duran
b. between 1738-1740
at
m.[3] Oct 21, 1767
at Santa Fe
d.
at

3. Maria Feliciana Sandoval
bap.[4] Sep 21, 1748
at Santa Fe
d.[5] May 26, 1811
at Pecos

4. Juan Jose Duran
b.
at
m. ca 1738
at
d.[6] Nov 23, 1789
at Santa Fe

5. Felipa Trujillo[7]
b. ca 1720
at
d.[8] May 20, 1806
at Santa Fe

6. Andres Sandoval Martinez
b. ca 1704
at Santa Fe
m.[9] Jun 29, 1729
at San Juan de los Caballeros
d.[10] May 30, 1785
at Santa Fe

7. Maria Marquez
b. ca 1712
at
d.
at

8. Sebastian Duran
b. ca 1675
at
m.
at
d.[11] Nov 20, 1761
at Santa Fe

9. Ana Martin
b.
at
d.
at

10. Bartolome Trujillo
b. ca 1699
at Santa Cruz
m.[12] May 1, 1719
at Santa Cruz
d.[13] after May 6, 1764
at Chama

11. Maria Margarita Torres
b. ca 1702
at
d.[14] Mar 27, 1742
at Santa Cruz

12. Miguel de Sandoval Martinez[15]
b.[16] ca 1678
at Mexico City
m.[17] Oct 28, 1697
at Santa Fe
d.[18] Nov 27, 1755
at Santa Fe

13. Lucia Gomez Robledo[19]
b. ca 1670
at
d.[20] Aug 20, 1758
at Santa Fe

14. Juan Marquez
b. ca 1684
at
m.[21] Aug 18, 1709
at Santa Cruz
d.
at

15. Josefa Apodaca
b. ca 1693
at Guadalupe Del Paso, NM
d. Mar 2, 1758
at Santa Fe, NM

Endnotes

1. Henrietta Christmas, extractor, *New Mexico Baptisms, Galisteo Marriages, 1776 - 1828*, AASF Roll #27, fr 237.

2. NMGS Volunteers, compiler, *Pecos, San Miguel del Bado & Ribera Burials, 1796 - 1850* (Albuquerque, NM: New Mexico Genealogical Society, 2014), p. 90.

3. Marie J. Roybal and Lila Armijo Pfeufer, extractors, Margaret Leonard Windham and Evelyn Lujan Baca, compilers, *New Mexico Marriages, Santa Fe - St. Francis Parish and Military Chapel of Our Lady of Light (La Castrense), 1728-1857* (Albuquerque: New Mexico Genealogical Society, 1997), p. 37..

4. Margaret L. Windham and Evelyn L. Baca, compiler, *Baptisms of Santa Fe, Parroquia de San Francisco de Asis, Vol. 1, 5 September 1747 to 17 July 1791* (Albuquerque, NM: New Mexico Genealogical Society, 2002), p. 6.

5. Henrietta M. Christmas, *New Mexico Burials, Pecos Mission, 1798 - 1829*, AASF Roll #35, frame 708.

6. Henrietta M. Christmas, Jeanette Gallegos and Patricia S. Rau, compiler, *New Mexico Burials, Santa Fe - St. Francis Parish and Military Chapel of Our Lady of Light (La Castrense), 1726-1834* (Albuquerque, NM: New Mexico Genealogical Society, 2007), p. 119.

7. 1598 New Mexico, online http://1598nm.blogspot.com/, Henrietta Martinez Christmas, Bartolome Trujillo will.

8. Christmas, Gallegos and Rau, *Santa Fe Burials, 1726-1834*, p. 177.

9. M. Eloise Arellanes, extractor and translator, Margaret L. Windham and Evelyn L. Baca compiler. *New Mexico Marriages, Church in San Juan Pueblo, 1726-1776, 1831-1855 & Church in Santa Clara Pueblo, 1726-1832.*. (New Mexico Genealogy Society: Albuquerque, NM, 1998.) p. 2.

10. Christmas, Gallegos and Rau, *Santa Fe Burials, 1726-1834*, p. 106.

11. Christmas, Gallegos and Rau, *Santa Fe Burials, 1726-1834*, p. 55.

12. Fr. Angelico Chavez, compiler, *New Mexico Roots Ltd., A demographic perspective from genealogical, historical and geographic data found in the Diligencias Matrimoniales or Pre-Nuptial Investigations (1678-1869) of the Archives of the Archdiocese of Santa Fe* (Santa Fe: Museum of New Mexico Press, 1982), p. 1929.

13. 1598 New Mexico, online http://1598nm.blogspot.com/, Christmas, Bartolome Trujillo will.

14. Henrietta Martinez Christmas, "Selected Santa Cruz de la Cañada Deaths, 1726-1859," *New Mexico Genealogist* Vol. 39, #4 (December 2000): p. 190.

15. Jose Antonio Esquibel and John B. Colligan, compiler, *The Spanish Recolonization of New Mexico, An Account of the Families Recruited at Mexico City in 1693.* (Albuquerque, NM: Hispanic Genealogical Research Center of New Mexico, 1999), p. 339.

16. Esquibel and Colligan, *Recolonization of NM, 1693*, p. 339.

17. Chavez, *DM's or Pre-Nuptial Investigations*, p. 1749.

18. Christmas, Gallegos and Rau, *Santa Fe Burials, 1726-1834*, p. 46.

19. Esquibel and Colligan, *Recolonization of NM, 1693.*

20. Christmas, Gallegos and Rau, *Santa Fe Burials, 1726-1834*, p. 52.

21. Chavez, *DM's or Pre-Nuptial Investigations*, pp. 1077/8.

Jose Antonio Ulibarri

8. Joseph de los Reyes
b.
at
m.[10] after Jan 10, 1672
at San Luis de La Paz
d.
at

4. Captain Antonio de Ulibarri
bap.[7] Dec 28, 1680
at San Luis de la Paz, Guanajuato, Mexico
m.[8] after Jan 25, 1725
at Santa Fe
d.[9] Nov 2, 1762
at Santa Fe, NM

9. Maria de Hinojosa y Robledo
bap.[11] Jun 17, 1652
at San Luis de la Paz, Mexico
d.
at

2. Jose Fernando Ulibarri
b.[5] ca 1736
at Santa Fe
m. Aug 17, 1762
at Santa Fe
d.
at

10. Captain Alonso J. Rael de Aguilar
bap.[12] Feb 14, 1661
at la Iglesia de San Mateo, Lorca, Spain
m. ca 1670
at
d.[13] Apr 10, 1735
at Santa Fe

5. Antonia Teresa Rael de Aguilar
b. ca 1706
at
d.
at

11. Josefa Garcia de Noriega
b. ca 1655
at
d.[14] Aug 12, 1734
at

1. Jose Antonio Ulibarri
bap.[1] Mar 29, 1767
at Santa Fe
m.[2] Sep 26, 1787
at Santa Fe
d.[3] before 1850
at

sp. Maria Rosa Garcia
bap.[4] Sep 7, 1770
at Santa Fe
d. before Mar, 1833
at

3. Maria Olalla Armenta
b. ca 1750
at Santa Fe, NM
d.[6] Jan 10, 1792
at Santa Fe

Endnotes

1. Margaret L. Windham and Evelyn L. Baca, compiler, *Baptisms of Santa Fe, Parroquia de San Francisco de Asis, Vol. 1, 5 September 1747 to 17 July 1791* (Albuquerque, NM: New Mexico Genealogical Society, 2002).

2. Marie J. Roybal and Lila Armijo Pfeufer, extractors, Margaret Leonard Windham and Evelyn Lujan Baca, compilers, *New Mexico Marriages, Santa Fe - St. Francis Parish and Military Chapel of Our Lady of Light (La Castrense), 1728-1857* (Albuquerque: New Mexico Genealogical Society, 1997).

3. 1850 United States Federal Census, Territory of New Mexico. . Ancestry Database, Provo, UT.

4. Windham and Baca, *Santa Fe Baptisms, Vol. 1, 1747-1791.*

5. Gerald Mandell, "A Second Look at Capitan Antonio de Ullibarri Alcalde de Santa Fe," *The Quarterly Journal of the Hispanic Genealogical Research Center of New Mexico* Vol. 4:2 (April 1996).

6. Henrietta M. Christmas, Jeanette Gallegos and Patricia S. Rau, compiler, *New Mexico Burials, Santa Fe - St. Francis Parish and Military Chapel of Our Lady of Light (La Castrense), 1726-1834* (Albuquerque, NM: New Mexico Genealogical Society, 2007).

7. Ernestino Tafoya, "More Information on the Genealogy of the Alcalde of Santa Fe, Captain don Antonio de Ulibarri," *HERENCIA, Quarterly Journal of HGRC* Vol. 10:2 (April 2002).

8. Fray Angelico Chavez, compiler, *New Mexico Diligencias* (Albuquerque: New Mexico Genealogical Society, 2010).

9. Tafoya, "More Information on the Genealogy of the Alcalde of Santa Fe, Captain don Antonio de Ulibarri," April 2002.

10. Tafoya, "More Information on the Genealogy of the Alcalde of Santa Fe, Captain don Antonio de Ulibarri," April 2002.

11. Tafoya, "More Information on the Genealogy of the Alcalde of Santa Fe, Captain don Antonio de Ulibarri," April 2002.

12. Jose Antonio Esquibel, et al. Beyond Origins of New Mexico Families, online https://sites.google.com/site/beyondoriginsofnmfamilies/.

13. Christmas, Gallegos and Rau, *Santa Fe Burials, 1726-1834.*

14. Christmas, Gallegos and Rau, *Santa Fe Burials, 1726-1834.*

Antonio de los Reyes Vigil

1. Antonio de los Reyes Vigil
bap.[1] Jan 8, 1749
at Santa Cruz
m. ca 1775
at
d.[2] May 12, 1832
at San Miguel del Bado

Spouses: (1st) Barbara Josefa Madrid
(2nd wife) Maria Antonia Benavides

2. Juan Bautista Montes Vigil
b. ca 1720
at
m. ca 1740
at
d.[4] Oct 21, 1785
at Santa Cruz

3. Maria Candelaria Medina
b. ca 1721
at
d.[5] Aug 26, 1771
at Santa Cruz

4. Captain & Alcalde Domingo Montes Vigil
b.[6] ca 1693
at Aguas Calientes, Zacatecas
m.[7] ca 1715
at
d.[8] Mar 11, 1771
at Santa Cruz

5. Pascuala Salazar
b. ca 1698
at
d. before 1725
at Santa Cruz

6. Soldier Jose Ysidro Medina[9]
b. ca 1695
at
m.[10] May 13, 1717
at Santa Cruz
d.[11] Mar 27, 1779
at Santa Cruz

7. Catalina "Catarina" Martín
b. ca 1700
at
d.[12] Jan 30, 1771
at Santa Cruz

8. Lt. Francisco Montes Vigil I
b.[13] ca 1666
at Zacatecas, Mexico
m.[14] ca 1683
at Zacatecas
d.[15] Sep 11, 1731
at Santa Cruz

9. Maria Jimenes y Anciso
b. ca 1670
at
d.[16] Nov, 1745
at Santa Cruz

10. Agustin de Salazar
b. ca 1665
at
m.[17] ca 1688
at El Paso del Norte
d.[18] Feb 17, 1741
at Santa Cruz

11. Felipa de Gamboa
b. ca 1668
at
d.[19] Oct, 1738
at Santa Cruz

12. Captain Diego de Medina
b.[20] ca 1674
at Durango
m.[21] Feb 7, 1694
at Santa Fe
d. before May, 1714
at

13. Maria Zapata 'Telles Jiron'
b. ca 1674
at
d.
at

14. Cristobal Martin Serrano II
b. 1678
at Santa Cruz
m.[22] Feb 24, 1699
at Bernalillo
d.
at

15. Maria Montoya Paredes

Endnotes

1. Margaret Langham Olmsted, transcriber, Margaret Leonard Windham and Evelyn Lujan Baca, compilers, *New Mexico Baptisms, Santa Cruz de la Cañada Church, Vol. 1, 1710-1794* (Albuquerque, NM: New Mexico Genealogical Society, 1994), p. 62.

2. Henrietta Martinez Christmas extractor, San Miguel del Bado Burials, 1829-1833, Film No. 0017002, frame 194.

3. Olmsted, Windham and Baca, *Santa Cruz Baptisms, Vol. 1, 1710-1794*, p. 10.

4. Henrietta Martinez Christmas, *Extracted Burial Records of Santa Cruz de la Cañada* , (AASF Microfilm, #39, May 2010), p. 192.

5. *Some Descendants of Domingo Montes Vigil*, Maria C. Martinez, Richard Dean Olivas, Brenda & LeeRoy Vialpando and et al, (San Pablo, CO: Self Published, 2001).

6. *Desc. of Domingo Montes Vigil*, Martinez, Olivas, Vialpando and et al.

7. *Desc. of Domingo Montes Vigil*, Martinez, Olivas, Vialpando and et al.

8. Henrietta Martinez Christmas and Patricia Sanchez Rau, compiler, *100 Years of Marriages, 1726-1826, Santa Cruz de la Cañada, New Mexico* (Corrales, NM: Self Published, 2001), p. 191.

9. Pat Sanchez Rau, "Ancestors of Pascuala Montes Vigil," e-mail message from leadville5@earthlink.net (unab22@att.net) to Nancy Anderson, 2003.

10. Fr. Angelico Chavez, compiler, *New Mexico Roots Ltd., A demographic perspective from genealogical, historical and geographic data found in the Diligencias Matrimoniales or Pre-Nuptial Investigations (1678-1869) of the Archives of the Archdiocese of Santa Fe* (Santa Fe: Museum of New Mexico Press, 1982), p. 1207.

11. Henrietta Martinez Christmas, "Selected Santa Cruz de la Cañada Deaths, 1726-1859," *New Mexico Genealogist* Vol. 39, #4 (December 2000): p. 191.

12. Santa Cruz de la Cañada Burials, 1726-1859, AASF Roll 39, Albuquerque Genealogy Center, Albuquerque, NM, frame 229.

13. Dr. Rick Hendricks & John Colligan "Beyond "Origins of New Mexico Families," Montes Vigil," *Herencia, Quarterley Journal of the Hispanic Genealogical Research Center of New Mexico.* Volume 4, Issue 2 (April 1996). Maria C. Martinez and et. al *Some Descendants of Francisco Montes Vigil II, Siero, Spain to "La Culebra".* (San Pablo, CO: Self Published, 2001).

14. *Desc. of Domingo Montes Vigil*, Martinez, Olivas, Vialpando and et al.

15. Christmas and Rau, *Santa Cruz Marriages, 1726-1826*, p. 190.

16. *Desc. of Domingo Montes Vigil*, Martinez, Olivas, Vialpando and et al.

17. Chavez, *DM's or Pre-Nuptial Investigations*, p. 1672.

18. Santa Cruz Burials, 1726-1859, AASF Roll 39: frame 114.

19. Santa Cruz Burials, 1726-1859, AASF Roll 39: extracted by Marilyn Britton.

20. Rau, "Ancestors of Pascuala Montes Vigil," e-mail to Nancy Anderson, 2003.

21. Chavez, *DM's or Pre-Nuptial Investigations*, p. 1206.

22. Chavez, *DM's or Pre-Nuptial Investigations*, p. 1096.

Index

Made in United States
Cleveland, OH
05 November 2026

47659886R00140